PORTRAITS OF CULTURE:
ETHNOGRAPHIC
ORIGINALS

PRENTICE HALL UNIVERSITY
PROFESSOR NANCY ROBERTS
DR. KATHLEEN BRITTON
ANTHROPOLOGY 101

D0225143

MELVIN EMBER
CAROL R. EMBER
DAVID LEVINSON

Prentice Hall, Englewood Cliffs, New Jersey 07632
Ginn Press, Needham Heights, Massachusetts 02194

Source One—Portraits of Culture
Prentice Hall, Englewood Cliffs, New Jersey 07632
Ginn Press, Needham Heights, Massachusetts 02194

Editorial: Nancy Roberts
Source One Editor: Andrea Shaw
Source One Project Editor: Kathleen Britton
Cover design and artwork: K.E. Roehr

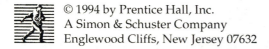
Printed in the United States of America
10 9 8 7 6 5 4 3 2 1

ISBN 0-131-46697-6

Prentice-Hall International (UK) Limited, *London*
Prentice-Hall of Australia Pty. Limited, *Sydney*
Prentice-Hall Canada Inc., *Toronto*
Prentice-Hall Hispanoamericana, S.A., *Mexico*
Prentice-Hall of India Private Limited, *New Delhi*
Prentice-Hall of Japan, Inc., *Tokyo*
Simon & Schuster Asia Pte. Ltd., *Singapore*
Editora Prentice-Hall do Brasil, Ltda., *Rio de Janeiro*

The first two . . .

From the Abelam to Yap. From researchers at work to global social problems and current controversies. Prentice Hall announces two revealing series that bring the current focus of anthropological study into the classroom.

PORTRAITS OF CULTURE: ETHNOGRAPHIC ORIGINALS, edited by Melvin Ember, Carol R. Ember, and David Levinson, and RESEARCH FRONTIERS IN ANTHROPOLOGY, edited by Carol R. Ember and Melvin Ember are resources that break new ground expressly for these series by experts and researchers that know anthropology because they do anthropology.

PORTRAITS OF CULTURE: ETHNOGRAPHIC ORIGINALS and RESEARCH FRONTIERS IN ANTHROPOLOGY open the door—open the world—to the diversity and possibility that anthropology teaches us.

. . . and the third

Prentice Hall and Ginn Press are pleased to introduce a custom publishing program for the anthropology course—SOURCE ONE. With the SOURCE ONE program, you choose the selections from PORTRAITS OF CULTURE: ETHNOGRAPHIC ORIGINALS and RESEARCH FRONTIERS IN ANTHROPOLOGY that fit your course, your teaching needs, and your interests. You determine the sequence in which these selections should appear, thereby keeping it consistent with the order in which you will cover them in class. And the professionally produced custom cover and table of contents provides you and your students with a perfectly tailored reader for the introductory course.

While leading researchers and anthropologists propel the study of anthropology in new directions, Prentice Hall and Ginn Press take teaching and learning resources in new directions as well.

SOURCE ONE.
See the "How to Order" section of this brochure for more details.

How to order

You and your Prentice Hall representative should fill out the SOURCE ONE order form. Order forms can be obtained by writing or telephoning Kathleen Britton at Ginn Press.

The order form should be mailed or faxed to:

KATHLEEN BRITTON
SOURCE ONE/GINN PRESS EDITOR
160 Gould Street
Needham, MA 02194
(FAX 617-455-1707)

Once SOURCE ONE receives the order, you and the sales representative will be notified. If you have any questions about your order, Kathleen Britton can be reached at **1-800-77-SOURC.**

The net price to the bookstores is determined by the total number of selections in the custom-designed textbook. (Each selection is approximately 30 pages and each reader costs a $4.00 base price plus $.04 per page.)

For the first order for any school, estimated delivery is 6–8 weeks from the day the order is placed. Subsequent reprint orders may take as little as 7–10 days.

Your Prentice Hall representative will call you to confirm the instock date with SOURCE ONE and follow up to ensure that the order reaches the bookstore safely.

☐ I would like to customize my own reader through the SOURCE ONE CUSTOM PUBLISHING PROGRAM for PORTRAITS OF CULTURE: ETHNOGRAPHIC ORIGINALS and RESEARCH FRONTIERS IN ANTHROPOLOGY from Prentice Hall and Ginn Press. Please send me an order form.

☐ I would like more information about the SOURCE ONE CUSTOM PUBLISHING PROGRAM for PORTRAITS OF CULTURE: ETHNOGRAPHIC ORIGINALS and RESEARCH FRONTIERS IN ANTHROPOLOGY from Prentice Hall and Ginn Press.

Please have my Prentice Hall sales representative contact me.

Name _____

Department _____ School/College _____

Address _____

City _____ State _____ Zip _____

Office Hours M _____ T _____ W _____ Th _____ F _____

Office Phone _____ Home Phone _____

FAX Number _____ Course Title _____

Total Enrollment For All Sections _____ Enrollment My Section _____

Current Text(s) In Use _____

When Are You Changing Texts?   ☐ For Spring   ☐ For Fall   ☐ Other

Adoption Decision Date _____ Text Decision ☐ Individual ☐ Committee

Committee Members _____

Do you have any textbook writing plans?   ☐ Yes   ☐ No

Are you interested in reviewing?   ☐ Yes   ☐ No

If yes, in what areas? _____

C-AY-143

Portraits of Culture: *Ethnographic Originals*

MELVIN EMBER,
CAROL R. EMBER, AND
DAVID LEVINSON
EDITORS

CONTENTS

EUROPE

- *Bulgaria: Anthropological Corrections to Cold War Stereotypes*, Gerald W. Creed, Hunter College, City University of New York
- *Abkhazians: Growing in Age and Wisdom*, Paula Garb, University of California, Irvine
- *Austrians: Development of a National Culture*, Robert Rotenberg, Depaul University, Chicago
- *Norwegians: Cooperative Individualists*, D. Douglas Caulkins, Grinnell College

SOUTH AND MIDDLE AMERICA

- *Miskito: Adaptations to Colonial Empires, Past and Present*, Mary W. Helms, University of North Carolina, Greensboro
- *Haitians: Dealing with Political Repression*, Robert Lawless, Wichita State University
- *Andean Mestizos: Growing Up Female and Male*, Lauris A. McKee, Franklin and Marshall College
- *Yanomamo: Varying Adaptations of Foraging Horticulturists*, Raymond B. Hames, University of Nebraska
- *Sierra Otomí: Guardians of the Eastern Mountains of Mexico*, James W. Dow, Oakland University

AFRICA AND MIDDLE EAST

- *Kurds: A Culture Straddling National Borders*, Annette Busby, University of California, Los Angeles
- *Efe: Investigating Food and Fertility in the Ituri Forest*, Nadine Peacock and Robert Bailey, University of California, Los Angeles
- *Yoruba: Political Representation in Old States and New Nations*, Sandra T. Barnes, University of Pennsylvania
- *Morocco: Adolescents in a Small Town*, Susan Schaefer Davis
- *Glebo: Civilizing the Anthropologist*, Mary Moran, Colgate University
- *Nandi: Cattle-Keepers to Cash-Crop Farmers*, Regina Smith Oboler, Ursinus College
- *Kalahari San: Sometime Hunter-Gathers*, Edwin N. Wilmsen, University of Texas, Austin

ETHNIC GROUPS IN THE UNITED STATES

- *Mexican Americans: Growing Up on the Streets of Los Angeles*, James Diego Vigil, University of Southern California, Los Angeles
- *Chinatowns: Immigrant Communities in Transition*, Richard H. Thompson, James Madison University
- *African-Americans: Getting into the Spirit*, George Brandon, City University of New York Medical School

CONTENTS

NORTH ALASKAN ESKIMOS: A CHANGING WAY OF LIFE

Ernest S. Burch, Jr.

"There it is," said the pilot of the small bush plane. "There is what?" I responded.

"It's the village, Kivalina," said the pilot. "We're practically there."

All I could see was an enormous expanse of empty space as we flew up the coast. The Chukchi Sea was on the left, and a broad, treeless flat area ringed with hills was on the right. The dividing line between land and sea was a beach of dark sand and gravel. It was mid-October. The rivers and lakes were newly frozen and covered with a light dusting of snow, but the sea was still ice free and dark under the overcast sky. I was so overwhelmed by the sensation of openness and space that I could scarcely identify the landscape's components.

Suddenly I saw some irregularities near the beach just ahead. Just as it dawned on me that they were buildings, we zoomed over them. Then we turned, descended, and landed on a small airstrip. The pilot deposited me and a few mailbags on the apron and left. Several villagers had come out to see the plane, and we stood there staring at each other as the plane's roar faded into the distance.

Kivalina in 1960 was a village of about 150 Eskimos, two white teachers and 175 sled dogs. Physically, it consisted of a school, a store, two churches, a National Guard armory, and twenty-four small houses. Of the houses, half were made of sod placed over a wood frame, and half were wooden shacks. There was no electricity or plumbing.

Just out of college, I was in Alaska as a research assistant on an environmental impact study. My job was to learn how dependent the Kivalina people were on local resources for their livelihood. My home was a small house rented from the Episcopal Church.

The day after I arrived I was invited to participate in a caribou hunt with three other men. I accepted, of course. Victor Swan told me to get in his sled. I was young and in reasonably good shape, and I responded that I preferred to trot alongside; I had read many times of how Eskimos travelled slowly across the country with two to three dogs pulling a heavily loaded sled. However, I could not reconcile my book-based vision with the scene in front of me.

3

Victor had fifteen dogs hitched to an empty sled, and they were so enthused at the prospect of going that they were leaping five feet (one and a half meters) into the air and screaming with excitement. So I got in the sled. As soon as I did, Victor raised the hook that had held it and the dogs took off so fast that I fell flat on my back in the sled.

The hunt was unsuccessful because Dennis, who had been my partner during the hunt, had apparently made some tactical errors. Sitting around drinking coffee afterward, Leonard and Victor expressed some negative opinions about his actions. They spoke in Eskimo, but swore in English. Leonard, in particular, uttered amazing strings of profanity. I asked him where he learned to swear, and he responded that he had just retired from the U.S. Army after many years as a master sergeant. It also turned out that, after living for many years in Japan while in the Army, he could speak fluent Japanese, as well as English and Eskimo.

The next day was Sunday, so I decided to see what a service was like in the local Episcopal church. It was led by an Eskimo from the village who turned out to be a fully ordained deacon (later priest) in the Episcopal hierarchy. The music was led by a pump organ, played by the deacon's brother, and a robed choir; the hymns were sung by the entire congregation in four-part harmony.

What was going on here? Were these people traditional Eskimos or modern Americans? On the one hand, they spoke almost exclusively in Eskimo among themselves. On the other hand, most of them could also speak English. They lived largely from hunting and fishing and ate traditional native foods almost exclusively, but most of the men also worked seasonally as carpenters, miners, longshoremen, or commercial fishermen in other parts of the state. All of the young men were members of the Alaska National Guard, which meant that they had had at least six months of military training at Fort Ord, Calif. Some of the young men and women had gone to school in southeastern Alaska, Kansas, New Mexico, or California. Every person had an English name, but also one or more Eskimo names.

The answer to the question "Were these people traditional Eskimos or modern Americans?" is that they were both, or, perhaps, neither. I became fascinated by this situation and decided to learn how it came about. That turned out to be more difficult than anticipated, involving hundreds of interviews with native elders and extensive library and archival research. I am still working on it

Point Barrow, the northernmost tip of Alaska. On the other hand, it does not get dark at all from mid-May to late July, and there is very little darkness for a month or so before and after that.

Iñupiaq country is also crossed by the treeline, or northern limit of trees, which angles irregularly west, then south across the region. North of the treeline the country is covered with tundra vegetation, which consists of a variety of grasses, sedges, and mosses, but with sizeable shrub growth along waterways and in well-drained or protected areas. South of the treeline the landscape is covered with patches of northern boreal forest (primarily spruce, with some birch and other species) along waterways and in well-drained areas, and by tundra vegetation elsewhere.

Northern Alaska is relatively warm for a region so far north, but it is still very cold compared to most regions of the world. Below zero temperatures Fahrenheit (below -17 degrees Celsius) last for weeks and often months during the winter, occasionally descending into the -40s Fahrenheit (-40s Celsius) along the coast, and much lower inland. Summers are cool along the coast, rarely getting above 60 degrees Fahrenheit (15 degrees Celsius), but it can get fairly warm—in the high 90s Fahrenheit (high 30s Celsius) inland. Rivers and lakes normally freeze in early to mid-October, and thaw in middle to late May. The ocean usually freezes in December. The ice starts to melt in May and breaks up in June. Precipitation is minimal, almost at desert levels. Most of what does fall comes as light rain in mid- to late summer. Snowfall is light, but because of the cold temperature snow accumulates on the ground for nearly eight months. Wind is an important fact of northern life everywhere, but particularly so beyond the treeline. In general, the southern part of the region is warmer and more moist than the north.

The animal life of northern Alaska is rich and diverse for a region so far north. Of particular importance to the traditional native economy were several kinds of sea mammal, bowhead whales, belukha whales, walrus, and several species of seal. Caribou (wild reindeer) were the most important land animals; others included polar bears, grizzly bears, and a variety of furbearing animals, such as wolves, wolverines, foxes, minks, beavers, otters, marmots, and ground squirrels. The region is favored with sizeable fish populations, including several species of salmon and whitefish, sheefish, char, ling cod, lake trout, grayling, pike, blackfish, and two varieties of small cod. Finally, northern Alaska is visited in summer by birds, such as murres, that nest on bluffs rising more than thirty years later. What follows is a condensed version of what I have learned so far.

THE IÑUPIAQ ESKIMOS

The Native residents of Kivalina belong to a larger group of people known as *Iñupiat* (pl.), or "North Alaskan Eskimos." The Iñupiat speak the Inuit Eskimo language, which is spoken across the northern part of North America from Bering Strait, on the west, to the coasts of eastern Greenland and Labrador, on the east. (Several *Yup'ik* Eskimo languages are spoken in south-central and southwestern Alaska and along the coast of easternmost Asia.)

At the beginning of the historic period, in the late eighteenth and early nineteenth centuries, the Iñupiat numbered about eleven thousand people and occupied an area of nearly one hundred thousand square miles (260,000 square kilometers). Their territory extended from the islands in Bering Strait to just east of the mouth of the Colville River, and included most of the drainages of the rivers reaching the sea between those two points (see Figure 1).

THE SETTING

Northern Alaska is characterized by a variety of landscapes. At one extreme are the rugged, glaciated peaks of the Brooks Range, which rise to altitudes of nearly nine thousand feet in their central portion. At the other extreme are extensive lowlands, the largest of which, the Arctic Coastal Plain, covers all of Alaska north of the Brooks Range. Much of the country is comprised of a mosaic of hills, flats, lakes, and streams. The coastline consists of a long sand and gravel beach bordered by lagoons in many areas, and broken here and there by capes and bluffs rising abruptly from the sea. Most of the country is underlain by permafrost (permanently frozen ground).

About 75 percent of Iñupiaq country lies north of the Arctic circle. The sun does not rise above the horizon for at least one day a year at the Arctic circle, and is not visible for nearly six weeks at

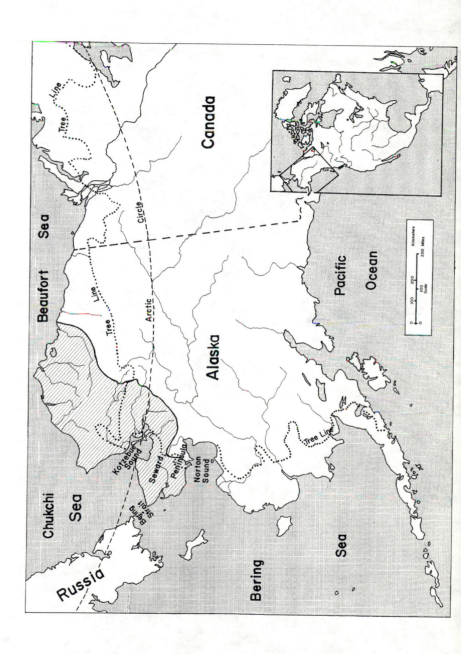

from the sea; huge numbers of migratory waterfowl (ducks, geese, swans, cranes); songbirds; and birds of prey. Ravens and two species of ptarmigan stay in the region year-round.

THE TRADITIONAL IÑUPIAQ WAY OF LIFE

Archaeologists have discovered that people have lived in northern Alaska for at least eleven thousand years. A number of prehistoric cultures have been identified, but for most of the period of human occupation it is difficult to assign ethnic or linguistic labels to them. However, the Iñupiaq Eskimos are clearly the direct biological and cultural descendants of the bearers of the Thule Culture, which emerged along the northwest Alaskan coast toward the end of the first millennium A.D. Over the ensuing centuries they expanded both inland and toward the south.

The first written accounts of the Iñupiat that have come down to us were made by English and Russian explorers in the late eighteenth and early nineteenth centuries. The latter is also the earliest time for which reliable oral historical accounts have been obtained. For these reasons, it serves as a useful ethnographic "baseline" from which to measure social change in the region, both backward into prehistoric times, and forward into the present. For convenience I refer to this time as the "traditional period," and to the social system that existed then as the "traditional" one.

The traditional Iñupiat were organized into twenty-six socioterritorial units that have been variously referred to in the anthropological literature as "tribes," "regional groups," and "societies." The boundaries of these societies are shown in Figure 2. Elders from whom I learned about these units characterized them as "nations, just like France, Germany, and England." Although I refer to them here as societies, it is useful to think of them as having been tiny versions of nations or countries as most of us understand those terms. Each society was characterized by a distinctive name, a discrete territory, a clearly identifiable subdialect of the Iñupiaq language, an ideology of distinctiveness, and a number of other distinctive features such as clothing styles, taboos, annual cycles of movement, and burial customs.

The estimated populations of the traditional Iñupiaq societies ranged from about 225 (*Ukiuvangmiut*, on King Island) to 1,340 (*Tikirarmiut*, at Point Hope), with an average of about 425. To modern readers, the idea that such a tiny social system can justifiably be considered the equivalent of a nation is ludicrous, but few modern readers are familiar with societies whose economy is based entirely on foraging (hunting, fishing, and gathering). They were very different from everything most of us have experienced.

The average area of traditional Iñupiaq societal territories was 3,850 square miles (9,970 square kilometers), but there was a considerable range of variation among them. The smallest territory was that of the Ukiuvangmiut, which consisted solely of the 4 square miles (10 square kilometers) that constitute King Island. The largest was that of the *Nunamiut*, in the northern interior, which encompassed some 19,000 square miles (49,000 square kilometers).

The village of Kivalina, where I first experienced northern Alaska, is located on the territory of a traditional society known as *Kivalliñarmiut*, which encompassed an area of approximately 2,100 square miles (5,400 square kilometers). The Kivalliñarmiut numbered about 320 people, making them one of the smallest Iñupiaq societies.

Families

The basic social unit in an Iñupiaq society was a large, bilaterally extended family (defined below). This large unit was comprised of several subfamilies.

The core of the system was a conjugal, or nuclear, family composed of husband and wife and their nonadult offspring. A conjugal family was created when a man and woman took up residence together and had sexual relations. That was all there was to it; Eskimos are among the few people in the world who did not recognize a marriage with some kind of ceremony. The Iñupiat had no system of preferential marriage by which certain categories of people were supposed to get married. They also lacked a system of arranged marriage, although in most cases parents seem to have tried to influence their children's choice of spouse. Incest taboos prohibited the marriage of siblings and close cousins, but in these small populations it was often difficult to find someone of the

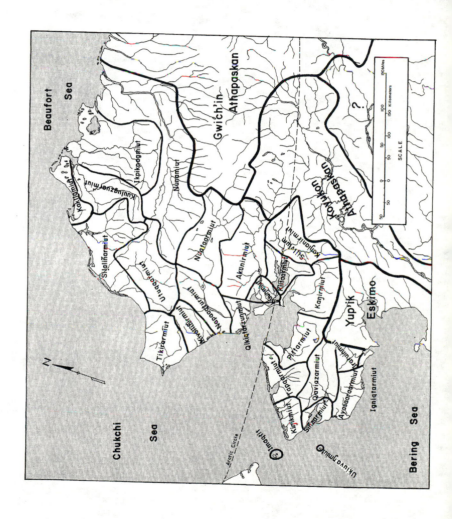

opposite sex and the right age to whom one was not rather closely related. Intersocietal marriage was one way to solve this problem. It did sometimes occur, but it usually led to so many conflicts that it was generally avoided. A few expert hunters had more than one wife (polygyny), the known record being five; having multiple husbands (polyandry) was also possible but extremely rare. Despite these possibilities, monogamy was the norm.

The division of labor along gender lines was sufficiently extreme as to ensure that most people did marry; it was almost impossible for an adult to live successfully without a spouse. Men hunted big game (caribou, mountain sheep, bears, and sea mammals) and most furbearers, and they manufactured tools, weapons, utensils, and most other paraphernalia that did not involve sewing. In some societies they did the fishing, at least at certain times of year, or else shared that activity with women. Except in special cases, women fetched big game animals that had been killed, butchered them, and processed the meat and skins. They also did most of the gathering of vegetable products, hunted small game (such as hares, ptarmigan, and ground squirrels), and in many societies did much of the fishing. Women were in charge of the storage, preparation, and distribution of all edible material from the time it reached the settlement until it was consumed. They also did all work involving sewing, which most notably involved the manufacture and maintenance of skin clothing, and they were the ones to make nets, pottery, and baskets. Child care was also largely the responsibility of women.

Conjugal families rarely lived by themselves. Most of the time they shared their dwelling with other relatives: the parents of one or (rarely) both spouses, married or unmarried siblings or cousins, their own married children if they were old enough to have any, or some combination of any of those possibilities. The families were "bilaterally extended" because they could include relatives from either the wife's or the husband's side, or both.

Extended family households were almost always located next door to other households of relatives of various kinds. Furthermore, the members of this larger unit acted as a single family under most circumstances. The men typically hunted and worked together, and the women spent most of the day together doing their chores. The children moved freely among the houses and felt at home in all of them. To distinguish these neighborhoods of related extended families from extended family households, I refer to the former as "local families" and to the latter as "domestic families." Thus, there were three levels of family in the Iñupiaq system: conjugal, domestic, and local.

Local families that I have been able to document for the late nineteenth and early twentieth centuries ranged in size between seven and nearly seventy members, with the majority involving between ten and twenty. According to elders with whom I discussed the matter, this was a very traditional pattern, except that in a few exceptional cases families had approached 100 members. For reasons that are not clear, couples seem to have had few children in traditional times, and in most households there were as many or more adults as children.

No matter how large or small they were, for all of the people most of the time local families constituted the social universe within which their daily lives were carried out. In one sense it is obvious that this would be so, since most settlements consisted of just one local family, and since settlements were situated several miles apart. But it was also basically true even in the largest settlements, where the houses of several local families were built close together.

Traditional Iñupiaq societies may be usefully conceived as being made up of a network of interrelated local families. Since in most cases the society as a whole involved just a few hundred members, it may be readily understood that most people were related by birth or marriage to practically everyone else. In addition, of course, there were friendships and various other relationships in which nonrelatives could interact, but family ties took precedence over all others to an overwhelming degree.

Economy

The economies of traditional Iñupiaq societies were based primarily on animate resources. The precise details varied from one society to the other according to the specific combination of resources available in their respective territories. At a general level the most critical resources were sea mammals, fish, and caribou.

Sea mammals were hunted with harpoons and spears; the precise techniques and the size of the weapons used varied according to the size of the animals being pursued and the ice conditions existing at the time. In northern Alaska, sea mammals range in size from the bowhead whale, which reaches sixty tons (54,400 kilograms) or more in size, down through walrus, belukha, and bearded seals to the hundred-pound (forty-five kilogram) ringed seal.

Sea mammals differ from land mammals in that their deposits of fat, known as blubber, are concentrated in a distinct layer located between the meat and the skin. Seal blubber renders easily into oil, and was served to the Iñupiat as food, fuel, medicine, and a medium within which dried meat and fish, and also some berries and greens, were safely stored without refrigeration for the better part of a year. Bowhead and belukha whales were a substantial source of meat, and their soft skin, rich in vitamin C, was relished as food. Walrus and bearded seals were also important sources of meat, and their skins were used for boat covers. Walrus tusk ivory was made into components of tools, weapons, utensils, and jewelry. Ringed seals provided meat, and their skins were made into rope, clothing (especially waterproof boots), tarpaulins, and bags. Finally, bowhead whale bones were used as structural members of the framework of sod houses in coastal regions north of the treeline.

Several varieties of fish are found in northwestern Alaska. They include lake trout, pike, burbot, grayling, and blackfish in freshwater; small species of cod and flounder in saltwater; and dolly varden char and several species of salmon and whitefish which move between salt water and freshwater seasonally. Fishing techniques varied according to season and species. In summer, the most productive technique in most areas was seining, whereby a long net made of rolled bark, baleen, or sealskin line was used to herd the fish toward a gravel bar and eventually scoop them up onto the bar. In the fall, when the ice is thin and many species of Alaskan fish move downriver, weirs were used. Otherwise, fish were caught with hook and line and with leisters (specialized fish spears). Although sea mammals and caribou receive most of the attention in the anthropological literature on northwestern Alaska, fish were a very important source of food for the members of practically all Iñupiaq societies, especially those whose territories were located inland.

The final primary animate resource in northern Alaska, and the only important terrestrial mammal, was the caribou. Caribou are a highly migratory species of medium-sized deer. Their meat resembles beef in taste and texture, and their hides can be made into tent covers, storage bags, and exceptionally warm but lightweight clothing and sleeping bags. Their antlers were made into the components of tools, weapons and utensils, and their back sinews (muscles) were made into excellent thread. The most productive way to hunt caribou is to build a circular enclosure, or corral, in an area they commonly cross when migrating and to herd the animals into it. Other techniques were snares set in passageways through forest or brush, pitfalls dug in the snow, bows and arrows, and spears wielded by kayakers chasing animals crossing rivers or lakes.

Vegetable resources ranked far below animate resources in general significance in Iñupiaq economies, although they were important in certain areas. Wood was used in the manufacture of boat and house frames, tools, weapons, utensils, sleds, paddles for *umiaks* (large open skin boats) and kayaks (small closed skin boats), and as fuel in some districts. Although most of northern Alaska is devoid of trees, driftwood formerly was common along the coast. Willows provided bark for net-twine, and the leaves, bark, and roots of various shrubs were used for medicinal purposes and for staining animal hides and some wooden objects. Finally, several kinds of berries, greens, and some roots were gathered and consumed as food or as medicine.

Minerals were used in a variety of ways. Chert ("flint") was chipped or flaked to make arrow and spear points, scrapers, knives, gravers, and other tools, and used with pyrite to start fires. Slate was made into knife blades, and nephrite (jade) was used to make adz blades, whetstones, jewelry, and occasionally knife blades or spear points. Two or three kinds of rock served as grinding material in the manufacture of slate and jade tools, in the manufacture of pottery, and, in conjunction with scrapers, in the preparation of skins. Clay was made into pottery, and certain kinds were eaten during periods of starvation. Finally, hematite, or red ocher, was made into paint to decorate paddles, the handles of weapons, and some items made from caribou skins.

All of the major animate resources of northern Alaska (including fish) are migratory, and they travel too far and too fast for people to follow. However, the various species take different routes and follow different schedules, so that every Iñupiaq territory had some important resources on hand most of the time except for late February and March. One way the people provided for seasonal variations in food supply was to overharvest in times of plenty and store the surplus for later consumption. They also undertook a series of annual moves themselves so that they could be in the best place to intercept each species of fish or mammal as it went through. As a rule, the members of local families stayed together during these movements, although during the lean season of late winter they often split up into domestic family segments and spread out. This spread the risk on the one hand, and increased the chances of someone finding game on the other.

For most of the year seasonal human movements were within societal territories. In summer, however, many involved trips to other territories as well. The residents of the islands in Bering Strait, for example, had alliances with the members of societies on the Seward Peninsula, which permitted them to hunt caribou on the mainland. In another example, the *Nuataarmiut*, whose territory lies far inland along the Noatak River, traveled to the coast every summer to hunt belukha; while they were away, hunters from the Kobuk River hunted caribou on the upper Noatak. All of the summer encroachments into foreign territory were undertaken at times or in ways that did not infringe upon the activities of the owners. It was a remarkable system of coordinated movements that must have taken centuries to develop.

Extensive movement was made possible by sled in winter and by boat in summer. Most domestic families had three or four large dogs to help haul their goods and possessions. People had to help pull and push when the sleds were fully loaded, but the arrangement still enabled them to transport much more than they could have otherwise. Extensive summer movement along rivers and seacoasts was carried out in umiaks. Umiaks built for travel—as opposed to those built for whale hunting—ranged from about 30 to 50 feet (9–15 meters) in length, and were made of wooden frames covered with seal or walrus skin. A 30-foot umiak could carry a ton of freight and a dozen people, yet was still light enough when empty for two men to lift out of the water. These large boats were sailed, paddled, or pulled along the beach or riverbank by dogs or people, as conditions permitted or dictated. Birchbark canoes served as the major form of transportation in a few inland districts where sealskins were not easily acquired. In the mountains summer travel was on foot, with the assistance of dogs as pack animals. Kayaks were used primarily for hunting in most areas.

People lived in cone or dome shaped tents in summer, during which time they needed no light (because of the midnight sun) and used wood as cooking fuel. In winter they lived in sod houses along the coast, and elsewhere in dome-shaped dwellings made of a wooden framework covered by sod, moss, or caribou-skin tarpaulins. Light and heat were provided by oil lamps. Cooking was done either over the lamps, or with rocks heated in wood fires and then placed in pots containing water and meat. In winter, most meat and fish were eaten raw and frozen except at the evening meal. When travelling, people took their skin-covered dwellings and frames with them, along with most of their other equipment and supplies. When they set up camp for the night they created a brand-new settlement.

The overwhelming majority of the goods and services required for survival in traditional northern Alaska were both produced and consumed at the local family level. Most raw materials, especially those used as food, were contributed to the general supply by the individual(s) who originally acquired them. The family stores were under the supervision of the wife (or main wife in the case of polygyny) of the local family head. She redistributed food to the domestic families as needed. However, since the men and older boys all ate together in one building, and the women and children all ate together in another, the redistribution of food was a simple operation.

The Political Process

Eskimos have been depicted in some anthropological texts as having lived in a state of anarchy. If, by anarchy, one means the absence of a formal government, that characterization would be correct. If, on the other hand, one means by the term a complete lack of order, an "every man for himself" type of situation, the claim is nonsense.

Local families, which formed the foundation of the Iñupiaq political system, were characterized by a pervasive hierarchical structure based on the factors of generation, relative age, and gender. With regard to generation, parents had authority over children. As long as children continued to live in the same local family as their parents, and as long as the parents were active, vigorous individuals, this authority continued pretty much throughout their lifetimes. With respect to relative age, the hierarchical system was even more pervasive: older people had authority over younger ones. In most families in our society, children are taught to resist attempts at dominance by older siblings that are not explicitly authorized by a parent (as when baby sitting); youngsters are taught to "stand up" for themselves. Eskimo children were taught just the opposite, to submit. While Eskimos did not record birth dates, they did know people's relative ages. With respect to gender, the picture is more complicated, but, in general, males had authority over females, at least over those of the same or lower generations. However, there were distinct domains, such as control over food supplies, where women's authority was superior to that of men.

Local family leadership was based on individual talent combined with the factors of generation, relative age and gender described above. A local family head was a highly competent hunter between the ages of about forty and sixty who had one or more wives, one or more married younger siblings and/or siblings-in-law and cousins, and one or more nonadult or married offspring living with him in the same local family. His authority over the others flowed almost automatically from his position in the kinship system. The successful head, or *umialik*, of a large local family was a wealthy man. He and at least his primary wife wore the most elegant clothes, ate the choicest food, and generally had the best of whatever they wanted. They bore themselves in a dignified manner, and were treated with deference by others. For these reasons, the first European explorers to visit northern Alaska could tell who the "chiefs" were from a long distance away.

The main check on an umialik's abuse of power was that compliance was voluntary. There was no legitimate source of coercion in the entire system. The various domestic and conjugal family subsystems of a local family could come and go as they pleased, and if an umialik became incompetent or demanding, everyone simply left. Effective umialiks were generous with their wealth and considerate of others in most of their dealings, and they consulted widely before making major decisions.

Disgruntled people had to consider their alternatives. If they left one local family, they had to join another, so they had to decide where they would be better off. Domestic and conjugal families did not realistically have the option of striking off on their own for more than brief periods. They would find it difficult to produce all of the goods and services they needed to survive, and they could not defend themselves against raiders from other societies or even against villains from within their own.

The counterpart of the problem of an ineffective or corrupt leader was a problem individual farther down the hierarchy. Such a person could be a nuisance, or someone who refused to perform his or her share of the work that had to be done in order for them all to survive. Such individuals were cautioned, exhorted, teased, admonished, and otherwise exposed to the sentiments of the other members of the family about their behavior. The ultimate sanction in this direction was to shun the offender. No one would talk to him or her, people would try to avoid him or her as much as possible, and they might even try to move the settlement without warning. In a world where social life and family life coincided, this was devastating treatment, and brought all but the most deviant individuals into line. Truly dangerous individuals were killed, preferably by their closest relatives so as to avoid the possibility of a blood feud.

Religion played a part in the political process in a way that crosscut the kin-based system just described. As discussed in the next section, the Iñupiat believed that the world is governed by a host of spirits. Some of them could control important things, such as the game supply and the weather. If the spirits were alienated by something people did, they sent the game to another country or visited upon the offenders some other kind of disaster. In order that this not happen, people had to obey an enormous set of prohibitions, or taboos, that were communicated to them by spirits via a shaman. This gave shamans considerable influence in daily affairs, since they could tell people what they had to do and when they had to do it in order to prevent hostile spirits from harming them. The authority of the shaman and that of the umialik ordinarily covered different sets of activities, but not always, and conflicts between them could be a source of stress within the local family.

Local families were very self-sufficient politically. Political integration above the local family level was weak, and this fact is what may have led to some of the claims of anarchy noted above. Iñupiaq societies did lack governments or other organizations above the local family level that could have mediated, influenced, or controlled relations between and among families. For most people most of the time, local families were located so far apart that this did not matter. However, in the larger settlements, where the members of two or more local families resided in close proximity to one another, there was often considerable tension, since there was no structured way to resolve interfamily disputes. The political process at this level operated essentially as it did within local and domestic families, through the voluntary cooperation of the people involved. When that did not work, the solution had to be either the departure of one of the contending families to some remote district, or bloodshed.

Religion

Iñupiat religion was based on the animistic belief that every living thing, and many things (e.g., mountains) that we do not conceive of as being alive, were imbued with souls. There were, in addition, a number of spirits who were not normally associated with any particular physical form. All spirits, including those associated with humans, could be temporarily disassociated from their related physical forms, either through their own volition, or through magical practices of some kind.

The Iñupiat believed that the world was basically a munificent place. Fish and game existed in infinite supply, the weather was good, and people were healthy—unless some spirit interfered. If one did, the result was famine, stormy weather, accident, or illness. Spirits were viewed as negative forces that had to be placated in order for people to survive. Unfortunately, spirits were also perverse, because they required people to obey an enormous number of taboos.

No one has ever compiled on paper a complete list of the taboos adhered to by the members of any Eskimo group, and no native elder living today knows more than a fraction of those followed in earlier times. However, some examples from northern Alaska illustrate their general nature:

1) If bear meat had been placed in a dish, the same container could not thereafter be used as a receptacle for belukha flesh;

2) Skins could not be deliberately wet while the salmon were running;

3) A young girl could eat meat from only certain ribs of a mountain sheep; when she was older she could eat only from certain other ribs; and when she was full grown she would have to abstain for a time from eating ribs which she had been allowed to eat up to that point.

If one understands that rules like these numbered in the thousands, one can begin to appreciate the significance of taboos in traditional native life.

The discovery of what activities were tabooed was the prerogative of the shaman. The shaman was a person, male or female, who, through mystical experiences or training, acquired an ability to communicate with spirits. If someone was ill, or the caribou failed to appear at the usual time of year, or the weather had been bad for weeks on end, a shaman was hired to intercede with the spirits to find out what caused the problem. The answer was always that one or more specific taboos had been broken, and the solution was typically the addition of a new one to placate the offended spirit. For the Iñupiat, religion meant avoiding trouble, not seeking a state of grace.

Intersocietal Relations

Hunter-gatherers in general, and Eskimos in particular, are some-times depicted in anthropological texts as being "free wanderers," as people who could go anywhere they wished. While that may have been true in some areas, it certainly was not in northern Alaska. In northern Alaska, anyone who ventured into foreign territory without permission was killed.

Alliances were arranged between individuals and families rather than between governments. They were of two basic types: trading partnerships and co-marriages. A trading partnership involved an arrangement between two individuals, male or female, to exchange certain basic products, and to provide general support in time of need.

A co-marriage involved the practice misleadingly called "wife trading" in the literature. It did involve two couples—usually from different societies—exchanging sexual partners for a night. But when a man and a woman engaged in sexual intercourse, they were considered married for the rest of their lives, even if they never had sex together again. They were married in a different way than residential spouses, but they were married nevertheless. The two women involved were considered related to one another in the same way that the women were in a polygynous residential marriage, and the relationship of two men was considered analogous to the one existing in a polyandrous marriage. All of the children that any of the four ever had, before or after, were considered siblings, with all of the rights and obligation implied by that status. Whether or not an exchange of sexual partners was undertaken for lustful reasons, the consequences were significant and long-lasting.

Ordinarily partners and co-spouses met at one or another of three large fairs that occurred each summer, and, less frequently, at special feasts that were held during the winter. In time of famine, people could go with their families and live under the protection of their partners or co-spouses in another society until the crisis passed.

Intersocietal warfare was common among the traditional Iñupiat. Usually it was undertaken to settle a grudge rather than to take prisoners or acquire territory. Participation in a raid was strictly voluntary, so resentment had to be widely felt before a fighting force could be mustered. The preferred tactic was a surprise night-time raid, but the Iñupiat knew how to form and maneuver battle lines, they knew how to construct defensive works, and they wore breast armor made from plates of ivory or bone attached together with thongs. Weapons consisted of bows and arrows, spears, and clubs. Although tiny operations by modern standards, battles often involved a significant proportion of the male populations of the societies concerned. They were also brutal affairs: neither women nor children were spared, and prisoners were tortured and killed. It is not surprising that men kept their weapons in good repair and close at hand at all times.

THE EXPLORATION PERIOD

Russian and British explorers began to make their way to northern Alaska in the eighteenth century, but their contacts were brief, and their reports of native life were not particularly informative. Both the number of contacts and the quantity of information increased dramatically in the early nineteenth century.

The natives encountered by the explorers were aggressive people. They were eager to trade, but only on their own terms and only during the traditional summer season of interregional travel. They were obviously experienced traders, for they brought forth their best wares only after the explorers rejected inferior work. When the Europeans tried to buy fresh fish to eat, the natives tried to sell them fish skins inflated with air.

Outside the summer trading season, which lasted from about late June to late August, or whenever the explorers were heavily outnumbered, the Iñupiat were hostile to them. Bloodshed was narrowly avoided on several occasions. For example, when Aleksandr Kashevarov's small party passed along the coast of Kivalina territory in late August 1838, it was frequently threatened

by a large number of Iñupiat. Only alert action and a hasty departure by the Russians prevented disaster. The English, under
Frederick Beechey, were threatened several times on Chamisso
Island in the fall of 1826, and again a year later. Finally, the Iñupiat
attacked the explorers with bows and arrows. They produced some
casualties but were repulsed, also with casualties, by the English
firearms.

After a hiatus of about a decade, exploration resumed in the
late 1840s with a number of British expeditions, all of which were
involved in a search for the missing explorer Sir John Franklin. For
the first time Europeans overwintered in northern Alaska: on the
western end of Seward Peninsula, on Kotzebue Sound, and near
Point Barrow, the northernmost point of Alaska. Several potentially violent confrontations were defused through wise action on the
part of the English captains and, by the time the British left in
1854, peaceful relations between Iñupiat and foreigners had been
established.

In 1848, the same year that the Franklin search ships arrived in
northern Alaska, an American whaling ship sailed north through
Bering Strait for the first time. The venture was so successful that
an entire fleet of ships soon began working in the Arctic Ocean off
Alaska. During the early years the whalers had little direct contact
with Iñupiat, but they had an enormous impact on the bowhead
whale population. Within a few decades they reduced it to a shad-
ow of its former self, and turned attention to walrus. It was not
long before the walrus population, too, was decimated.

American trading vessels followed the whalers north of Bering
Strait. Their initial goal was to supply the whaling fleet, but they
soon found a lucrative trade with the natives. They cruised the
coastline and, in exchange for furs and various items of native
manufacture, they traded whisky, firearms, knives, and various
other goods. As the whale and walrus populations declined, some
of the whalers also turned to trading as a way to turn a profit.

While these developments were taking place north of Bering
Strait, the Russians, who "owned" Alaska, established permanent
trading posts just south of Iñupiaq country. Shortly afterward a
smallpox epidemic struck the region served by the Russian posts,
killing at least half of the native population. For some reason the
epidemic did not reach Iñupiaq country, but it almost eliminated
the Yup'ik Eskimo population living between it and a Russian post
on the south side of Norton Sound. That post lured a number of

Iñupiat southward, and the loss of the former native population removed the chief obstacle to expansion. When the United States acquired Alaska in 1867, Americans took over the St. Michael post and began selling firearms and other goods to the Iñupiat.

The cumulative effect of these developments was disaster. The whalers' near extermination of whales and walrus eliminated two major sources of food and other important raw materials. Rifles made caribou hunting much easier than it had been previously. Firm in the belief that caribou existed in infinite supply, with access to them only controlled by the whims of the spirits, the Iñupiat themselves proceeded to wipe out the herds. The U.S. Revenue Marine (now the Coast Guard), which began regular summer cruises to northern Alaska in the early 1880s, unsuccessfully attempted to prevent this by halting the trade in rifles.

Between 1870 and 1890, famine and newly imported diseases such as influenza and measles combined to reduce the Iñupiaq population by some 50 percent, more in some districts, less in others. Faced with disaster in their homelands, and no longer fearing the few remaining defenders of other territories, people began to move around in search of food, not only within the traditional Iñupiaq area, but beyond it as well. These trends continued into the twentieth century.

Missionaries arrived in the 1890s to attack traditional Iñupiaq beliefs and replace them with new ones. The gold rush of 1898, especially to Nome, but to several other areas as well, temporarily brought in tens of thousands of outsiders, with a number of disruptive effects on native life. The U. S. government imported domesticated reindeer from Eurasia to replace the now nearly extinct caribou, and built schools in most of the places where there still was a resident Iñupiaq population.

By 1910, the demographic basis of the traditional societies was destroyed. The economy had been fundamentally altered by the loss of important game animals (walrus, whales, caribou), the introduction of rifles and the new hunting techniques they required, the importation of reindeer and new types of food, and the introduction of money. Native political independence was lost when the U. S. government imposed its control over the region. And, finally, the traditional cognitive and belief systems were under attack by the teachers and missionaries. The traditional way of life was gone.

THE MISSION-SCHOOL
VILLAGE PERIOD

The years from about 1910 to 1970 were a time in which Iñupiaq life was focused on settlements built around missions and schools. It was a time in which the demands of the new and old ways were in constant conflict. I was fortunate enough to begin my own work in northern Alaska before this period had quite run its course.

Physically, a mission-school village consisted basically of a one-room government school (with dwelling quarters for the teacher and his or her family), a Christian mission of one denomination or another, and a number of native dwellings. Later on, independent traders established stores in many of the villages.

The reason that there was only one mission per village is that representatives of the several denominations had agreed among themselves to divide the Alaskan "field" so that they would not come into conflict with one another. Missionaries met with considerable resistance during the early years, but after a few converts publicly flouted taboos without bringing harm to themselves or their families, conversions came fairly quickly.

Initial composition of the Native populations of these villages varied to some extent from one to another. In Point Hope, for example, most of the people were direct descendants of the traditional Tikirarmiut. In Kivalina, however, the first residents included descendants of traditional Kivalliñirmiut, as well as immigrants from five other societies.

In Point Hope, the mission-school villages were organized along traditional family lines. In the Kivalina-type situation, where there was a mixture of people from different areas, local families initially were few in number and small in size, and many of the domestic units were isolated from other relatives. It was only after several marriages had taken place that local family neighborhoods began to emerge.

Interestingly, about this time couples began having more children than they had had traditionally. Since heating requirements strictly limited house size, this development eventually led to overcrowded houses. Over time, what had been extended family households became conjugal family units. Houses still had five to ten people living in them, but that number now included a married couple and their nonadult children. Married siblings lived next door to one another, not in the same dwelling.

During much of the mission-school village period the natives were faced with a major dilemma. On the one hand, they were legally required—and for the most part genuinely wanted—to keep their children in school during the winter. Most of them also wanted to be near the church and the store. These considerations meant they had to stay in town. However, since they still derived their sustenance almost entirely from hunting and fishing, and since most of their cash income (required to buy rifles, ammunition, and such new staples as flour, coffee, tea, and sugar) was derived from trapping, they also had to be out on the land. Some families were involved in reindeer herding, which required that they, too, live out of the village.

The dilemma was resolved in a number of ways. Several families did spend the winter a long way from the mission-school villages, usually in traditional-style local family settlements. They left their school-age children with relatives in town, and returned periodically to pick up supplies, and during major holidays such as Christmas. The people who stayed in town, on the other hand, started using larger teams of smaller, faster dogs to pull their sleds. Instead of hunting on foot, as they had traditionally, village-based men started going out to hunt with dogs and empty sleds. They could cover much more country in one day this way than they could have on foot. During the early fall and late spring, the major hunting and fishing seasons when the entire village emptied out, teachers accepted the inevitable and closed school.

Mission-school village affairs tended to be dominated by the teachers, or the head teacher where there was more than one. Teachers were the representatives of the federal government in most villages. Much of their influence stemmed from this and from their knowledge of contemporary American affairs and the natives' ignorance thereof. If the teacher told people they should do something, they thought they had to do it. After the government forced the native herders to place their reindeer under government control, for reasons too complicated to discuss here, teachers were placed in charge of herd administration, and also in charge of the cooperative stores formed by the new government reindeer companies to reduce the cost of imported goods.

Disputes in many villages were settled by elected village councils. Most of them were established initially by teachers to show the natives how American democracy worked. The councils generally had no legal authority, but the threat of filing a complaint with a federal marshall (in one of the regional centers) if a troublemaker got out of hand gave their demands some force. Some councils were shamelessly manipulated by teachers, but others—especially those comprised of several local family heads—were effective in managing village affairs.

The situation described above is broadly accurate for the entire 1910–1970 period, but a number of changes also occurred. For example, the Great Depression of the 1930s ruined the fur market, and severely restricted the government's ability to pay the salaries of reindeer herders. In addition to increasing the general poverty level, these developments reduced the need for families to spend winters in small, isolated settlements. They also introduced the Iñupiat to government welfare.

In another, more positive development, the caribou population recovered, beginning in the late 1930s. By the time I arrived on the scene in 1960, caribou were abundant. Moose arrived in the area for the first time in the 1940s, and quickly became an important source of food.

A third important change was the growth of opportunities for men to work at seasonal wage employment. Most of the time this was in places far from the villages, which took them to cities such as Fairbanks and Anchorage for the first time. Other avenues for wage labor came through government programs, such as the Civilian Conservation Corps during the Depression, exploration of the Naval Petroleum Reserve south of Barrow after World War II, and the construction of the Distant Early Warning (DEW line) system of radar sites all along the coast in the 1950s. Other opportunities for Iñupiat to learn about the world at large were provided by the military, by boarding schools and training centers, and by the Bureau of Indian Affairs relocation program.

Disease remained a major problem until the very end of this period. There were two catastrophic flu epidemics early in the century, and tuberculosis became almost universal. At a church conference in Noatak in 1961, all those who had been in a sanitarium were called forward to sing a hymn together. Of the several hundred people present, only about a dozen adults and the children were left in the audience. If, in 1960, one asked a woman just past her childbearing years how many children she had, a typical response was "fourteen, five living."

By 1960 most Iñupiat still preferred village life, their traditional foods, and their native language. However, the formal education provided by the schools, and the informal learning acquired via radio, books, and magazines, and experiences in places outside the villages combined to produce a native population that was reasonably knowledgeable about modern American ways.

During the late 1950s and the 1960s, a number of development schemes were proposed for northern Alaska as well as for other areas of the state. All were conceived without consultation with natives. Nor did they include provisions to compensate natives for losses they might bear because of the plans. That angered not only Iñupiat but natives all over Alaska. Armed with their new knowledge of American society, they formed a number of regional organizations and the statewide Alaska Federation of Natives. Working through the courts, these organizations brought the proposed development of the Prudhoe Bay oil field to a halt. Then, using classic, American-style pressure politics, they effectively pursued their claims with the U. S. Congress. The result was the Alaska Native Claims Settlement Act (ANCSA) of 1971.

THE LAND CLAIMS ERA

ANCSA granted to Alaska natives fee simple title to 40 million acres of land and $962.5 million in return for their dropping all aboriginal claims. Both the money and the land were to be received and administered by twelve regional corporations and 204 village corporations established under the act. Shortly before ANCSA was passed, hundreds of claims were filed by individuals for allotments, the equivalent for natives of the homesteads by which whites had taken possession of much of the western United States. In 1980 the Alaska National Interest Lands Act (ANILCA) was passed, establishing national parks, monuments, and preserves over huge areas of the state, particularly in northern Alaska. Two boroughs have been created in the region, the North Slope Borough across the northern part of the state, and the Northwest Arctic Borough in the country draining into Kotzebue Sound.

For the first time since the breakdown of the traditional societies, land ownership became a major issue for the Iñupiat. In 1960, one could travel for days in almost any direction without bothering anyone; by 1990, one could hardly go anywhere without trespassing on someone else's property. Even the villages have been surveyed and divided into plots.

ANCSA has had a major impact on life in northern Alaska. The natives had to staff and operate the regional and village corporations despite the fact that a corporation was an alien organizational form to most of them. Although the corporations provided more opportunities for local employment than had ever existed before, more trained people than the native population could supply were required to staff them. Outsiders had to be hired to fill the gaps, leading a number of non-natives to immigrate to the region. Similarly, both the new oil field at Prudhoe Bay, near the Beaufort Sea coast, and the Red Dog Mine, about 50 miles (80 kilometers) inland from Kivalina, employed Iñupiat and brought in lots of outsiders.

Iñupiat are now more in control of their own affairs than they were during the mission-school village period. They run the regional and village corporations, and in most cases the village and local governments. School districts are now under local control, and most church congregations are led by native clergy. Villagers complain that their lives are controlled by the regional corporations and people in the regional centers, but that is very different from having them controlled by an agent of the Bureau of Indian Affairs.

In 1990 there were nearly sixteen thousand people residing permanently in traditional Iñupiaq territory, 74 percent of whom were natives.[1] Slightly more than half of the Iñupiat were distributed among 23 predominantly native villages having an average of 290 inhabitants. The rest lived in the regional centers of Barrow, Kotzebue, and Nome, which had average populations of about three thousand.

The physical aspects of community life have been transformed through a process that began shortly before ANCSA. Several projects sponsored by the state, and later by the new local governments and regional corporations, provided much larger houses for almost everyone. They are heated by oil stoves and/or by very efficient factory-made wood-burning stoves. All the villages have electricity, television, and telephone service, and almost all of them have plumbing. In 1960 Kivalina was lucky to get one small bush plane bringing mail and passengers three times a week; thirty years later ten flights a day was not considered unusual. Dog teams are gone, having long since been replaced by snowmobiles and all-terrain vehicles. In 1960 an eighteen-horsepower outboard motor was the biggest thing around; now boats have ten times that. Every village now has a high school, so no one has to attend boarding schools in some other place if they want a high school education. Physically, life in northern Alaska is much more comfortable than it used to be.

Modern life apparently has been acquired at significant psychological cost, however. Alcoholism, drug abuse, suicide, accidental death, and domestic violence occur at unusually high rates in Alaskan villages. The precise causes of these problems remain unknown, and so, unfortunately, do the solutions.

Local families continue to be important in village life, but they are gradually yielding to domestic and conjugal families. People may no longer build a house anywhere they want. With each passing generation, it is becoming more difficult to maintain local family neighborhoods, and closely related conjugal families are increasingly spread all over the village. However, telephones and the ubiquitous citizen's band radios make keeping in touch a simple matter, and snowmobiles in winter and all-terrain vehicles in summer make it easy for relatives to get together no matter how far apart their houses might be.

Traditional food is still preferred by most of the Iñupiat, and people still have to hunt and fish to get it. But many have full- time jobs, and they must either buy their food or hunt on weekends. Many women hold full-time jobs, and more than one erstwhile hunter has to spend most of his time baby-sitting. English is the preferred language in many homes, but Iñupiaq remains the language of choice in others, and is now being taught in the schools.

Anecdotes may capture the flavor of modern village life in Iñupiaq Alaska better than any generalizations can, and I conclude this piece with two of them. Both occurred in June, 1983, when I was doing a follow-up of the 1960–1961 Kivalina study.

The first event occurred one beautiful day when I was standing outside enjoying the view. About ten women were scattered along the shore butchering seals their husbands had taken the night before. Suddenly, as if by some signal, they all stood up, put their things in order, and went inside. Curious, I started visiting around to see what they were doing. Every one of them was watching General Hospital on TV. As soon as the show was over, they returned to their work.

The second event occurred a few days later. This time I was visiting a local family at its sealing camp about fifteen miles (twenty-five kilometers) southeast of the village. Its members lived in tents complete with floors, beds, stoves, stereo systems, and lots of tapes. A CB radio was used to maintain contact with the village, and also with hunters boating among the loose pans of sea ice. After a dinner of seal meat, rice, and seal oil, we listened to world news on the radio. The broadcast concluded with the stock market report, which stimulated among my Iñupiaq friends a discussion of the state of the world economy, particularly on the effect that lower oil prices might have on it. Then they went out and resumed seal hunting. By 1990, the place where their camp was located had become the port site for the Red Dog Mine.

NOTES

1. These figures do not include the many places to which Iñupiat have spread to the south and east (including northwestern Canada) of traditional Iñupiaq territory.

SUGGESTED READINGS

Burch, Ernest S., Jr. *Eskimo Kinsmen: Changing Family Relationships in Northwest Alaska.* St. Paul, Minn.: West Publishing Company, 1975. A comprehensive study of changing family life from traditional times to the 1970s.

Burch, Ernest S., Jr. "Traditional Eskimo Societies in Northwest Alaska." *Senri Ethnological Studies* 4 (1980): 253–304. The only comprehensive summary of traditional societies in northern Alaska, although somewhat out of date.

Chance, Norman A. *The Iñupiat and Arctic Alaska: An Ethnography of Development.* Fort Worth, Tex.: Holt, Rinehart & Winston, 1990. A summary of recent changes, especially in the northeastern portion of the Iñupiaq sector of Alaska.

Ray, Dorothy Jean. *The Eskimos of Bering Strait, 1650–1898.* Seattle, Wash.: University of Washington Press, 1975. A comprehensive account of the traditional and exploration periods in the Bering Strait/Seward Peninsula area.

Spencer, Robert F. *The North Alaskan Eskimo: A Study in Ecology and Society*. Washington, D.C.: Smithsonian Institution, 1959, republished in 1969 by Random House. A highly regarded general ethnography of the northern portion of the Iñupiaq sector of Alaska during the exploration period.

Van Stone, James W. *Point Hope: An Eskimo Village in Transition*. Seattle, Wash.: University of Washington Press, 1962. The best description of an Iñupiaq village during the mission-school village period.

MISKITO:
ADAPTATIONS TO COLONIAL EMPIRES, PAST AND PRESENT

Mary W. Helms

INTRODUCTION

In the late twentieth century the people known as the Miskito "Indians," possibly numbering as many as 150,000 persons, are one of the largest ethnic groups in Central America.[1] They inhabit the eastern lowlands and Caribbean coastal regions of Honduras and Nicaragua, the so-called "Mosquito Coast" of eastern Central America.

I first learned of the existence of the Miskito Coast in the early 1960s when I was a graduate student in anthropology. At that time a member of my family, a medical doctor, was serving as director of a small clinic and hospital operated by the Moravian Church in Puerto Cabezas, the major port town of the northern Nicaraguan Miskito Coast, south of the Río Coco, the boundary between Nicaragua and Honduras. Knowing nothing about Nicaragua or the Miskito Coast, I prevailed upon my uncle's kindness and spent a summer with his family in Puerto Cabezas, occasionally accompanying Moravian missionaries on visits to nearby Miskito villages.

On my return to the university I began to research the history of the coast and the Miskito Indians. I pieced together the general features of colonial history and of native life during the colonial centuries from historical reports and travelers' accounts and read a very useful monograph of Miskito customs that had been published some thirty years earlier.[2] However, no contemporary anthropological work had been done. Consequently, when in a few years it came time to decide upon a location for fieldwork and a subject for a dissertation, a return visit to the Miskito Coast was the logical and obvious choice. I decided to pursue a general village study that would afford me the chance to observe basic economic, social, political and ideological features of Miskito everyday life as it was in the mid-1960s. So it was that I found myself once more in Puerto Cabezas and, in a few weeks time, again with the assistance of Moravian missionaries, resident in the Miskito community o Asang, a settlement of about 600 persons located approximate

33

two hundred miles upriver on the Nicaraguan side of the Rio Coco, a few miles short of the rapids that severely reduce river travel. I lived in Asang about ten months (from 1964–1965), residing in the home of the Moravian lay pastor and his family (who are Miskito), learning to speak Miskito and involving myself as best I could in daily Miskito life. I describe life in Asang as I found it in the 1960s, and also recount the considerable influence of European contact in the colonial period and the turmoil brought about by recent political events in Nicaragua.

The Miskito are an example of what has been called a "colonial tribe," meaning an ethnic population whose sense of group identity and many customs resulted from contact with European or European-derived colonial powers.[3] In fact, it is likely that the names "Miskito" and "Mosquito Coast" are derived from seventeenth century Spanish, English, or French terms since the spellings used in the earliest European accounts of the coast (Mosqueto, Mosquito, Musketo, Mustique) compare closely with contemporary European terms for musket (mosquete, mousquet, musket). As we shall see, access to guns during the seventeenth and eighteenth centuries allowed the Miskito to become the most powerful population on the coast.

Prior to European contact the coast was occupied by numerous small groups of natives who hunted, fished, and cultivated small plots of land. In contrast with many other indigenous peoples, Western contact did not lead to the cultural disintegration of these native forebears of the Miskito. Neither did association with European colonial agents force the Miskito to become a rural peasantry living within a larger colonial polity, forced to pay taxes or rents or provide labor services. The Miskito have never paid taxes to a more powerful government and were never subject to forced labor, such as army drafts, though they have, at times, fought vigorously in pursuit of their own interests. In short, though the Miskito have been strongly influenced by Western or European contacts for approximately 300 years, to date they have maintained considerable social and cultural autonomy and political independence.

Can such autonomy continue? This question is the major issue currently facing the Miskito. It is particularly acute for Miskito living in eastern Nicaragua where pressures that could force them to lose valuable land and become more closely affected by laws and policies of the state of Nicaragua have become much more intense as a result of the Sandinista Revolution that began in 1979. Prior to that time, however, life in eastern Nicaragua and eastern Honduras (the entire region known as La Mosquitia) was only minimally affected by dictates of the governments of Nicaragua and Honduras.

This extensive eastern region has long been more closely affiliated with the Caribbean region as the western edge of the Caribbean sea. As such it has also been a frontier region, geographically part of the Central American mainland but historically facing to the east and the Caribbean world rather than to the rest of Central America lying to the west.[4]

The reasons for this situation are geographical and historical. The territory of Central America (Guatemala through Panama) is divided by a central chain of mountains that runs the length of the land, creating a western or Pacific zone, a central mountain zone, and an eastern or Caribbean (sometimes called Atlantic) zone. Since the valleys, plains, and foothills of the western zone are relatively dry and temperate in climate they were found suitable for settlement by Spanish conquistadors and colonists who subdued the indigenous population and developed several Hispanic colonies.[5] These colonies became the contemporary countries of Central America, whose populations speak Spanish and are predominantly Roman Catholic and whose capital cities and major population clusters are still located in the western zone.[6]

The eastern zone on the other side of the mountain chain, however, is a hotter and wetter tropical lowland of forests, swamps, and savannahs. Spanish conquistadors found nothing of interest here, and did not settle. Instead, they long regarded the eastern regions and its native peoples as a very "savage" and inhospitable "backwoods." Because the Spanish ignored this region and because this land was adjacent to Spanish settlements, the English, long colonial competitors of the Spanish Crown, eventually became interested in the east coast as a vantage point for watching and sometimes harassing their Hispanic rivals. Consequently, the English became the predominant colonial power there.[7]

The English presence was relatively low-key. Only a few settlements were established, and contacts with the local native population were basically friendly, cooperative, and mutually satisfactory. On the Miskito Coast the native peoples came to admire the English and made some attempt to imitate their customs and even learn some English. Consequently, though the native language remained the mother tongue, the predominant colonial language was English. Eventually various denominations of Protestantism, most notably (by far) the Moravian Church, became the accepted religions.

During the seventeenth, eighteenth, and nineteenth centuries, therefore, the cultural climate of the east coast of Nicaragua and Honduras was strongly differentiated from that of western Central America. In fact, adopting the attitude of their English associates, the native population of eastern Nicaragua-Honduras developed a strong aversion toward the Spanish-speaking peoples of western Central America. Many of them have maintained a strong dislike and distrust to this day.

ORIGINS OF THE MISKITO

During the latter decades of the seventeenth century the Miskito Coast was a quiet and secluded backwater region. Consequently, it became a zone of refuge for African and mulatto slaves and freed slaves, including survivors of a wrecked slaving vessel and freed slaves from a short-lived English colony on the Caribbean island of Providencia. Many of these new arrivals, presumably mainly men, settled in the vicinity of Cape Gracias a Dios, at the mouth of the Río Coco (known also as the Wangks or Segovia River), the current boundary between Nicaragua and Honduras. There they intermingled with local native women and established a small (perhaps 1,000) population of mixed African-Indian descent known in the colonial literature as the Miskito (Mosquito)-Zambos. This was the beginning of the ethnic group now known as the Miskito Indians, many of whom still consider the Río Coco to be the heartland of their territory.[8]

Because of its isolation and proximity to the Caribbean Sea, the Miskito Coast also became a favorite rest and rendezvous locale for French, English, and Dutch privateers and buccaneers, who could remain safely hidden in its numerous coves and inlets between raids on Caribbean shipping and on Hispanic settlements of the Caribbean region (the Spanish Main). During the late seventeenth and early eighteenth centuries the Miskito became willing allies of these pirates, who also enjoyed the amenities of Miskito village life. Miskito men accompanied buccaneers to sea, serving mainly as provisioners because they were excellent hunters and fishermen.[9]

They also received muskets and ammunition (and other types of European goods) from the buccaneers. Armed with these weapons, the Miskito began their own military expansion to north and south of Cape Gracias, along the Caribbean coast of Honduras and Nicaragua, absorbing some local natives (who had only traditional weapons for defense) and driving others away, farther into the interior, to seek sanctuary in the wilds of the central mountains. These interior people, whose numbers have gradually declined, are known to us now by the collective term, Sumu.[10]

The Miskito also found allies in English planters and traders who settled at river mouths along the coast (including surviving buccaneers who had opted to settle down to a safer, if duller, lifestyle). These settlers used the Miskito as trading "middlemen" vis-à-vis interior natives who hesitated to come to the coast themselves now that Europeans and militarily powerful Miskito were on the scene. In return for forest products acquired by the Miskito from "upriver" Sumu Indians, the English provided the Miskito with a range of European goods, some of which the Miskito returned to their interior trade partners. These goods further strengthened the identity and dominance of the Miskito.[11]

Their English contacts also enabled the Miskito to range even farther afield during the first half of the eighteenth century and to conduct damaging raids against other native populations in the mountains of central Honduras and Nicaragua, in the coastal areas of Costa Rica to the south, and, to the north, in eastern Guatemala and Yucatan. The goal of these raids was primarily to obtain native people as war-captives. Some of these captives (mainly the women) were kept by the Miskito themselves and adopted into their own families, helping greatly to increase the Miskito population. Other war-captives were sold to British settlers for use as laborers on English plantations on the island of Jamaica.[12]

These raids were greatly feared both by Spanish frontier colonists and Central American native peoples, and the Miskito received a long-standing reputation as fierce fighters. During this time the Miskito were frequently referred to, especially by Hispanic Central Americans, as Miskito-Zambos. The term "Zambo" emphasized the Indian-Black admixture of the population. This mixed ancestry was reputed, by Europeans, to explain some of the ferocity of Miskito raiders. The Miskito continued their depredations until about 1740, by which time labor requirements on Jamaica were adequately met by African slaves who were preferred as laborers by plantation owners. As this market for native laborers declined, Miskito raids ended, too.[13]

During the remainder of the eighteenth century and throughout the nineteenth century the Miskito population consolidated their hold over the coast. Their settlements extended up the Río Coco for several hundred miles and along the Caribbean coastline from Río Negro (Honduras) in the north to Pearl Lagoon (Nicaragua) in the south. The Miskito generally lived in proximity to rivers and European trading stations at river mouths and maintained regular interaction both with English-speaking traders and settlers and with interior natives.

The Miskito adjustment to coastal life was made possible only by continuing to serve, as in prior centuries, as middlemen between Europeans and interior tribes. Coastal territory provided excellent fishing conditions but was poor for agriculture, except for manioc, a tuber that can grow in the sandy coastal soils, and a few varieties of fruit trees. The coast proper also lacked forest resources needed for the local manufacture of numerous household items. In order to acquire the necessary range of foodstuffs and domestic products the Miskito tended agricultural plots located along river banks some distance upstream from the coast, periodically traveled south to coastal Costa Rica to harvest quantities of sea turtles from nesting sites on the beaches, traded European goods (axes, adzes, beads, mirrors) and coastal products (salt, turtle meat) with interior tribes in exchange for forest products (game, rough-hewn dugouts, gourds and calabashes, skins, net hammocks, sarsaparilla) and obtained European goods from coastal trading posts in exchange for local coastal resources (turtle shell, skins).[14]

By the late nineteenth century and during the twentieth century Christianization was begun under the guidance of German and, later, American missionaries of the Moravian Church, who operated small trading posts and eventually introduced small clinics where Western medical care could be obtained. The missionaries developed a written form of Miskito, translated hymns and the Bible, and introduced literacy and Western modes of schooling to train native lay pastors.[15]

During these years the Miskito Coast also attracted various Western business enterprises interested in the natural resources of the region. Commercial rubber tapping was profitable during the last half of the nineteenth century. Then lumber companies cut valuable mahogany and pine. Mining entrepreneurs sought precious metals in the interior mountains (as colonial Spaniards had done before them), and banana companies established commercial plantations on the lowlands. Banana companies also introduced, as laborers, a population of English-speaking "creole" persons from Jamaica and the Grand Cayman Islands, whose descendants still form an important component of the few port towns that were established on the Coast.[16]

These businesses, which replaced the small colonial trading enterprises of earlier centuries, now provided the Miskito with opportunities for wage labor. Miskito men worked as cutters for lumber companies, provided river transport for India rubber traders, worked at the mines, and grew cash crops—rice and beans and bananas—for sale to Europeans. However, these operations were highly speculative, meaning that the businesses remained viable only so long as an immediate profit could be made and were readily abandoned when the resources became depleted or when better investment opportunities beckoned elsewhere for Western owners and investors. Consequently, wage labor opportunities (and the coastal money economy) were of the "enclave" or "boom-and-bust" variety common to frontiers like the Miskito coast. When a foreign company was operating, jobs and money would be available for native laborers; but when a company stopped operation and left the region jobs and money would suddenly be gone. Because foreign companies came and went rather regularly, periods when jobs were available alternated frequently with periods when jobs were scarce or nonexistent.

The Miskito handled this situation well, however, by continuing to maintain their own traditional subsistence economy based on horticulture, hunting, and fishing. It was possible to do so because, in spite of centuries of involvement with foreigners, the Miskito had never lost access to the basic land and water resources that provisioned them. Foreign settlements were small and the number of resident Europeans and other non-Miskito limited. Foreign businesses did not obtain permanent land rights but were interested only in movable forms of natural resources such as wood products and metals. Consequently, traditional subsistence continued year in and year out regardless of the vagaries of Western enterprises. Women tended to most of the agricultural work. Men alternated between wage jobs, when they were available, and traditional hunting, fishing, and farming when wage labor was gone. Lack of money meant store-bought items would be in short supply at times, but basic survival was never threatened since the traditional economy continued to flourish.[17]

Flexibility under boom-and-bust economic conditions was also facilitated by matrilocal marital residence, meaning that married couples lived either under the same roof as the wife's parents or in a separate dwelling located in the same village as the wife's parents. This arrangement may have developed in earlier centuries as a response to contact situations in which former slaves and freedmen, settled buccaneers, and other foreign planters and traders took native women as wives. It may also have developed when Miskito men were frequently away from home as buccaneer assistants or as raiders themselves, activities that caused men to be absent for many months or even years at a time.[18]

When men were away matrilocal residence allowed domestic and village life to continue without disruption as related groups of kinswomen—mothers, daughters, sisters—remained together in residence in their home villages, maintaining traditional language and customs, socializing their children in Miskito ways, and maintaining agricultural production. As a result, no matter what the nature of their later wanderings (particularly with reference to boys), there was always a solid base of Miskitoness firmly established in a child's formative years of village life. The core of family women remaining at home also meant that there were functioning households for husband-fathers to return to when adventures farther afield were unavailable and that these same men could easily leave at a later time if new work opportunities became available on the coast.

A VILLAGE ON THE RIO COCO

When I lived in Asang in the mid-1960s the Miskito Coast was in an economic depression. Pine lumbering, the latest economic "boom," had declined and wage labor was hard to find.[19] One of the consequences of that decline was seen in the increasing isolation of communities as logging roads fell into disrepair and small-plane service ended. Travel was mainly by water, as it had been for prior centuries. Although I was able, on a few occasions, to fly by small plane in about thirty minutes from Puerto Cabezas on the coast to a landing strip a few miles short of Asang, about 200 miles upriver on the Río Coco, the more usual mode of travel took several days at best; a few hours by land transport over a lumber road from Puerto Cabezas to the Río Coco followed by river travel to Asang—a trip of several days by poled dugout canoe.[20] (Canoes were powered upstream not by paddling but by pushing against the river bottom with a long pole; the work is easier and faster if several men pole at once. Travelers, enduring sun or rain, sit cross-legged on a narrow plank or, more likely, on several sections of bamboo wedged between the narrow sides of the craft.) The canoe trip took a mere eight hours if the dugout were equipped with a small motor. Alternately a seat might be found on one of the commercial barges that traveled from village to village serving as floating commissaries.

The Río Coco is one of the longest rivers in Central America, flowing approximately 760 kilometers (470 miles) from interior sources near the Pacific coast to the Caribbean shore (Cape Gracias a Dios). Like many tropical rivers, its length is a function of numerous meanders. Traveling upriver from close to the coast, as I did, the river initially winds through flat, open savannah where fertile alluvial banks are lined with mangrove, bush, or bamboo groves. Sometimes a cleared area appeared where manioc, maize, rice, and beans were growing, or a small banana or plantain patch appeared. When a curve loomed ahead a village usually appeared, with houses strung along the edge of a high bank overlooking a gravel and sand beach where cattle and a few horses might be standing knee-deep in the water to escape swarms of mosquitos.

It was a peaceful scene, enlivened perhaps by a kingfisher flashing by with rasping calls of annoyance or a chain of brightly colored butterflies suddenly erupting from the bush along the river bank or by a glimpse of a woman fishing as she knelt quietly in the bottom of her dugout anchored at a sheltered spot. Other dugouts occasionally might drift past on their way downstream, men relaxed, freed from the chore of poling, but alert for submerged debris as the current swept them along. Such a canoe was held steady by a woman kneeling in the stern and trailing a paddle as rudder. Once I saw a bamboo raft float by carrying a family of Sumu Indians who were traveling down river from the isolated interior. They had built a fire on their raft for cooking and quickly hid their faces behind hands or hats or sleeves when they saw my camera.

As the river winds inland the land gradually rises and low mountains form a constant backdrop for the riverine panorama. Eventually, not too far beyond Asang, the character of the river abruptly changes. Instead of mud banks draped with greenery,

stretches of bush and gardens, beaches and a quiet river, the landscape alters to show huge black rocks jutting from the middle of
the river, which now roars and churns and foams. More rocks line
the banks, the river follows a torturous, twisting path, and swift
boiling rapids take control of the dugout, leaving bowmen and
motorman little to do except to try to protect the motor from the
stones and prevent a broadside crash against the rocks.

Very little traffic is found in these stretches of the river. Those
who attempt it generally do so during the dry season, January
through April, when there is virtually no rain, the river level drops,
and the rapids are more subdued. On the lower river, though, dry
season travel can be difficult if the shallower river uncovers extensive sections of gravel beach and loaded dugouts run a greater risk
of running aground. This situation alters in May, when rains begin
and the heavy downpours turn the river into a ranging torrent carrying huge trees and mobile dams of debris in its swirling path.
One blow from a hurtling log can easily capsize a dugout or raft.
But a flooding river has its advantages, for as it overflows its banks
low-lying gardens and small fields are covered with a muddy liq-
uid carpet that fertilizes and rejuvenates the soil with silt.

Like most Miskito river villages, Asang was situated high
above the flood line on top of a small (fifteen to twenty foot) bluff
with a mud and grass embankment which was climbed by a series
of twisting, slippery, narrow paths. It was one of about forty
Miskito settlements extending from Cape Gracias to Bocay, above
the rapids. The name Asang is a Sumu word meaning "hilly land
covered with forest." When I lived there it was a large community
with a population of 665. Some ninety inhabited dwelling units
had been built, standing in several parallel rows all facing the river,
in addition to a school, a small commissary, and two churches (the
larger and dominant one Moravian, the other, Church of God).

It was a picturesque community. Tangled growths of forest
and uncleared bush surrounded the village on three sides but grazing animals and periodic work parties kept grass low in the village.
Numerous citrus trees provided shade and fruit. A few coconut
palms added character along with a considerable variety of other
trees: cashew, rose-apple, papaya, mango, pejivalle palm, zapote,
soursap, calabash. Small herb gardens, fenced with rough wood or
bamboo against cows and pigs, were cultivated close to homes.
Garden flowers and flowering bushes, including gardenias and a
wonderfully scented night-blooming lily, were valued for orna-

ment. Slab benches were built along the edge of the bluff, affording a magnificent view of the country across the river. This was a popular spot where young people could "hang out" in the evening. Asang residents also had access to a dozen or more natural springs that flowed from the river bank and afforded clean fresh water, greatly preferable to using impure river or creek water (and one of the reasons Asang was a good choice for me).

A typical dwelling unit was composed of two buildings. One, the larger, approximately 18–19′ by 22–24′, was divided into sleeping compartments for the household, typically a couple with growing children and sometimes the husband's or wife's parents. Most of the time people sat or worked on a porch stretching the width of the house or in the cleaned yard in front. A smaller building (about 14 by 19′) served as kitchen and produce center and contained a clay cooking platform—a table-like structure standing on legs with raised sides and filled with white clay on which a fire could be built. Cooking refuse could be tossed out a nearby window where the family's pigs hurried to eat food scraps. (It was thanks to the pigs as well as to people's efforts that Asang was a very clean and pleasant village.) The kitchen was joined to the sleeping quarters by a plank and both structures stood about four feet above the ground on wooden pilings. Access to the house was by steps or a notched log. Dwelling units were constructed either of wood planks or of flattened bamboo, and most had thatched roofs, though a few well-to-do families had roofs of corrugated metal, which was prestigeful but very hot on sunny days.

The wooden, red-roofed Moravian Church dominated all, and could be seen from several miles downriver. The mission also included a wooden house and kitchen unit built for the use of the lay pastor and his family. The interior of this structure was built along European lines with several separate bedrooms surrounding a large central hall. The lay pastor and his wife and family of young children preferred to sleep together in the largest of the bedrooms, leaving three smaller ones unoccupied. One of these was used for storage, another as the lay pastor's office. The third became my home.

FAMILY AND KINSHIP IN A
MISKITO COMMUNITY

Asang was founded about 1910 by a family whose original home had been destroyed in a flood. The move was not without some danger, for the river below the high bank where Asang was to be built was believed to be the home of an evil spirit (apparently an area prone to whirlpools then), and it was necessary for a shaman to exorcise the malevolent being before the bush could be cleared and a few houses built.

The nucleus of the new village formed around five daughters and two sons of a prominent man. The families of these siblings constituted the major kinship groups of Asang when I lived there. Several of the sisters' spouses were non-Miskito, and illustrate well the mixing of Miskito women and non-Miskito men that has been a characteristic of the Miskito in general since their origins. One sister was married to an Englishman who originally came from Cornwall, England, and had operated a general store and owned some cattle before settling in Asang. After his death his widow married a Nicaraguan reportedly from Managua. Another sister married a Spanish-speaking Honduranean man, while the only child of a fourth sister married a merchant of Jewish background. Another foreigner who settled in Asang soon after its founding was an American (United States) Black originally from Ohio who was involved in mahogany lumbering and owned a chain of three commissaries along the river (one in Asang). This man had two Miskito wives, one of whom had several sisters who, along with their spouses (at least one of whom was a non-Miskito Honduranean), moved to Asang, too. Several Creole men eventually moved from the coast to the growing community, married Miskito women, and settled down. Most Asang residents were related either to the original five siblings or to the family of the American; members of these two family groups have intermarried over the years.

One of the social practices that most directly expressed the interrelatedness of individuals and families was the use of teknonymy, the practice of referring to an adult by the name of his or her eldest child or sometimes, spouse. Girls and women in particular used this type of reference, referring to another adult or directly addressing that person not by personal name but as "so-and-so's mother" or "so-and-so's father" or "so-and-so's spouse." For example, a woman might call out from her kitchen to her husband, "Alonso *popika*, dinner's ready"; Alonso being their eldest child and popika being an anglicized term for father. Men were more likely to use personal names, especially when dealing with other men, probably due to their experience in wage labor jobs where personal names were necessary for payroll and other work relationships.

In the formal kinship system in use in the mid-twentieth century, an individual would use the terms for brother and sister not only for all of his or her siblings but also for all first cousins. Separate terms were used for mother and father, but instead of lumping mother's and father's siblings into two categories (aunt and uncle) as English-speakers do, separate terms were also used for mother's sister, mother's brother, father's sister, and father's brother. This custom was fairly new. In the late nineteenth century terms for father and father's brother and father's sister had been basically the same (father was called *aisa* and both father's brother and father's sister were called *aisa diura,* meaning "father's sibling"). Similarly, terms for mother and mother's sister had been basically the same (mother was called *yapti* and mother's sister was called *yapti diura,* meaning "mother's sibling"). There was a separate term—*tahti*—for mother's brother. At that time brother-sister terms were extended only to certain first cousins—the children of father's brother and mother's sister (what anthropologists call "parallel cousins"). Other first cousins, the children of mother's brother and possibly father's sister (what anthropologists call "cross-cousins"), were given different terms and were considered as possible marriage partners.

In Asang the terms for brother and sister were used in a different way than English-speakers do. Although two terms are used, one—*moini*—means "person of same sex same generation as the speaker" and the other—*lakra*—means "person of opposite sex same generation as the speaker." Thus, a boy or man calls another boy or man *moini* and a girl or woman calls another girl or woman moini, but boy and girl or man and woman address each other as lakra. These terms were also extended to include the children of any persons whom an individual's parents called brother and sister, which included the children of all persons whom *their* parents had called brother and sister. As a result, brother and sister actually referred to many persons whose specific kin ties to an individual might not be well known, especially since kinship reckoning for an individual generally stopped at about the great-grandparent generation. Stated more accurately, the names of the dead were not mentioned, keeping specific kin-reckonings quite abbreviated.

Use of brother or of sister in effect became a respectful way of addressing even strangers, and could be seen to unite all Miskito into a network of mutual "brotherhood" and "sisterhood." This practice was also compatible with the traditional Moravian practice of addressing other church members as brothers and sisters. For Moravian Miskito, the majority today, use of brother and sister thus connotes a general social and ideological communality with all Miskito.

Matrilocal residence, in which an Asang woman married a non-Asang man who came to live in his wife's community, probably in the same household as her parents, had been followed by many Asang families, particularly in older generation marriages. But there was a definite trend toward village endogamy among the younger generation, who preferred to find a spouse within Asang. These marriages also showed a distinct preference for virilocal or neolocal residence within the village. Residence for newlyweds was tending to be with the husband's family with the expectation that they would eventually build homes of their own near the husband's parents' home or at the back of the village where more land could be cleared. To help co-resident families keep the peace, mother-in-law and son-in-law as well as father-in-law and daughter-in-law avoidance was practiced (meaning that these persons officially did not speak to each other) after the birth of a child.

People were somewhat defensive about village endogamy, saying that by seeking a mate from within Asang a person at least knew the type of individual he or she would be marrying and could expect a more stable marriage. Asang residents, in fact, were quite proud of their orderly community. Outsiders as spouses were often perceived as potential troublemakers, perhaps prone to drinking or generally unfriendly. Some of this attitude reflected the reality that alcoholism, especially among teenagers, was a major problem in many Miskito villages but not in Asang, where the strict practices of Moravianism were stringently enforced by church and village elders. Adult villagers simply did not tolerate unruly or drunken behavior, and I saw virtually none. Asang was renowned along the river for this sobriety, and other villagers often had mixed feelings about Asang's insistence on strict and righteous behavior.

Until the early twentieth century marriage between cross-cousins was the rule, meaning an individual married a father's sister's child or a mother's brother's child. The children of two brothers or of two sisters were definitely not to marry, but the children of brothers and sisters were encouraged to do so. (These persons would not have been living in the same village if matrilocal residence were followed, as it generally was then). The prohibition of marriage between offspring of two brothers or two sisters was still followed in Asang when I lived there. People were also troubled if the couple who wished to marry stood as "brother" and "sister" to each other, as was increasingly the case as village endogamy continued. Preference for the security of a spouse from within Asang thus could clash with ideas about proper social or kinship distance between prospective spouses and/or their families.

Wage labor opportunities plus missionary pressures have also increased the age at marriage. Girls used to be betrothed by their parents while still children, perhaps eight or nine years old, and married shortly after reaching puberty. In Asang, however, men married at about 20 to 26 years of age and women at about 16 to 22, when they felt they could adequately support a family. Having children is important to Miskito families and a girl was thought to have reached adulthood when she bore a child, regardless of marital status. In fact, since divorce was frowned upon by the mission churches, couples frequently delayed a church wedding until their family was well established and the compatability of the parents beyond doubt.

Secular marriages were more common among young people, however, who could be married by the village headman, the official representative of the village to the Nicaraguan government. (The headman of Asang was empowered both to conduct civil marriages and to record births and deaths.) Prior to missionary influence polygyny was possible, though not so very common. Well-to-do and influential men were most likely to have two or (rarely) more wives. In Asang, although the days of polygyny were remembered, all families were monogamous. Families in Asang were large, not only because women bore many children but also because in half the Asang households two or more families lived together. Eighty percent of the women of child-bearing age had borne from seven to twelve children apiece, with the number of living children averaging about eight. Sixty percent of these women had lost children under the age of six either from disease or as still-births probably caused by the hard physical labor involved in women's household and field work.

Respect should be shown between all relatives and was expressed through food sharing. Proper Miskito hospitality required that food be offered to anyone, relative or stranger, who was in the vicinity when food was being prepared or eaten. Food sharing thus served as an integrating mechanism for village society. There was a constant exchange of small amounts of food between relatives and neighbors every day. A cup of coffee and an extra flour tortilla or some *wabul* (a staple beverage made of mashed boiled bananas or plantains mixed with water) might be sent to the house next door anytime. Portions of the catch were also distributed after a successful hunting or fishing expedition or when a cow or pig was slaughtered. The role of women as guardians of the social core was given particular expression and support by food sharing. Although it was the man who was theoretically responsible for providing food for the household, it was the woman who was responsible for distributing food among relatives. Thus it was usually to other women that food was sent, and when food was sent directly to men it was likely that they would be related to the giver on the maternal side.

VILLAGE ECONOMIC LIFE

Within the operation of the household and related activities there was a general division of labor between men and women. Men were expected to chop wood, clear fields, and build houses but not to carry water, wash clothes, or cook. These were women's duties. Women, however, were fully capable of almost every type of task either at home or in the field. A husband's periodic trips to other villages, his absences while working downriver, or desertion by her husband forced many women to learn to take care of themselves and their families almost singlehandedly.

Men as a group were casual, laughing, and independent. They did not complain much about daily matters. They joked readily. Women, on the other hand, usually had something to complain about—health, overwork, general poverty. Women didn't joke as much, were more serious, and gave the impression of hard and steady work. Men had definite periods of free time, too, after they returned from the day's work in the fields and they enjoyed longer respites from their work by occasional visits to other villages. Women's work, in contrast, seemed endless, and they rarely had a chance to enjoy a change.

Much of women's work involved agriculture. Agriculture was focused on subsistence crops (sweet manioc and other tubers, plantains, and bananas with maize, cacao, pineapple, sugarcane and tree fruits cultivated on a smaller scale) and on potential cash crops (rice, beans, certain varieties of bananas). Bananas had been cultivated widely when the commercial banana business was booming and dry rice and apparently also beans began to be grown to feed foreign lumber workers. By the mid-1960s production of rice and beans had added a major component to the agricultural year and had become food staples for the Miskito, especialy since the economic depression had effectively removed the foreign customers for these cash crops. Women, who worked in the fields eleven months out of twelve, handled most of the daily agricultural chores, including the tedious job of weeding rice, while men's agricultural labor centered more on briefer periods of clearing and, together with women, planting and harvesting rice and beans.

Agriculture in Asang was conducted by slash-and-burn techniques in which fields were cleared by machete, allowed to dry, and sometimes fired. Details of crop rotation and field fallowing were determined by type of crop and field preparation. Annual crops of rice, manioc and maize were planted in fields that had been burned. Perennial crops of bananas and plantains were planted in unburned fields. Beans, a major annual crop, were also planted in unburned fields, sometimes alone or sometimes among banana and plantain plants. Rice, bean, and maize fields were generally planted for one year and then allowed to lie fallow for one or two years. Manioc fields were used for several years before allowing a year's fallow period.

Land by itself had no monetary value—to buy or sell land was inconceivable. It was free for the taking. Once cleared, however, a plot of land belonged to the person who had cleared it, who alone directed its use. Sometimes, however, people tried to "steal" another's land by planting perennial plants, a procedure which was a frequent cause for quarrels.

All agricultural work was done by hand with only digging sticks and machetes as tools. Each nuclear family was basically responsible for its own agricultural plots, though there was considerable cooperation between households of relatives and neighbors during crucial periods of field burning, planting, and harvesting.

Cultivated foods formed the basis of daily meals. Generally two main meals were eaten, one in the early morning shortly after dawn and the other in the late afternoon. A typical meal included rice and beans, boiled green bananas or baked plantains, boiled manioc, perhaps a small fish, coffee or wabul. Wabul provided a warm and satisfying drink, and no Miskito meal was complete without it. Maize, the Mesoamerican staple, was mainly used in beverages and played only a small, though constant, role in Miskito diets. A piece of meat or fish or perhaps a flour tortilla was a treat, and not available every day.

Domestic animals—horses, cattle, pigs, chickens, turkeys, and an occasional muscovy duck—were raised by the villagers, but with little care and in a rather casual manner. Sale of pork or beef or of a fowl brought in a bit of cash. Cattle were kept mainly as an emergency source of money, and because they represent wealth, cattle were also prestige items. An average family had one or two head. Most cattle roamed the bush and often died of old age. Pigs provided more meat and were slaughtered on special occasions, especially to reward people who had helped with cooperative agricultural activities or at Christmas and New Year celebrations.

Agriculture provided most food, but many men still enjoyed hunting and fishing although game, once abundant, had decreased as human population grew and hunting and fishing had become largely recreational activities. Wild game was still considered the best form of meat, however, much superior to that of domestic animals. A wide range of honeys, fruits, and seeds were gathered casually in the bush as people came and went about their tasks, and were eaten as between-meal snacks. Some households kept hives of stingless bees in large bamboo joints suspended from the house porch roof, and enjoyed the honey, which they prepared as a beverage.

A number of forest products were also still used around the house. For example, annatto provided food coloring and was applied to the face for protection against the sun. Hair oil was made from oil palm seeds. The juice of a variety of sour orange was used to scrub floors and tables and was applied as a bleach to bark cloth as the bark was beaten over a log bench with a grooved wooden mallet. Bark cloth was made from the inner bark of a tree closely related to the rubber tree. It was used for bedding and, before the turn of the century, as clothing particularly for women, who wore a bark cloth wrap from waist to knees. (Under missionary influence cotton dresses replaced the bark cloth wrap.) Gourds and calabashes were used as water carriers. Thin strips of tree bark fiber were invaluable for carrying lines and for tying things together. Large leaves were used for wrapping food packages and made impromptu umbrellas in a sudden downpour. Silk-grass fibers could be rolled into an extremely durable thread and a pierced thorn made a serviceable needle if such sewing supplies were not available at the commissary. All manner of household utensils and furniture were made of wood, and torches of pine provided the only light on dark nights for most families. (Kerosene lanterns were the other lighting option, but were used mainly for community and church events.) Baskets of various sizes were made of vines and twisted fibers.

Wage labor opportunities were limited when I lived in Asang. Work in gold mines in the interior offered the best possibility, but with a surplus of labor available due to the decline of other wage-paying jobs there were many men who simply stayed in the village and did agricultural work. For the same reason cash was scarce. (I found it almost impossible to get change for large bills.) Store purchases either at the two small shops in Asang or in other villages were sharply curtailed. Many people felt frustrated and personally deprived by the decline in the cash economy. They complained frequently of hard times and of the absence of cash and even of food. Although there was plenty to eat, the basis of the diet was the cash crops—rice and beans—which people would much rather have sold in order to be able to buy salt, sugar, lard, flour, and various manufactured household and personal items (soap, cigarettes, cloth, kerosene, tobacco). To have to eat the cash crops because there were no foreigners to buy them epitomized both the economic depression affecting the cash economy and the personal disquietude of the jobless populace.

POLITICAL INTEGRATION

The people of Asang directed their personal lives and community affairs according to traditional Miskito custom, mission church regulations (primarily Moravian), and statutes of the Republic of Nicaragua. Traditional guidelines for behavior were most important, and were enforced mainly by gossip—highly effective, though productive of a lot of tension, in a rather small face-to-face community. Most traditional behavior involved appropriate fulfillment of kinship responsibilities, and most gossip dealt with alleged infringements of these responsibilities. Accusations of theft of small property were frequent. Snatching chickens at night as they roosted beneath houses in order to sell them outside the village was a frequent charge directed at young men, while children were said (perhaps with some truth) to be stealing eggs to sell to me for meals. Property inheritance at death was another potentially delicate matter that was of relatively recent significance since before the introduction of missions all personal property, including livestock, fruit trees, plantation crops, and personal possessions, were destroyed at the death of the owner or buried with the deceased.

If a problem required additional arbitration, most villagers preferred to consult the Moravian lay pastor (a Miskito man, though not originally from Asang) for advice. The community influence of the lay pastor varied greatly from community to community depending on the strength of individual missions and the personalities and personal abilities of individual lay pastors. In Asang the lay pastor was respected and his advice both sought and heeded. The lay pastor frequently utilized the church Helpers—a group of respected church members acting as community elders—as a community forum for hearing and settling disputes, whether they related to secular or church-related matters.

The importance of the role of the Moravian church as focal point for community affairs in Miskito communities in general can hardly be overstated. Prior to the introduction of the missions in the late nineteenth century Miskito settlements were very fluid but tended to form around foreign trading stations at river mouths. Missions provided a comparable focal point, especially when the missionary operated a small commissary, too. In addition, the Moravian missionaries themselves were very community-oriented by virtue of the history of their church, a self-sufficient, separatist, and utopian-oriented communal organization that developed in Europe in the eighteenth century with roots in the fifteenth century Czech Reformation.

On the Miskito Coast, the Moravian congregation, with its assembly of Helpers, served as focal point for community stability.

The church building itself, both as material symbol and as meeting place for community activities, became the social core of many Miskito villages. Certainly in Asang, which had become Moravian shortly after its founding only a few generations earlier, to be a good Miskito person and to be a good community member coincided closely, for most people, with being a good member of the Moravian church. The church, in turn, emphasized traditional Miskito respect for kinsmen along with community responsibility and sober living. (A parallel sense of personal worth combined with community and church membership was expressed by the few families forming the small Church of God congregation, too).

Historically the influence of the Republic of Nicaragua had been negligible on the Miskito Coast and was still very limited in the mid-1960s. Most Miskito preferred to avoid representatives of the central government, and government officials detested assignment to stations on the Miskito Coast. A few police stations were kept along the river and Miskito headmen, answerable to the police commandante, kept census records and performed civil marriages. Public schools, taught in Spanish, were staffed by Spanish-speaking Nicaraguans in most villages, but attendance was poor and such schooling was rather ineffectual overall due largely to teachers' lack of understanding of Miskito culture and to the continued primacy of Miskito as mother tongue. Asang's school had classes one through six with attendance falling rapidly after grade two. School-learned information seemed very little utilized outside the classroom.

Yet Miskito parents had a high regard for education and wanted their children to become literate, but in English and Miskito rather than in Spanish. Before government schools had been established (in 1952), formal education had been handled by the Moravian church with lay pastors (trained by missionaries) as teachers. Reading and writing of Miskito was taught so that the Bible and hymns (translated into Miskito) could be read. Villagers greatly preferred this system and wished they could return to it. Generally children and adolescents were the most literate members of the village. Most adult women had forgotten how to read and write and men's knowledge, though better, varied in functionality largely because there was not much call for literacy skills in general. Most men spoke Spanish as well as Miskito and some also spoke English; women usually spoke Miskito alone.

THE FATE OF ASANG
AND THE FUTURE

On January 15, 1982, in the middle of the night, Asang was burnt to the ground. For several weeks previous people had been killed, personal belongings confiscated, food supplies destroyed, livestock slaughtered, and the population generally terrorized by Hispanic militia. The Nicaraguan Sandinista Revolution, begun in 1979 with the ouster of the last dictator of the ruling Somoza family, had reached the village. The destruction of Asang, along with the other Río Coco Miskito villages, by Sandinista soldiers was intended to create a "sanitized" zone, totally devoid of life and resources, along the river so as to prevent opposition guerrilla forces from establishing any footholds there. In the confusion of that dreadful night families were separated and children lost as some of the residents of Asang fled across the river to Honduras, ultimately to find safety in refugee communities operated under the aegis of the United Nations High Commissioner for Refugees, while others were marched across country by Sandinistas to refugee communities in Nicaragua. They joined the tens of thousands of Miskito dislocated by the bitter fighting of a revolutionary war.[21]

The Sandinista revolution, which opposed the longstanding and repressive national government of the United States-backed Somoza dynasty, embroiled the Miskito Coast in harsh and predominantly military activity for several years (especially 1981–1984) as revolutionary leaders sought to strengthen government influence in the extensive Atlantic Coast hinterland that had remained outside the national life of Nicaragua for so long. The Miskito resented this intrusion,[22] and became actively involved (with considerable United States funding and logistical support) in opposing the revolutionary forces.[23] As the Miskito and other coastal populations became increasingly politicized and as life on the Coast became thoroughly disrupted and traumatized by the violence of war,[24] the issues they pursued came to include not only counterrevolutionary goals per se but also growing demands for government recognition of their distinctive ethnic identity and for the right of coastal peoples to administer their territory and its resources themselves.

Peace was largely restored by the late 1980s, and the demands for regional autonomy and political self-government accorded a hearing by the new Nicaraguan government. A difficult process of forging a political arrangement by which Miskito self-government and Nicaraguan sovereignty might be made compatible has now begun.[25] The villages along the Río Coco are gradually coming back to life, too. The people of Asang have returned to begin the rebuilding of their community. Like many other returning refugees, they have started the slow and difficult process of shaping their lives for an uncertain future.

NOTES

1. Philippe Bourgois, "The Miskitu of Nicaragua," *Anthropology Today*, 2 (1986): 4; Mary W. Helms, "The Society and Its Environment," in James D. Rudolph, ed., *Honduras: A Country Study* (Washington, D.C.: United States Government, 1984), p. 95.

2. Eduard Conzemius, *Ethnographical Survey of the Miskito and Sumu Indians of Honduras and Nicaragua*, Smithsonian Institution, Bureau of American Ethnology, Bulletin 106. (Washington, D.C.: United States Government, 1932), pp. 14–16.

3. Mary W. Helms, "The Cultural Ecology of a Colonial Tribe," *Ethnology*, 8 (1969): 76.

4. John P. Augelli, "The Rimland-Mainland Concept of Culture Areas in Middle America," *Annals of the Association of American Geographers*, 52 (1962): 119–129.

5. Murdo J. MacLeod, *Spanish Central America: A Socioeconomic History*, 1520–1720 (Berkeley, Calif.: University of California, 1973), Part 1.

6. Robert C. West and John P. Augelli, *Middle America, Its Lands and Peoples* (Englewood Cliffs, N.J.: Prentice Hall, 1966), chapters 9, 13, 14; Mary W. Helms, *Middle America: A Culture History of Heartland and Frontiers* (Washington, D.C.: University Press of America, 1982), chapter 9.

7. Helms, *Middle America*, chapter 13; Troy S. Floyd, *The Anglo-Spanish Struggle for Mosquitia* (Albuquerque, N.M.: University of New Mexico, 1967).

8. Mary W. Helms, "Coastal Adaptations as Contact Phenomena among the Miskito and Cuna Indians of Lower Central America,"

in Barbara Stark and Barbara Voorhies, *Pre-historic Coastal Adaptations* (New York: Academic, 1978), pp. 128, 136; Mary W. Helms, *Asang: Adaptations to Culture Contact in a Miskito Community* (Gainesville, Fla.: University of Florida, 1971), pp. 15–18; Carlos M. Vilas, *State, Class, and Ethnicity in Nicaragua* (Boulder, Colo.: Lynne Rienner, 1989), p. 17.

9. Helms, "Coastal Adaptations," p. 131; Floyd, *Anglo-Spanish Struggle*, chapter 3.

10. Mary W. Helms, "Negro or Indian? The Changing Identity of a Frontier Population," in Ann M. Pescatello, ed., *Old Roots in New Lands: Historical and Anthropological Perspectives on Black Experiences in the Americas* (Westport, Conn.: Greenwood Press, 1977), pp. 159–160. Conzemus, pp. 14–16.

11. Helms, "Negro or Indian?"

12. Mary W. Helms, "Miskito Slaving and Culture Contact: Ethnicity and Opportunity in an Expanding Population," *Journal of Anthropological Research*, 39 (1983).

13. Helms, "Negro or Indian?"

14. Helms, "Coastal Adaptations"

15. Helms, *Asang*, p. 185–86; Helms, "Coastal Adaptations," pp. 134–36; Vilas, *State, Class, Ethnicity*, p. 33–36.

16. Helms, *Asang*, pp. 27–29; Vilas *State, Class, Ethnicity*, pp. 44–51.

17. Helms, *Asang*, pp. 110–115; Helms, "Coastal Adaptations," pp. 142–45.

18. Mary W. Helms, "Matrilocality, Social Solidarity, and Culture Contact: Three Case Histories," *Southwestern Journal of Anthropology*, 26 (1970).

19. Vilas, *State, Class, Ethnicity*, chapter 3.

20. All information regarding life in Asang is derived from Helms, *Asang*, which should be consulted for full particulars.

21. Ibid., p. 5.

22. Philip A. Dennis, "The Costenos and the Revolution in Nicaragua," *Journal of Interamerican Studies and World Affairs*, 23 (1981), pp. 288–89; Vilas, State, Class, Ethnicity, chapter 4.

23. Bourgois, "Miskitu"; Vilas, *State, Class, Ethnicity*, chapter 5.

24. Vilas, *State, Class, Ethnicity*, pp. 165, 181–82.

25. Ibid., pp. 170–84.

SUGGESTED READINGS

Bell, C. Napier, *Tangweera: Life and Adventures among Gentle Savages* (Austin, Tex.: University of Texas, 1989, first published 1899). Remembrances by an Englishman of his boyhood on the Miskito Coast in the mid-nineteenth century.

Conzemius, Eduard, *Ethnographical Survey of the Miskito and Sumu Indians of Honduras and Nicaragua,* Smithsonian Institution, Bureau of American Ethnology, Bulletin 106. (Washington, D.C.: United States Government, 1932). A compendium of Miskito cultural practices in the early twentieth century.

Helms, Mary W., *Asang: Adaptations to Culture Contact in a Miskito Community* (Gainesville: University of Florida, 1971). History and lifestyle in a riverine Miskito community in the mid-1960s.

Nietschmann, Bernard, *Between Land and Water: The Subsistence Ecology of the Miskito Indians, Eastern Nicaragua* (New York: Seminar, 1973). Utilization of material resources in a coastal community in the late 1960s.

Vilas, Carlos M., *State, Class, and Ethnicity in Nicaragua* (Boulder, Colo.: Lynne Rienner, 1989). Historical background and the impact of the Sandinista Revolution on the east coast of Nicaragua.

ABKHAZIANS: GROWING IN AGE AND WISDOM

Paula Garb

Woe and ruin to a people whose young
do not honor the old.

(Abkhazian proverb)

INTRODUCTION

The people whose ancient and modern story I tell in this chapter are, as I write in May 1993, dying in battle, fighting off cold, hunger and fear in territory occupied by the forces of their Georgian foes. Refugees from the warfare who are living in the unoccupied parts of Abkhazia and Russia are sharing cramped quarters and anxieties over relatives and friends with whom they have lost contact. So it is highly unlikely that any of these people are leading lives that resemble pieces of the culture I am about to describe.

When I originally contemplated introducing to anthropology students this tiny corner of the world where I did my first field work, I was reluctant to dwell on peacetime life knowing that such a devastating war was raging. Friends and colleagues developed over twelve years of frequent visits have seen their lives shattered, loved ones tortured and killed, and all primary sources of Abkhazian culture and history destroyed by fire and pillage. Clearly, physical and cultural genocide is under way, while only a handful of linguists, anthropologists, and historians watch helplessly in horror.

As I listened to tapes of my conversations in Abkhazia, dating back to my most recent visit there in the summer of 1991, my protest grew against depicting a life that may never more exist. I wept at hearing the birds chirping in the background as 91-year-old Grisha Aiba, sitting in his peaceful rural homestead, recounted his life's experience solving community disputes. I agonized as I listened to the voice of my guide, Yermolai, and remembered the shy, awkward manner of this fifty-year-old man, his refusal to take pay for his work on grounds that it was his duty as an Abkhazian

61

to open up to me all avenues to information about his people. I couldn't bear to visualize the story I had been told about him being shot in the foot by occupying forces as he wept in front of the fire that demolished the Abkhazian history archive in October of 1992.

It was precisely this surge of passion that ultimately showed me the way to this chapter. I realized it was imperative to explain the powerful aspects of this culture at peace that had so thoroughly impacted my life, that had lifted this floodgate of emotions. The wisdom of the culture that I was reminiscing about through my tapes and notes persuaded me that, indeed, this story did have to be about Abkhazia in a more normal time.

People in every culture have children, parents, lovers; they experience everyday sorrows and joys. This is what they all lose in time of war, and we accept it as a given that this is a tragedy. However, when we read about foreign peoples at war, we usually know few specifics about their peacetime lives. Perhaps this ensures a certain level of indifference. In the case of Abkhazia, a society on the verge of extinction, I thought it all the more necessary to know about what world culture stands to lose if genocide prevails.

THE LAND

Abkhazia covers 3,300 square miles between the eastern shores of the Black Sea and the crestline of the main Caucasus range; from the rivers Psou (in the north) and Inguri (in the south). To the north Abkhazia is bordered by Russia, and to the south by the Georgian provinces of Svanetia and Mingrelia. Around seventy-four percent of the territory is mountains or mountain approaches. The coastal valleys are humid, subtropical. At higher altitudes the weather ranges from moderately cold to such freezing temperatures that the snow never melts. The relatively small distance between seashore and mountains lends Abkhazia a striking contrasting landscape.

The area is best known by non-Abkhazians for its prime resorts for vacationers from all over the former Soviet Union; and for its major cash crops of tea, tobacco, and citrus fruits. There are two cities: the capital Sukhum,[1] with a population of 100,000, and Tkvarchel, an industrial center. There are three urban resorts— Gagra, Gudauta, and Ochamchira; two rural spas—Pitsunda and Novy Afon; and 575 villages.

Abkhazians describe their country as harsh but beautiful. A legend they often tell is about how God was distributing land to all the peoples of the earth while the Abkhazians were entertaining guests. Since it would have been impolite for the hosts to leave before their guests, they arrived late. All that God had left for the Abkhazians were some stones out of which he created a land that was hard to cultivate but paradise-like in its beauty.

THE PEOPLE

The Abkhazian language belongs to the northwest Caucasian family spoken by only a few other peoples in the world—the Abazins (or Abaza), Adyghey, Kabardians, and Circassians, all of whom live in the North Caucasus. Historically these peoples and other related groups in the North Caucasus maintained close ties until they were divided by modern transportation lines that made direct travel to one another impossible. Until this century they could ride their horses to each other through the mountains. However, plane and train routes developed under the Soviet government were designed so that each of these peoples had to first travel all the way to Moscow, then transfer to get back to the other parts of the Caucasus.

The closest neighbors of the Abkhazians (they were not related linguistically or ethnically) were the Mingrelians, Svans and Georgians.[2] After Abkhazia was incorporated into Russia in 1810 large numbers of migrants came from other parts of the empire—primarily Russians, Armenians, and Jews. These settlers were also joined by Greeks fleeing religious persecution in the Ottoman Empire and Iran.

HISTORY

Abkhazians hold on to their history for dear life, dreading the same fate as a now extinct related group, the Ubykhs who were their northern neighbors around Sochi (now in Russia). All Abkhazian children for millennia have been taught their family's history at least seven generations back, as well as the legends and history

depicting Abkhazian mores, heroes and villains, friends and enemies. The war today is essentially over that history, contested by
Georgians who perceive Abkhazians as guests on their land.

According to Abkhazian legends the people originated in pre-
historic times on the territory they now occupy. The people have
no collective memory of having ever lived on another territory.
Archeological evidence of proto-Abkhazian tribes in the Western
Caucasus dates back to 4,000–3,000 B.C.[3]

The Abkhazian people were first mentioned by Pliny Major in
the first century A.D. The territory that Pliny Major assigned to the
early Abkhazians was in the same area as contemporary Abkhazia.
This had been the site of several Greek colonies from the sixth and
fifth centuries B.C.[4]

The Abkhazian principalities were subsequently controlled by
Rome, the Laz Kingdom, and then Byzantium. Under Byzantine's
Justinian I (543–6) the Abkhazians adopted Christianity (Russia
adopted Christianity in the late 900s). Byzantium lost its power
over the area in the late eighth century. At that time, Leon II, poten-
tate of the Abkhazians, seized the land, thus establishing the
Kingdom of Abkhazia (the whole of today's Western Georgia).
This kingdom lasted for 200 years during which time the ancient
Abkhazian tribes consolidated into one ethnic entity.

In the late tenth century Abkhazia lost its independence, and
became part of the united Georgian state. After central power in
Georgia collapsed in 1245, with the appearance of the Mongols, the
whole region became a conglomeration of princedoms. From the
early sixteenth century Abkhazia is mentioned as an independent
entity. It is also during this century that the Ottoman Turks gained
considerable influence in Abkhazia and converted part of the population to Islam.

When Czarist Russia conquered Ottoman Transcaucasia in the
first half of the nineteenth century, Abkhazian and other northwest Caucasian peoples fought for their independence in fierce
and unequal battles. Their resistance was finally put down in the
1870s, when the North Caucasus came under imperial Russian
domination.

This prompted the tragic exodus to Turkey of around half the
Abkhazian population (100,000),[5] which left whole villages and
vast areas of Abkhazia vacant. The mass exodus was of enormous
consequence to the Abkhazian and other recalcitrant mountain
peoples forced out of their ancient homelands, either by assaulting
Russian troops or by their Turkish rulers. The vacated territories

(primarily the middle part of Abkhazia around Sukhum) were settled by Russians, Georgians, Armenians and other ethnic groups. Consequently, the Abkhazians were reduced to a small majority on their own territory, making them culturally and politically vulnerable.

The Russian Revolution brought the Abkhazians a degree of political autonomy and cultural resurrection. Within the Soviet state Abkhazians originally governed their own republic (from March of 1921). This was short-lived, however. In 1931, Stalin and Beria (both from Georgia), changed the status, designating Abkhazia a republic within Georgia.

For all practical purposes Abkhazian affairs were administered by Georgia until the collapse of the USSR. In those few decades, primarily due to the Stalin-era mass deportations, executions and major population-transfer programs for the settlement of Georgians, the Abkhazians dwindled to 17.1 percent[6] of the population on their own ancestral territory.

The Khrushchev period brought the Abkhazians relief from the Stalinist terror, and gave them the appearance of control over their government. The most significant decisions, however, were still made in Tbilisi (capital of the Georgian republic) and Moscow (building permits, land rights, language policies), and most of the economic resources (revenue from the port, resorts, cash crops) were lost to Tbilisi and Moscow.

Nevertheless the 1960s and 1970s brought new opportunities for reviving Abkhazian culture—schools that offered instruction in the native language, the cultivation of dance, drama and music, limited publishing rights, the promotion of the local Institute of Abkhazian History, Language and Culture.

This was the time when I began working in Abkhazia and found a relatively peaceful multiethnic society. I discovered a thriving ethnic pride that people openly exhibited. Relations between ethnic groups, including Georgians, appeared to be quite healthy.

The only people who expressed hostility were Georgians from outside the Abkhazian autonomous republic, and a few local Georgians who clearly thought of Abkhazians as ungrateful guests occupying their land. These Georgians did not hesitate to express to me their indignation. They maintained that there was no such ethnic group as Abkhazians. The argument offered was that Abkhazians were actually Georgians who had been assimilated by some "Abkhazian-speaking mountain tribe" arriving there in the seventeenth century from an unspecified place, and were essentially "pretending" to be Abkhazians for the "benefits" they reaped in the Soviet system for being a demographically small nationality—special affirmative action rights to higher education, and during the war exemption from military service (which was a myth). These Georgians also complained of reverse discrimination by the local Abkhazian leadership.

Despite these animosities, there was no bloodshed between the two groups. Furthermore Abkhazian-Georgian marriages were not uncommon.

The policies of political openness and decentralization efforts that characterized the Gorbachev years unleashed the latent forces of discontent among all the country's ethnic groups. This new energy was first focused on the restoration of neglected historical sites and an honest examination of the black holes in history left by the legacy of the Stalin period. Abkhazia was no exception.

As the Soviet Union collapsed this movement among the various ethnic groups grew into a struggle for resources and power, eventually leading to warfare in some former republics. When Georgia separated itself from the Soviet Union in 1992, its leaders tried to incorporate the Abkhazian Autonomous Republic into an effectively unitary Georgian state, controlled from Tbilisi. All the minorities in Abkhazia, including the Abkhazians, who together constitute a narrow majority, resisted. In response to the Georgians' measures to "Georganize" Abkhazia (all too reminiscent of the Stalinist period when the Abkhazian language and cultural institutions were banned) Abkhazia declared its sovereignty, and attempted repeatedly to negotiate a federal relationship with Georgia.

On August 14, 1992, the Georgian government, led by Eduard Shevardnadze, moved troops into Abkhazia. Georgian forces terrorized Abkhazian civilians as a group. Additionally, Georgians either pillaged or destroyed every Abkhazian cultural institution in the Abkhazian capital of Sukhum, including its history archives and museum. The primary sources of Abkhazian history and culture no longer exist.

If there are any remnants of Abkhazian culture after the war, it will require miraculous healing measures for Abkhazians and Georgians to live once again as peaceful neighbors.

A careful examination of Abkhazia in peacetime may point to the society's internal healing forces. I personally count on the wisdom of the elders in a country most famous for its centenarians.

Let's more closely examine this phenomenon of active old age in Abkhazia where the elderly are the primary decision makers and resolvers of conflict in their families and communities.

THEORIES ABOUT THE LONG-LIVED PEOPLE OF THE CAUCASUS

If we are to believe the journalists of the 1970s and 1980s who brought this phenomenon to the world's attention, centenarians (100 years or older) are really old people who till the land from sunrise to sundown, dance and sing in professional folk ensembles, and look no older than sixty. I found this image was not a reality. Centenarians look like very old people; some of them have no teeth, are shriveled with wrinkles, and move about slowly like all very old people. Nevertheless, they work in the fields and around the house, even if at a slow pace, and they are mentally alert. (Later I will discuss how scholars verify an elder's approximate age when documents are lacking.)

All the long-lived people of Abkhazia have varying opinions about the secret of their "fountain of youth." This is what I learned from them during my visits between 1979 and 1985.

Elizaveta Shakryl (114 years old) thought that she passed her century because she never allowed herself to fret. Timur Vanacha (102)[7] was sure it was because he had worked all his life. Jgug Chamagua (95) believed her habit of walking long distances and her even disposition helped her reach a ripe age. Arutan Gitsba (95) had no doubts about Allah's intervention. Other elders explained that Abkhazian food, the mountain air, or the home-made wine and vodka made the difference. A few told me the Abkhazians lived longer because they married later than most other peoples,[8] hence waiting longer for their first sexual experience (pre-marital sex was and still is taboo). According to this theory, Abkhazians can continue sexual activity many more years and this, they say, is an important reason for better health in late adulthood. One man explained that his good health despite his advanced age was due to his satisfying marriage and happy family life.

The scientists who have been studying long-lived people, not only in Abkhazia, but in other parts of the world as well, also hold different theories about the factors that may promote longevity, such as genetic, physical environment, and lifestyle factors. What all experts agree on, however, is that there are certain territories, or ethnic groups, with a higher percentage of people over 90 than others. Abkhazia, Azerbaijan, and Yakutia in the former Soviet Union are just such territories. There are also pockets of large centenarian populations in Pakistan (the Hunzas northeast of the Khyber Pass) and Ecuador (the valley of Vilcabamba in the Andes). This information tends to reinforce the genetic hypothesis, that longevity is inherited.

There has been some controversy over whether the centenarians of the Caucasus really are as old as they say. After all, most of the elders of the 1970s and 1980s, when this phenomenon gained worldwide attention, did not have birth certificates to prove their claimed distinguished age. The Soviet-American program on longevity that I participated in was careful to verify the ages of the elders, contrasting our information with the age stated in their Soviet internal passports. We did this by interviewing elders, members of their families and their neighbors. These people did not know the intent was to verify their age because questions about age would come up only once in a while in a wide-ranging conversation about the person's diet, work habits, and life history.

My own study of Abkhazian longevity focused on lifestyle. I believe that one of the most basic factors is the inherited potential to live long. But having the potential does not guarantee its fulfilment. This is where other factors come in, such as diet, work, sex, and social environment; factors we can modify in our lives to one degree or another.

Perhaps one of the most popular theories is that the secret to long life is in one's diet. The everyday diet of all Abkhazians consists of homegrown and home-processed foods, abundant raw fruit and vegetables, moderate meat consumption, and even less fish, low fat, low calorie intake.

Despite a relatively limited assortment of foods and the predominance of plant products, in particular grain and beans, the diet contains a balance of almost all the main nutrients. The proportion of the main nutrients remains constant for the people studied over sixty, irrespective of their overall reduction with age.

The following alimentary factors may play their part in the longevity of the given population: a diet relatively low in tryptophan; low consumption of raw vegetable oil; and an adequate content of food antioxidizers (vitamins C and E).

Eating habits are formed in early childhood and have persisted consistently throughout the lifetime of the elderly, thus ensuring the necessary period of time to exert an effect on prolongation of life.

The diet of the population appears to have elements thought to be associated with low heart disease and low risk of cancer. These features include: low consumption of sugar and salt; a high proportion of plant products, hence fiber; moderate alcohol consumption; low calorie food intake; optimal fat content in general and vegetable oil in particular; a high content of vitamins and antioxidizers possessing antiatherosclerotic properties.

Another theory put forward by some experts and endorsed by several centenarians I met is that waiting until the age of 30 to 40 (historically common ages of marriage) to begin sexual relations is related to longevity. The hypothesis of later introduction to sex, however, does not explain longevity in Azerbaijan, where most centenarians married before the age of twenty, according to local traditions; nor among the long-lived people of the Andes where there is no indication of late marriage.

As for attitudes to sexual relations, among the Abkhazians sex is considered to be a strictly private matter. Any manifestation of affection or sexual desire in the presence of others is scorned. Yet private attitudes to sex appear to be quite healthy. Sula Benet, the first American to do fieldwork in Abkhazia, summed up these attitudes:

> Despite the elaborate rules—perhaps, in part, because they are universally accepted—sex in Abkhazia is considered a good and pleasurable thing when it is strictly private. As difficult as it may be for the American mind to grasp, it is also guiltless. It is not repressed or sublimated into work, art, or religious-mystical passion. It is not an evil to be driven from one's thoughts. It is a pleasure to be regulated for the sake of one's health—like good wine.[9]

Dr. Benet also recorded the results of a medical team investigating the sex life of the Abkhazians. It was learned that men retain their sexual potency beyond the age of seventy and 13.6 percent of the women were found to continue menstruation after 55 years of age. "Late menarche and late menopause for women," writes Dr. Benet, "are both expressions of the same biological principle of the slow aging process. Biologically speaking, they are 'late bloomers'."[10]

The Soviet anthropologists who worked in Abkhazia with me were also looking into the psychology of the people to see if it had any important contributions to make to the science of stress allevia-tion. They believed that the extensive and close family ties in Abkhazian communities—and hence traditions of mutual assis-tance—may help to minimize stress. They particularly emphasized the prestige of growing old in Abkhazia, and the active participa-tion in family and community life by centenarians as a possible explanation for the relative absence of senility.

Galina Starovoitova, a Moscow psychologist (who later became Russian President Boris Yeltsin's aide on ethnic relations), made a statistical study of the contact between the elders and the younger members of rural communities in Abkhazia. She learned that elders, including those over 90, converse daily with relatives and close neighbors, and at least once a week with friends. Over 80 percent of the conversations the youth and middle-aged had with their elders were for advice on important everyday matters.

In a 1980 conversation I had with Sula Benet she emphatically stated her belief that the honored position of the elderly is respon-sible for the self-respect so notable among them. "In the United States," she commented, "getting old is not exactly a good thing; people like to stay as young as possible. The same thing, I suppose, holds true in many other contemporary groups, but the position of the Abkhazian elders in the family and in the society helps them want to live long and be in good health."

As for wanting to be healthy, I noticed that most of the elderly I interviewed qualified their state of health as good. They men-tioned an ache here or there, but were basically people not accus-tomed to complaining about their health. On the contrary, the sub-ject did not seem to be of interest to any of them.

In Abkhazia there are no seniors who do not enjoy the every-day care of relatives and neighbors and there is no Abkhazian senior who lives in a nursing home because, no matter what the ill-ness, the patient will be cared for by someone in the kinship group if there are no close relatives. A doctor or nurse will come to the house daily if necessary to administer medical care. An Abkhazian family will only agree to hospitalization for their elderly if an oper-ation is required, or round-the clock medical care is in order, such as intravenous feeding. Otherwise, they believe love and care to be the best medicine.

Anna Petrova, a Moscow psychologist I worked with in Abkhazia, had trouble getting any clear answers to her questions about mechanisms for coping with stress. It was not because there is little stress as we know it in these rural communities. "I believe that there is psychological stress in any society, even in rural communities," said Petrova.

> A death in the family, for instance, creates plenty of anxiety. Or what about marriage, the birth of a child? The emotions are positive, but this is still stressful. Nobody in Abkhazia, at least the elders I have interviewed, thinks of stress consciously, so they do not always know how to explain the coping mechanism that apparently comes naturally to them.

Galina Starovoitova revealed one aspect of the centenarians' psychology that may have some bearing on coping with stress and on longevity. She discovered by testing the rural population in Abkhazia, using methods devised by I. B. Phares, that the long-living people tend to interpret the events in their lives as the result of their own doing rather than external forces. She found that this type of personality was most common among the elderly who were most healthy physically and psychologically. Therefore, it is possible that people who accept responsibility for what happens to them in life, feel they are masters of their own destiny, are more likely to live longer.

To me the most striking factor in Abkhazian culture was the place of honor the Abkhazian elderly hold in their communities and the resulting strong will to go on living active lives. So I turned to study childrearing customs because the foundations of old age, attitudes to the elderly, and psychological well-being are laid in childhood. I wanted to see how these practices perpetuate in the culture a process of growing old in which people become increasingly important and gain power and honor in their families and communities the older they become. So let us take a look at what it was like growing up in Soviet Abkhazia.

SUSANNA'S STORY

In 1980, when I first met Susanna Jinjolia in an Abkhazian village named Jgerda, she was twenty-three. She was a typical young woman of her generation brought up in the countryside during the mid-fifties, when most traces of the difficult years of World War II had been erased. Susanna's story of her childhood, which follows in her own words (translated by me), reflects the changes as well as the constants in the Abkhazian system of child-rearing. She describes her life most eloquently.

I was born prematurely, two months before I was due. The doctor who pulled me through in our local hospital was an Armenian. She asked my parents if she could choose my name. She wanted me to be Susanna. After I was brought home from the hospital the doctor visited every day for several months, and then at least once a week she came to see how I was doing. She loved me very much. My grandfather worked at that hospital then. I remember the doctor would ask him to have me come and visit her when I was a toddler. Now she works in Sukhum, but we still keep in touch.

I was a few years old when my middle brother was born, and remember as though it happened yesterday how excited the family was when he was brought home from the hospital. In Abkhazia a boy in the family has always brought great joy because so many men were killed in fighting in the old days. Now it is a habit to celebrate a boy's birth more than a girl's. All the neighbors came to see him, and as the baby was carried into the yard my father, who likes to hunt, picked up his rifle and shot it into the air twice in keeping with the old custom when a boy is born. I was so excited. I don't think I was jealous; I gave my new brother a doll to welcome him home. Grandma walked around his cradle three times, and said, "May all your illnesses be mine." My grandmother is a very kind woman, and loves children. Of course, every grandmother loves her grandchildren but our grandmother has been especially fond of us.

When my brother was brought home from the hospital my mother did not go near him if my grandfather was in the room. If my grandfather entered the room where she was taking care of the baby she would leave at once. This is an old custom, a sign of deep respect to the head of the household and her father-in-law.[11] A woman who disregards this old custom might as well be saying to her father-in-law, "you see, your son and I were intimate and had this baby." Some women today don't pay attention to that custom, but I think such people just show disrespect for themselves because they don't appear to care about preserving our Abkhazian traditions.

After the child is given its name at a special ceremony, usually three weeks after its birth, the mother can take care of her baby in front of her in-laws, or other elders, but she will still refrain from kissing or hugging the child in front of elders.

This name-giving ceremony used to have religious meaning: it was a time to pray for the protection of the gods so the child would grow up happy and healthy. In the past only women attended the ceremony and ate the sacrifical food, chicken and cheese pie. But now even men come and eat at the banquet that is given in the newborn's honor. The elders, of course won't come. They still are strict about following the old ways. But the rest of the community comes to the celebration because it is a time for relatives and neighbors to get together and mark the birth of a new member of the community.

Traditionally the mother was not involved in selecting the child's name which was made public at the ritual. This right was reserved for the head of the family. And the child was never named after an ancestor, because its mother had no right to pronounce such names. Now no one pays attention to these rules, at least not anyone I know. But a person's name is still quite significant in our culture. In Abkhazian the world for "name" also means "fame."

The people who come to the ceremony bring presents and the women give their blessings to the child. An old woman in the community with a gift for oratory supervises the festivities and says the main blessing.

I don't think this custom will die out. Almost everyone has such a party after the baby's birth. When I am older I am sure my children and their children will organize such a gathering for the sake of the elders who want to keep the old traditions. The same goes for our weddings, which are so beautiful and so necessary to give a young couple the right start in life. A family that would not follow these customs would be considered quite strange in the community.

The cradle that my brother slept in until he was about a year old is the traditional Abkhazian cradle that our people used for centuries. The baby is strapped into it, and he eliminates through a hole in the bottom of the cradle. I remember as a toddler asking my mother if I could sleep in my brother's cradle. Of course, she wouldn't let me because it was for my brother, so I slept in a small bed by myself in my parents' room. Later I slept in my grandmother's room. When my brother got a little older I moved to my own room and he slept in my grandmother's room. It was very warm sleeping with her, and it made her happy to have one of us so close.

My younger brother was born a few years after my middle brother. We repeated the same ceremony for him. The youngest son is usually a family's favorite although we all felt we were wanted and loved by everyone in the family and by our other relatives.

For instance, my uncle on my father's side lives nearby. Before he married and had his own children he became very close to my brothers and me. To this day if he sees something we might like he buys it for us, clothes and what-not and treats us like his own children—even better, because with us he can show his affections more openly. He will not be affectionate with his own children if others are around.

When we were little my brothers and I played together in our yard or with our cousins who also lived nearby. Until I went to school these were my only playmates. I would only leave the yard to go to the neighbors or with my grandfather to the hospital where he worked or to the store in the center of our community. So our world was small, and the people we knew best were our own relatives.

Mama was always affectionate with us. She would give us a hug, or say what good children we were every day. Papa rarely kissed us, but we knew he cared about us very much. It's customary for a father to keep his distance from his children when his parents are around.

Neither of my parents went to college, but they brought us up well. I think we were good children, although sometimes we got into trouble. Because I was the oldest child, and a girl, I was hardly ever punished. I was supposed to look after my brothers, and they were supposed to mind me since I was the oldest. If my parents had punished me my brothers would not have respected me so much and would not have minded me.

Nobody ever hit us. The worst punishment my parents had was to stand my brothers in the corner. But that was only a few times that I can remember. Once the boys had climbed our cherry tree to get some fruit after being told not to. Grandma was afraid they could have fallen, and she was very upset. She told my father when he came home so he put them in the corner for half an hour or so.

We were afraid of Papa even though he never hit us, and never even raised his voice with us. But when Mama would threaten us that Papa would come home and punish us "*severely*," we begged her not to tell him and promised to mind her. I don't know why we believed Mama that Papa would be so hard on us! He never was. Maybe after seeing how he put the boys in the corner once was enough for us to believe he was capable of punishing us even more harshly.

Some parents, I know, promise their children candy or some small favor when they want them to run an errand. But my mother did not have to. We were always willing to help. What she would promise us was to read or tell us a fairytale about a little boy who grew up with a deer. We also liked the stories she told us that came from Bulgaria. (The book we had was in Abkhazian, a translation from Russian, in turn a translation from Bulgarian.) Mother would tell us about the customs of other peoples and how they live in different countries.

I knew more fairytales than my brothers and many of my friends. I would go to my cousins and tell them the stories I knew and would correct the little ones when they made mistakes in telling the stories they had heard. My mother also taught my brothers and me how to dance and sing our folk songs. She plays our folk instruments very well; now my brothers play the guitar and sing for the family when we are all together.

We learned how to work around the house and on the farm before we went to school, but it was like play for us. We never had to do anything beyond our abilities. I would help wash the dishes, and my brothers would help my father with his work. Starting from the fifth grade, we helped the farmers with the harvest as a class and it was there that we learned the real skills of farming. The work was never hard work and we enjoyed it. Besides, grandmother taught us that work was good physical exercise. Our families and our schools believe work is good for children, and the earlier we learn work skills the easier it is to get used to regular work habits.

I went to our local school in the center of Jgerda. My first teacher had the title of "Honored Teacher of the Georgian Republic." She really deserved that honor, too, because she approached each child as an individual. She was my best teacher. My worst teacher taught German: she knew the language well, but did not have the gift to teach. I studied with her for six years, but cannot say that I know the language. Our math teacher, on the other hand, was a talented teacher. She taught us everything, not only math, because she shared with us her ideas and philosophy about life. The literature teacher we had when I was in my last few years of school was brilliant. His classes would begin and end and we wouldn't even notice the time pass.

Not all schools are the same, of course; some are better, others worse. I would say that our school was a little better than average. Our students were also capable; I don't remember any children who were difficult to handle. If someone was doing badly in school, or perhaps misbehaving, the teachers, or principal, would call in the child's parents and ask them to talk to the child. This measure was used only in extreme cases, but it was always effective, because the family exerts the strongest influence on a child.

Many of my friends go to college, and some have already graduated. The others remained on the farm to work in the fields. I cannot do this because of a back injury from a childhood accident falling off a tree, so I help out at home and spend my time reading.

I was close to all the girls in my class. If you follow the Abkhazian customs, you will win lots of friends. If you don't, people are less likely to respect you. For girls this means dressing modestly and not wearing makeup. Abkhazian boys do not like girls who try to stand out: in our class there was one girl who, under the influence of the older sister, insisted on wearing makeup, not realizing how ridiculous she looked. Her parents finally stopped her.

I also had about five close friends among the boys. They would tell me their secrets, their problems, and would come to me for help or advice; when they had some good news they would share it with me too. I call myself a closed archive: any secret I am told goes no further. You could threaten to kill me and I would not give away any of the secrets people have told me.

I appreciate most of our Abkhazian traditions, the fact that we value modesty, generosity, hospitality, respect for elders and elders' respect for those younger. Most of our bad customs have died away, such as feuding, blood revenge, and the limited mobility of women. We still have many complicated rituals that we should simplify, such customs as the taboo against a daughter-in-law speaking in the presence of her father-in-law, or a son handling his child in front of his father. Of course, one should feel some restraint around elders, out of respect, but it is not necessary in our modern world to keep to the letter of the old traditions. We see these customs being modified today, especially in the cities, but I do not know one Abkhazian family that is willing to give up all those traditions which make us Abkhazians, which give us our unique identity.

We have always been concerned about the fate of our people and our traditions. For example, the first toast at an Abkhazian celebration is always to "the people."[12] Perhaps because we were on the verge of extinction in the nineteenth century we are anxious to hang on to our traditions and care more about them than we otherwise would. When a person is guilty of some particularly serious misbehavior, the relatives say, "You are shaming your people." At that first celebration after a baby's birth the guests who come to look at the baby say, "May you become a son or daughter of your people." This is supposed to guarantee that this new human being should never do anything to shame the Abkhazian people.

This was always the ideal of the people, yet in old Abkhazia, only 100 years ago, people killed each other for a piece of land. When a man did not have enough food for his family, and someone stronger tried to take away the only source of income he had, he was ready to kill to protect it, and vice versa. The strong were greedy, and stopped at nothing to get more.

I have lived for nearly a quarter of a century, but I have never heard of such a thing in Jgerda, in Abkhazia, or anywhere else in our country. There is work for everyone, and land for anyone who is willing to farm it. Some of us are better off than others, but basically we in Jgerda are all farmers with the same privileges, and the same obligations. No one feels that they are on the outside of society and I suppose that is why our community is so peaceful.

HOW TYPICAL IS SUSANNA?

Susanna's story, told in her own words in the last section, provides a glimpse into the mental set that ensures a process by which Abkhazians gain in stature as they grow older. This advance up the social hierarchy is gradual and sure. Each age group has authority over all those younger and must follow completely the wishes of all those who are older. This natural sequence of acquiring power and prestige is, perhaps, what minimizes the resentment a person from our culture might expect of individuals who are compelled by tradition to acquiesce to elders.

To be sure, not all young people share the same outlooks as Susanna. Increasingly, juvenile delinquency has been on the rise among Abkhazians, indicating a serious breakdown in the old system. Educators there explained that one of the reasons is that the school system, standardized in Moscow by a totally different culture, does not adequately inculcate the specifically Abkhazian value system. The code of behavior learned at home by implicit instruction is not reinforced in the schools. For instance, not only are younger people supposed to honor and obey those who are older, but those older are, in turn, supposed to treat their juniors with respect, and not abuse their power. In the schools this approach is not observed. Older children take advantage of younger children. This kind of school environment, point out Abkhazian educators, disrupts the traditional dynamics of interaction between the generations.

However, the vast majority of young people I observed, starting from the time they could walk, were well-behaved, demonstrated obvious respect for their elders, and seemed incapable of offending an adult.

Even more astounding to me (having agreed with the prevailing philosophy of my generation of the sixties, that you can't trust anyone over thirty) was the wisdom and inner energy I encountered in the elderly. I concluded that when you know that people look to you for the answers to important questions, you grow to meet the community's expectations. When a society defines "elderly" as synonymous with being sage, as in Abkhazia, the individual is more likely to strive to fit that profile.

ELDERS AS MEDIATORS OF CONFLICT

Since the elders are considered the society's most experienced and wise people, they are regarded as the primary mediators of conflicts. They are usually males, ordinarily around fifty and older, and among the most respected. Elderly women may also be mediators, but they are a minority. When a woman is called in to resolve a conflict it is because she is especially highly regarded. As one male mediator explained, "For a man it's almost enough for him to have lived long to serve as a mediator, but if a woman is involved it means she is a person of particular wisdom."

The formal mediation institutions are the Councils of Elders[13] that function only when the members are called upon to settle a conflict. However, any elder, not necessarily serving on a council, may be asked to mediate. They may even be relatives of the conflicting parties, if the dispute is not major. Several mediators usually serve together, the more the better, and preferably those who live a good distance from the disputants or are not among the interested parties.

Mediators must have certain qualities. They are supposed to be objective, wise and knowledgeable about traditions; they are influential people and eloquent speakers. The following reflects the typical statements I heard about the desirable qualities of mediators: "He was the ideal mediator because of his personal qualities. Each side knew him to be objective, not a politician. A good mediator is someone who is respected by both sides and is untainted, not hypocritical."

Abkhazian mediators are not called upon to resolve conflicts subject to a criminal suit. They are usually responsible for civil disputes which the involved individuals or the community do not want to be escalated. These disputes are typically feuds or potential feuds over an accidental murder (usually automobile or hunting accidents), cases of juvenile delinquency, and family conflicts.

The period that precedes the actual mediation is the most critical because this is when the parties decide that they are ready to cease hostilities. In the case of a feud, this decision usually seems to be voluntary and arises when both sides feel they have taken even revenge. In some instances the side that has caused the greatest damage to the adversaries is the one that calls in mediators in order to preempt a severe counter blow.

In all my conversations about feuds involving deaths[14] it was clear that combatants are motivated to seek a resolution not just to save one's own family, but also out of an awareness of the small numbers of Abkhazians and a concern for the nationality's endangered status. So a sense of self-preservation as a group was found to be a strong motive for settlement if the conflict could result in loss of life.

Sometimes the decision to mediate a dispute is due to the pressure of public opinion exerted by the future mediators, or perhaps,

by neighbors, family members, etc. One elder told me that mediators and members of the community talk to recalcitrant parties one
at a time to get their agreement to begin negotiations. During these
caucuses an experienced and eloquent elder cites to the parties
many cases of conflicts as instructive examples of how to improve
relations. Other influentials may also enter the effort to persuade
the antagonists.

Fear of becoming an outcast is a strong motivation in such a
closely knit culture as Abkhazia, so this kind of public pressure is
highly effective. The threat of ostracism and exile is ordinarily the
method used to deal with juvenile delinquents. In these cases
elders make the threats gently, knowing that the mere mention of
such an action is taken seriously by the youth. Often this is done at
annual meetings of the surname group (*azhvala* which means
"those who belong to the same root"),[15] when influential members
of the group summarize, as it were, the accomplishments of outstanding individuals, as well as the failures of others.

When mediators begin the actual mediation procedures, a
standard opening, reflecting the power of public opinion, is as follows: "We've come at the request of society. Have you anything
against us?" By this time, the parties are ready for mediation and
will answer in the negative, thus confirming their willingness to
bow to the authority of the mediators.

Use of the concept of *apsuara* has traditionally been the most
important element of mediation procedures. If I were to translate
this term into one word it would be "Abkhazianism." However, it
does not really explain this extremely broad notion. Apsuara
embraces all the components of the entire, complex ethical code for
Abkhazian behavior. Thus, an appeal to the parties by mediators to
remember apsuara is essentially an appeal to ethnicity, to
Abkhazian values, and to the very existence of the group. *Alamys*, or
"conscience," is another related concept that is utilized. It is actually
also encompassed by apsuara. These two words are integral to the
main thrust of the mediators' arguments for reconciliation.

Mediators also commonly say: "Are you an *apsua* (Abkhazian)? If so, then you must do this," whatever the mediators suggest. Or mediators may ask this rhetorical question: "How can you
do that to another Abkhazian; there are so few of us as it is?" This
mechanism of conflict resolution clearly serves to preserve an
endangered ethnic group, so it works best within a group that uniformly shares common values, as is the case with the Abkhazians.

This was how 91-year-old Grisha Aiba (whose father and grandfather had also been well-known mediators) managed to end a long-standing feud in his village of Otkhara. He told me how he and his co-mediators used these considerations of Abkhazian group survival to persuade a father to forgive his son's killer. Aiba told me of the intensive three-day negotiations (no one eats throughout the negotiation period) with the father and the killer. Meanwhile mediators were negotiating with the murderer. When the man was ready to repent for his crime and agreed to go to the graveyard to be tied to his victim's tombstone, the negotiators who were with the father began persuading him to go also to his son's grave. Finally the father realized the killer must be waiting at the graveyard and gave in, saying: "Since all of you insist I have no choice." When they arrived at the grave the murderer was guarded by several men to protect from any harm from the other side. After being untied the man approached the father and kissed him on the chest, making them father and son for life. This is a modern version of an ancient Abkhazian practice in conflict resolution.

Traditionally a feud could be ended either by fosterage, the custom of giving up a child to be raised temporarily (months or years) in another family, or by the adoption of a child or an adult as a means of uniting two families as relatives. In this case the hospitality ritual was combined with bringing the child or adult into the new home. Fosterage and adoption were widespread in the Caucasus until the nineteenth century and in Abkhazia it was practiced at the beginning of the twentieth century.

Even if one side did not agree to adoption as the solution, there was still hope. If a woman from the family which offered the adoption could get access to a child from the reluctant family and put the child to her breast, even symbolically, the relationship was sealed. No more blood could be shed between the two families. If no child was accessible, another alternative was for a man to find an opportunity to somehow steal into the home of the reluctant family and put his lips to a woman's breast, perhaps the wife or mother of the revenging male. Although the adoption was forced, it was fair and had to be recognized.

Although the appeal to ethnicity, to Abkhazian ethical codes and conscience, is the strongest means of persuasion among a group of people so acutely aware of their fragility, other techniques are also used, depending on the conflict. One approach is to persuade parties that the conflict is not worth the antagonism. For instance, in the small resort of Novy Afon, a conflict began when members of two families had a fist fight after drinking heavily at a party. Within four days, because of growing hostility between the families, all the respected elders in the town gathered together. They contacted the relatives, and appointed a day, time and neutral site to discuss the conflict. Dmitry Smyr, a member of the local Council of Elders, recalled how he initially addressed the two families: "How could you fight over such a matter. Aren't you ashamed? Won't it be ridiculous if the dispute has to be heard in court?" After eloquent pleas by all the mediators the parties finally agreed, he said: "They shook hands and hugged, and then we held a feast where we had gathered. Some time later one side invited the other side to their home for a banquet, treating them like honored guests." An important conflict, explained Smyr, "is over something that has economic value, something having to do, for instance, with agriculture."

It is important to the mediation outcome that both sides emerge from the conflict with their dignity intact, which is so highly valued in the Abkhazian culture. Thus, face saving measures are part and parcel of the mediation process. In the 1950s and 1960s, Shalva Inal-Ipa, an Abkhazian anthropologist extensively interviewed long-lived Abkhazians who provided rich oral history on conflict resolution going back to the nineteenth century. Inal-Ipa found that the goal of the mediators was not to establish who was right or wrong in the conflict because that would just exacerbate the circumstances. Instead, mediators emphasized the need for peace. He explained that, "It was felt that the guilty party had essentially discredited itself; it wasn't necessary to rub in the guilt."

The mediators I met with expressed varying opinions about whether mediators are supposed to determine the guilty parties in a conflict. Some said that the only way to solve a conflict is to ascertain which side is in the wrong. A fifty-year-old mediator stressed, "Of course the mediators must get to the bottom of the conflict, or it can't be resolved. The mediators' goal is not to smooth over the conflict, but to protect the honor of the victims."

Grisha Aiba said that it is imperative to determine the guilty party in order to get an apology, which in his experience, is absolutely necessary for a settlement to occur. The trick is to orchestrate an apology that is face saving, and that allows both sides to feel completely at ease with the final agreement.

Others claimed that determining guilt is not important. Dmitry Smyr maintained that "In court it's important to determine who's guilty. But when elders are involved in conflict resolution, they're more interested in keeping the conflict from continuing. We say to the parties: 'We don't care who is right and who is wrong, that's past history. What we care about is that you make up, that you let bygones be bygones'."

This approach in interpersonal disputes is made easier in the Abkhazian culture because public expressions of pride in one's own family and children are culturally unacceptable. Therefore it is unusual, for instance, for parents to take the side of their child in a conflict with another family, even if the child is clearly in the right. One informant told me of how, as a ten-year-old, he seriously injured a neighbor boy with a knife during a fight. The father of the victim did not fault the assailant, but his own son. He preferred to assume that his son had provoked the assault, rather than display what would have been considered undignified fatherly pride.

This is how close relatives can exert pressure on members of their family to take blame for their wrong-doing in the conflict. Public opinion favors such relatives over those who are more protective, because the former are behaving more within the confines of the traditional values of apsuara.

Abkhazian diplomacy, also referred to as Caucasian diplomacy, was a term used frequently to explain the actual style of mediation. Informants had a strong sense that this style is distinctly different in the Caucasus than in other cultures. Often people told me that the art of persuasion required mediators "to start from afar," to gradually work their way toward a mutual agreement. Humor was also cited as an important element of this diplomacy. How mediators express themselves, even in subtle ways, is as important as what solutions they propose. As an informant explained, "Caucasian diplomacy can be expressed in a particular gesture, facial expression, reinforced by the right words said at the right time."

When I came to this part of my conversations with informants it was hard to learn details because apparently so much of the art of mediation is spontaneous and creative. Mediators had difficulty recounting their exact words, the eloquence of their expressions, and as an outsider I was never able to witness these sensitive negotiations.

Once the mediators persuade the antagonists to reconcile, the next step is to finalize the agreement. Usually this is done by an offer of hospitality and, if applicable, material compensation for whatever the losses were, "the price of blood," as the compensation is called. The initiator of the hospitality might say: "I want to get rid of these hard feelings and invite you over to say some kind words, to apologize, and give gifts."

Acceptance of hospitality has an even more binding effect than a modern contract, signed and sealed in a court of law. Eating someone else's food precludes any animosity. A solemn ritual oath of reconciliation is sacred and cannot be broken.

Can such traditions of conflict resolution, that work so well within a group with the same values and concern for survival, operate effectively in settling disputes between ethnic groups with different values? Of all the elders I met only Aiba had any experience mediating conflicts involving Georgians. All of them, however, took an acute interest in the conflict that was brewing between Abkhazians and Georgians the last time I met with them in the summer of 1991.

Some elders believed this was not a conflict that they could solve because the roots of the dispute reached too far out of their cultural experience—all the way to the government bodies of Moscow (the capital of Russia) and Tbilisi (the capital of Georgia). "This is a problem to be tackled only by politicians," was a common refrain.

Other elders clearly wanted a role in resolving the dispute between the Georgians and Abkhazians before it escalated into war. Grisha Aiba was certain that he could manage a settlement based on his experience living peacefully with Georgians and Svans in his village. But he complained, "nobody will let us elders get involved in this conflict."

Eventually the traditional peacemaking customs of the Caucasus will find their place into the contemporary arena. These practices appear to have been set aside, but I believe they are being utilized to varying degrees behind the scenes. The Caucasian peoples now at war are not so far removed from their cultural heritage that they are completely ignoring the lessons of their past. The whole Caucasus, including Abkhazia, has known frequent warfare throughout its history. But, in the process, these peoples have also fine tuned their practices of resolving even the most protracted conflicts.

They will find their way to return, once again, to life without trenches, tanks and machine guns. I hope at that point anthropologists will be welcome to work in this area which is one of the last frontiers for understanding traditional cultures, the role of the elderly, and the mechanisms for conflict resolution and cultural change.

NOTES

1. On most modern maps these cities are denoted as Sukhumi and Tkvarcheli. The i's were dropped by the Abkhazian government in 1991 as part of a general campaign to restore historical toponyms that had been Georgianized during the Stalin period.

2. In the Soviet census all three of these related peoples, with distinct dialect and cultural differences, are referred to as Georgians.

3. Shalva Inal-Ipa, *Abkhazy: istoriko-etnograficheskie ocherki* [Abkhazians: Historical-Ethnographic Essays], (Sukhum: Alashara Publishers, 1965).

4. B. G. Hewitt, "Abkhazia: a Problem of Identity and Ownership," paper presented for the PHRG, 1991. The colonies were Pitiunt (contemporary Pitsunda), Dioscurias (contemporary Sukhum), and Guenos (near contemporary Ochamchira).

5. Georgy Dzidzaria. *Makhadzhirstvo i problemy istorii Abkhazii XIX stoletiya* [Emigration and the Problems of Nineteenth Century Abkhazian History], (Sukhum: Alashara Publishers, 1975).

6. 1989 Census data.

7. When I met Vanacha in 1980 his passport (Soviet identity papers) said he was 135 years old, but one year later when I went to a performance of the Nartaa Amateur Folk Company where he was the oldest member, the master of ceremonies proudly announced that Vanacha was 117. Anthropologists who verified his age by a methodology explained in this section have him on record as a few years over 100.

8. Traditionally it was not uncommon for men to marry in their forties and fifties (after they had established a homestead nearby their parents), and for women to marry in their thirties. Even today, early marriages are not the norm.

9. Sula Benet. *Abkhasians: The Long-Living People of the Caucasus* (New York: Holt, Rinehart & Winston, 1974), p. 86.

10. Ibid.

11. When couples marry the wife always moves to the husband's home and often lives in the same house with her in-laws or nearby. The youngest son is obligated to remain in his parents' home with his family. Three-generation households are prevalent.

12. "The people" spoken as a toast in Abkhazia is an all-inclusive concept that simultaneously refers to the Abkhazian people, to each individual group of people, and to all people of the world as a whole.

13. The traditional institutions were banned during the Stalin period, but restored in the 1960s. Under the republic's constitution the councils can mediate civil disputes.

14. A feud may begin between two families when a member on one side is killed by a member on the other side, even if the death is accidental. This is because it is culturally imperative in the Caucasus to avenge any injury or death. It is not even enough that the guilty party has been tried, convicted and is serving time.

15. The traditions of these meetings have roots that go back millennia, before Christianity and Islam, when each surname group had its own sacred site where it prayed to its patron spirits for the group's well-being. Almost every surname group in Abkhazia revived this practice in the 1970s and 1980s, using the opportunity to praise its outstanding members and scold in public all those who could blemish the reputation of the *azhvala*.

SUGGESTED READINGS

Benet, Sula. *Abkhasians: The Long-Living People of the Caucasus.* New York: Holt, Rinehart & Winston, 1974.

Garb, Paula. *Where the Old Are Young: Long Life in the Soviet Caucasus.* Palo Alto, Calif.: Ramparts Publishers, 1987.

KURDS:
A CULTURE
STRADDLING NATIONAL
BORDERS

Annette Busby

D o you know why I have so many children? Because everywhere, they are killing Kurds. I am doing what I can to be sure there will still be some Kurds left (A Kurdish man in the late 1980s).

The Kurds have lived in the rugged mountains and high plains at the headwaters of the Tigris and Euphrates rivers for over two thousand years. They believe themselves to be de-scended from the Medes, who ruled the area until 550 B.C.[1] In 375 B.C. the Greek, Xenophon, recorded his encounter with the fierce "Karduchi", and the Arabs first used the term "Kurd" in the seventh century A.D. The region called "Kurdistan" (the land of the Kurds) is currently divided by the borders of Iran, Iraq, Turkey and Syria. There are also pockets of Kurds living in the former Soviet republics of Armenia, Azerbajijan, Georgia, Kasakistan, Kirighiz and Turkoman.[2] The policies of these countries toward their Kurdish minorities have changed over time, and differ from one country to the other. They have, however, affected many aspects of the lives— and deaths—of the Kurds. Little anthropological research has been done on the Kurds, in large part because the national governments have often been at odds with the Kurds. These governments have not encouraged or allowed anthropologists to study their Kurdish populations. Those anthropologists who gain permission from the governments may be suspect to the Kurds, who are fearful of gov-ernment spies. My research was carried out among Turkish Kurds during the late 1980s. If this sounds vague, it is meant to protect the identities of the people I studied.

Estimates of the numbers of Kurds living in the Middle East are not reliable because the government censuses vary from one country to the other. The census surveys tend to underestimate the Kurdish population for political reasons. The Kurds themselves tend to estimate much higher numbers in accordance with their own political agenda. In the mid 1970s the number of Kurds living in Turkey, Iran, Iraq, Syria and the Soviet Union was estimated to be between 13.5 and 21 million.[3] By the 1990s the number has doubtless increased due to the high birthrates among the Kurds.

Traditionally, the Kurds were nomadic pastoralists, herding their sheep and goats back and forth from summer pastures high in the mountains, to winter pastures in the lower river valleys. Although the Kurds were predominantly nomads, today most are settled in villages where they grow crops for their own consumption and for sale as cash crops. The raising of sheep and goats continues to be a strong focus in their lives. Many Kurds also live in larger towns and cities in Kurdish areas as well as the major cities of the Middle East. In addition, there are Kurds living in exile in Europe and the United States. In 1966 only 5.5% of the population of Turkish Kurdistan was employed in industry; 72.2% lived in the country and made their living growing crops and raising sheep and goats. The other 22.3% worked as shopkeepers, teachers, truck drivers, public officials, etc.[4]

Kurdish language is of Indo-European origin, and is most closely related to Persian. There are numerous subdialects of Kurdish (such as Gurani, Leki and Kirmanshahi), but the major dialects are Kurmanji, Sorani (also called "Kurdi"), and Zaza. There is some disagreement about whether these are in fact major dialects or distinct languages.

While the Kurds' language and origins are similar to those of the Persians, their religion distinguishes them from one another. Whereas the Persians are predominantly Shi'ite Muslims, most of the Kurds are Sunni Muslims. (Sunni and Shi'a are the two branches of Islam. The fundamental difference between them is their views on who should have been the caliph—i.e., the religious and political leader of the Muslims—after the Prophet's death. Sunni Muslims acknowledge the first four caliphs as rightful successors of the Prophet Mohammed, while the Shi'ites reject the first three caliphs, and hold that Ali—the fourth caliph, and son-in-law to Mohammed—was the rightful successor to Mohammed.) Some Kurds adhere to Shi'ite-inspired sects or other religions, including those of the Yezidi, Alawite, Christian, and Jews.

Although current Kurdish political organization is complicated by their incorporation into political parties within different nation-states, traditionally the Kurds organized themselves into lineages, clans and tribes—kinship groups which often acted in political ways. In some areas the tribal structure continues to have political relevance, in others only the lineages remain. In the Kurdish tribal system, several generations of one man's descendants through the male line make up a lineage. Several lineages, going back further to an assumed ancestor, make up a clan, and several clans make up a tribe. The members of a lineage join together in response to conflict between one or more lineage members, and members of other lineages within the clan. If the conflict is not resolved it can lead to a blood feud between the two lineages. Clan membership entails rights to use the pasturage owned by the clan within the territory of the tribe. When the Kurds moved from one area to another, their migration was organized at the tribal level and disputes over territory were fought out between tribes. As one tribe became larger and more powerful, it would attempt to take over territories belonging to other weaker tribes.

For most of their history, the Kurds have had a crucial relationship with various state-level governments. Beginning in the 11th century, several tribes united to form emirates (or principalities) under the hereditary leadership of an emir—the political equivalent of a feudal prince.[5] Between the 15th and mid 19th centuries, the emirates were incorporated into the Ottoman Empire and, to a lesser extent, the Safavid (Persian) dynasty. They were able to maintain local self-rule, due to their distance from the centralized governments and the rugged terrain in a buffer zone between the Ottoman Empire and the Persians. Their reputation as fierce warriors was doubtless also a factor. As long as the emirs controlled their subjects and defended their territory from the advances of the neighboring Persians, the sultan and his forces didn't interfere. If the Ottoman demands for tribute became too great or the Persians made concessions which were more advantageous, tribal leaders and emirs would change loyalties in accordance with their interests. During the eighteenth and nineteenth centuries the Ottoman government extended its influence from the center to the periphery of the empire by assigning regional governors to control and tax its subjects. The regional bureaucrats began to deal directly with the tribal and clan leaders (called *aghas*). The aghas were required to provide taxes and warriors in the service of the empire. By the mid-1800s the last emirates had collapsed and the Kurds were well incorporated into the bureaucratic structure of the Ottoman Empire, despite several revolts lead by individual emirs.[6] As the point of contact with the government, the aghas were able to control trade between the tribe and the outside world.

By the early 1900s the Ottoman Empire began to collapse. Kurdish intellectuals living in Istanbul at the turn of the century came into contact with European ideas. They organized several Kurdish associations and published journals dealing with specifically Kurdish issues. These were the first Kurdish nationalists.

Eventually similar activities caught on and became quite popular in the cities of Kurdistan. A series of Kurdish revolts occurred. Having more or less taken over the government, the Turkish nationalists were hostile to non-Turkish schools, organizations and publications. Prominent Kurdish leaders were imprisoned, exiled, or forced underground.[7]

During World War I the Russians invaded the Ottoman Empire and encouraged the Armenians (who were fellow Christians) to revolt and demand the establishment of an Armenian state. The Turkish nationalists, with the help of the Sunni caliph, rallied the Muslim population in a "holy war" against the "infidels", i.e., the invading (Christian) Russians, and the Armenians. More than a million Armenians were massacred. Many, but not all, of the Kurds took part in this slaughter. The Ottoman Empire finally surrendered to the Allied forces in 1918. The Kurdish desire to create a Kurdish nation-state from the ruins of the Ottoman Empire seemed possible, especially after the Treaty of Sevres was signed in 1920. In dividing the remains of the Ottoman Empire, the Allies and the Turks recognized the right of the Armenians and Kurds to establish independent states. But the Sevres Treaty was never ratified.[8]

Meanwhile, Turkish nationalists engaged in a fight for independence from foreign rule. Fearing that the Turks would side with the newly created Soviet Union, the Allies recognized the Turkish nation-state. In 1923 the Treaty of Lausanne was signed. The Kurds were not represented. Turkey, Britain and France were all eager to control Kurdish areas which had been discovered to contain a good deal of oil and other mineral deposits. The end result was that Turkey was granted the largest section of the Kurdish area. Iraq (under the British Mandate) was granted the oil rich area of Mosul. The French were granted a slice of Kurdistan in addition to other territory elsewhere, and a 25% share of the proceeds of the Mosul oil fields. Thus, Kurdistan was sliced up by the borders of five different countries: Turkey, Iran (formerly Persia), Iraq (under the British Mandate), Syria (under French rule), and the Soviet Union. As a result, the Kurds—despite their majority status in Kurdistan—became an ethnic minority in each of these countries, and were subject to their divergent laws.[9]

Before considering the differences in policy between these countries, let's first get to know the Kurds. In Kurdish villages and towns, the houses are often built on the slopes of the hills so that the roofs form flat terraces lining the hillsides. A well, stream or spring provides water for the village and may also be directed into a walled garden area. The garden is walled to keep out the animals which are herded or allowed to wander near the village. A typical family will own goats and sheep, a cow and a donkey, chickens, and turkeys. They might also own a horse and cart for transportation, a dog for protection, and cats to eat small rodents. In the summer when the temperatures rise to 115 degrees F., the Kurds may eat the evening meal, socialize, and sleep on the cool rooftop under the stars. The animals find whatever shade they can near the village in the heat of the day, and are herded to nearby pastures to graze in the cool of the night. During the harsh winters, some villages are isolated for several months by heavy snowfall. Temperatures drop to -22 degrees F. and people huddle indoors around coa- or dung-burning stoves for heat. The animals spend the winters nearby in stables which, from the outside, resemble the houses. Inside the stable floors become covered with dung several inches thick. After the winter this dung is allowed to dry and then broken into pieces, which are stacked to be used as fuel for cooking and heating in the winter.

If you were invited into a Kurdish home in a village, you would find the rooms lined with colorful bolsters, filled with cane or reeds, and dried mud floors covered with oriental carpets or straw mats, depending upon the wealth of the inhabitants. With the exception of a modern dresser or two, the furniture would consist of the bolsters and three square cushions (called *minder*) which are placed in the corners and the center of the wall farthest from the door. The inhabitants and guests would be seated on the minder and carpet, leaning back against the bolsters along the walls. As you entered, some of the people would stand and offer you a place to sit. They would remain standing until you were seated. Your age, gender and whether or not you were an honored guest, would determine which people stood up and where you were asked to sit.

The honored guests and older men, and sometimes women, sit on the minder along the far wall. The younger men sit along the side walls, with the youngest men farthest from the back wall. The young women sit along the side walls, further yet from the back wall. Relative age takes precedence over gender, when there is a substantial difference in age. A young man would relinquish his place to an older woman, but not to one who was his elder by only a couple of years. If an older man enters the room, everyone rises and one of the corner cushions is offered to him. Everyone moves one space closer to the door and once the elder is seated, everyone else sits. If a young woman enters, everyone remains seated and continues their conversations. This seating arrangement is a demonstration of the respect young people show their elders, and women show to men. This formalized respect is central to all relationships and activities. Thus, the oldest men and women may speak, joke or argue amongst themselves and the younger people show their respect by listening silently unless addressed by their elders. The younger women find their positions close to the door convenient for quietly leaving and entering to make and serve tea, or to carry out other duties, such as tending unruly children, straightening the shoes left at the door by entering guests, preparing meals, etc. If there are no women present, or if the men and women are gathered in separate rooms, the youngest man or boy serves tea to the men. If the young women have no more tasks to perform, they may slip away to another room where they can visit freely with one another. In one village, when the relatives from the city came to visit, the talk was dominated by the elders. The young, unmarried women motioned me to follow them, away from the serious talk of their parents to the other room where they were free to chatter, giggle, try on the city clothes of their cousins, and have me photograph them.

Small children stay with their mothers or play nearby with their siblings and cousins. A child of six or seven is often given the responsibility of supervising younger siblings and cousins. Indoors, valuable or breakable items are stored high out of the reach of children, and outdoors there is plenty of open space in which the children can play in relative safety. Infants sleep in low wooden cradles, or on a minder placed over their mother's outstretched legs. By rotating her legs from side to side under the minder, the mother is able to rock her child and keep her hands free for other things. At night children are rocked to sleep or encouraged to curl up on a minder and fall asleep next to their mothers while the family drinks tea and socializes.

As a young girl grows up, she takes on more and more of the household duties. Her mother is thus gradually freed from the tedious or strenuous tasks she performed as a daughter, or young bride and mother. The girl is not merely helping her elders, but also learning the skills she will need as an adult bride, daughter-in-law and mother. She learns how to prepare and serve a variety of dishes, to care for and milk the family's sheep and goats, to make yogurt from the milk and butter from the cream. She learns to care for younger siblings and cousins, to wash clothes at the stream or spring, to sweep and dust the floors and bolsters, to serve meals and tea, and to clean the dishes. As she nears marriageable age, she also learns to embroider, sew and crochet items for her future home, and to weave the knotted covers for the bolsters and cushions. She spins wool from the sheep using a hand-held spindle. Each year the dyer comes to the village and dyes the yarn into rich colors. In the winter when other chores are light, the young woman weaves the yarn into beautiful intricate patterns using a simple floor loom. A young woman learns to be modest and submissive— i.e. show respect—toward her elders. She must behave appropriately to protect her reputation (for which her entire family is responsible). She is expected to be a virgin on her wedding day. It is also important that a young woman establish a reputation as a healthy, demure, hardworking housekeeper and hostess. One morning, after sleeping on the roof in a village we were visiting, a young Kurdish woman awoke with a start and roused her sisters and myself. "Hurry, get up! The sun has almost reached us!" She then told me of the Kurdish saying that if a woman sleeps when the sun is shining on her, she will never marry. She explained that if a woman had not arisen before the sun reached her bedroll, she was indeed lazy, for there were many things to be done in the morning. Thus if she was known to sleep after the sun reached her, no one would want her for a wife or daughter-in-law.

When a young man decides to marry he will ask his mother to find him a bride. His mother is responsible for suggesting the names of suitable brides for her son. Since the bride goes to live with her husband's family, a woman is most concerned that her son's bride have the qualities to make her a helpful, capable daughter-in-law who will do nothing to bring shame upon the family. The groom's mother is in the best position to choose a bride because she has many opportunities to see the daughters of her friends and relatives. Over the years, on her visits, she can observe how the young woman behaves as hostess toward her mother's guests, whether she makes good tea and coffee, how demurely and attentively she serves the guests, whether she is sloppy or clumsy, and whether she shows respect toward her elders. Having seen the young woman grow up, the prospective mother-in-law also has a good idea of the young woman's personality and whether she is a compatible match for her son.

Among the Kurds, the preference is for a man to marry his father's brother's daughter. Since sons live with or near their parents, this helps keep the daughter in the same lineage, living close to her own family. It also allows her to benefit from her family's inheritance, since daughters do not inherit. Sons inherit equal shares of their father's property. A woman's father's brother's inheritance is thus equal to that of her father, and she benefits from it through her marriage to her cousin. Traditionally, a young man has first right-of-refusal over his father's brother's daughter, and a father who wishes to marry his daughter to another man must first ask permission from his nephew. When the sisters-in-law of a family socialize, they may observe and comment upon their children's compatibility:

> Dilan's mother: "Your Zeki [a toddler] is very sweet. See how nicely he plays with his little cousins. When he grows up he may have my little Dilan as his bride."
> Gule's mother: "Yes, Zeki is sweet. But his brother. . . . No, he is too rough. I will never let him have my Gule [an infant]!"
> Zeki's mother: "Oh! My boys are too good for your girls! My boys are going to marry Aisha's [possible future] daughters! We don't need your girls!"

These conversations are mostly in jest, but they reveal something of the future expectations and negotiations which will be taken quite seriously. As the children grow older, the topic may become too sensitive to joke about.

After the groom's mother suggests a possible bride for her son, the groom-to-be and his parents pay a formal visit to "meet" the bride. She will serve tea or coffee to the guests, but remains silent unless spoken to. If the groom likes what little he sees, the fathers of both families begin formal negotiations over the amount of clothes and gold jewelry that will be given to the bride by the groom's family. The cost to the groom's family is substantial. The amount varies depending on the social and financial status of the families involved. Between poor families, the groom's family will be expected to buy a complete set of clothes, including shoes, and perhaps a dresser. They must also provide at least one each of the following items of gold: a bracelet or watch, a ring, a neckchain, a pair of earrings, and a gold coin to be hung from the chain. The proceeds from selling animals and hides are used to buy the gold, (at least five to ten sheep are required to pay for the gold listed above). If the families are wealthy, more gold is required. The number of rings, earrings and bracelets, lengths of chain and number of coins are all stipulated and may cost several thousand dollars. The gold signifies the groom's family's respect for the bride and her family, and acts as insurance for the bride in the event that the marriage fails or she runs short of funds to pay doctors, to feed her children, etc. The bride's family provides her with a cow or a couple of sheep, and the bride brings her woven *minder* and bolsters, and embroidered linen to use in her new home.

Once the fathers reach an agreement, a formal settlement is drawn up and a time for the wedding may be set, if the future bride and groom are of marriageable age. The prospective bride is expected to marry the man her father chooses for her. A kind father will ask the daughter's opinion before agreeing to a marriage, but he makes the ultimate decision. A well-raised daughter does not question her father's authority. I was told of a case in which two young people were in love, but the father refused to consider the man's request for his daughter's hand. The girl's mother and siblings carried on so much, exerting pressure on the father to allow the marriage, that he finally consented. A girl may be betrothed a few years before she is old enough to marry. She will remain in her parents' home until the marriage and will receive gifts of clothes, or cloth, and gold jewelry from her future father-in-law. Once an agreement is reached and gifts accepted, a change of heart may lead to great animosity between the families. If a man fails to provide the full amount agreed upon, or if he does not support and clothe her according to the standards to which she was accustomed in her own family, a bride has grounds for divorce. Unless otherwise stipulated in the marriage settlement, the wife must repay the gifts in full in order to obtain a divorce. A man, on the other hand, need only renounce his wife three times to divorce her: "I renounce you. I renounce you. I renounce you!" The bride then returns to her natal family. She may keep the children of the marriage only while they are small. The children belong to their father's family, and when they reach the age of seven they return to live with their father, who has sole custody.

Enough talk of divorce, let's return to the marriage at hand! The evening before her marriage, the bride's family hosts a henna party attended by her female friends and relatives, and the groom's female relatives. In addition to dancing and singing, the women rub the bride's palms with henna. A woman who has had a happy and successful life is the first to rub henna into the bride's palms. The idea is that the woman's good luck will rub off and bring good luck to the bride in her new life. The bride may at first refuse to open her hand. A member of the groom's family will then entice her to open her hand by presenting her with a ring or some other small gift. The women have a good time dancing and singing and they all rub henna into the bride's palms to make her beautiful for her wedding. They may apply henna to the soles of the bride's feet and—less often—to her hair. The participants at the party also henna their own palms, and the stain remains for several days. If you see a Kurdish woman with henna-stained hands, you may ask, "Who was married?" Chances are the woman has been to a henna party. If the bride's family lives in another village, and the groom's female relatives must travel far, fewer of them will make the journey. In this case, they are expected to stay the night and the bride's family serves their guests a generous meal, and provides bedding and places to sleep for everyone. In the morning the guests are served breakfast before returning home. If they have traveled far, the women of the groom's family are accompanied by a few male relatives, since women avoid traveling alone without the protection of a male relative. These men bide their time while the women enjoy themselves at the henna party.

At the groom's home, the groom's family hosts a party for friends, neighbors and relatives. Food is served, and everyone dances to the music of a drum and reed instrument. The music and dancing continues until the groom and his father and brothers leave to bring the bride home. The guests all follow the groom to help fetch the bride. While the groom's family is joyous to be receiving a new bride, the bride's family is expected to be sad at the loss of their daughter. The bride's young brothers station themselves at strategic spots along the route, and at the door, demanding small coins in exchange for letting the entourage pass. After dispensing a fair amount of change, the groom and his father and brothers are allowed in to take the bride. The bride is sad to leave her family and go to her new home. If she is not sad, she is expected to act as though she were. As a modest young woman, she is expected not to show affection toward her groom. Before the bride crosses the threshold of her husband's house, a ceramic pitcher full of water is broken on the threshold, and the bride throws an egg to break upon the ground. This is to ensure that the marriage will prosper.

Even after the wedding, the bride and groom are expected not to display affection when others are present. In fact, their daily lives do not overlap much. The groom works with his father and brothers. The bride begins her new life helping the unmarried daughters and her sisters-in-law who married into the family, under the guidance of her mother-in-law. The groom's family will refer to her as "our bride," for she is now a member of their family. A good bride never argues with her mother-in-law, but seeks to be helpful and pleasant, and shows her respect by quietly accepting advice and suggestions. A good mother-in-law is not a "slave-driver", but is kind, supportive and even protective of her "bride." She recognizes that the bride will bear and raise her grandchildren, and so she seeks to ensure the bride's health and fertility. If she overworks her or lets her catch a chill, she may jeopardize the bride's chances of conceiving and bearing healthy children. By showing her new daughter-in-law kindness when she is a new bride, a woman ensures herself of a willing helper and a happy family life for herself in the future. A childless marriage is a tragedy for all concerned, for children are considered the only insurance against loneliness and poverty in old-age. A man may then take a second wife who will—hopefully—be more fertile than the first.

The Koran allows a man to have up to four wives, provided he can support them all and spends equal time with each. In fact, few men can afford more than one wife, but in the case of a childless first marriage, taking a second wife is considered a necessity, regardless of the affection between man and wife (or mother and daughter-in-law). Each wife will usually have her own section of the house to run independently. The relationship between the two wives is not automatically hostile. Although the second wife should show respect to the first, it is in the best interest of the childless first wife to help care for and develop an affectionate relationship with her husband's children by his second wife. This ensures that the children will love and care for her in her old age, just as they do for their real mother. Two middle aged women who have cooperated to share the work of raising one's children may be very close friends by the time the children are grown. In some cases, however, a man may take a second wife despite the many children born by his first wife. Unless he is a wealthy man, he may be open to gossip and criticism for this. When the two co-wives each have their own children, they are more likely to see one another as the source of competition for their own children's prospects. If a man neglects his first wife, he may also have to answer to her father and brothers. In fact any woman's best protection against an unkind husband is to have a caring father and many strong protective brothers.

One family I visited prepared a meal in honor of their daughter-in-law's father. There was much joking and visiting, but at one point the father saw that his daughter was unhappy. "Why is my daughter crying?" demanded the father. "What have you done to her? Have you worked her too hard?" He turned to his daughter and asked her why she was upset. She wouldn't tell him, and he asked, "Has your husband's family treated you badly?" She shook her head no and told him it was nothing, not to blame her in-laws because they treated her very well. Her father gave the in-laws one last threatening glance and said, "Okay, but you tell me if they ever mistreat you, it doesn't matter how far away you live, I will send your brothers after them!" The fact that this man was powerful in the village and had many sons meant that this threat of physical violence was taken seriously. Since the daughter assured her father of her good treatment, the visit was concluded amicably.

The bride may tease or joke with her husband's younger brothers, or even send them on errands, but she must show respect to and remain somewhat distant from his older brothers. Toward her father-in-law she shows particular respect. She will not eat, drink, smoke or sleep in his presence. She will serve meals to her husband's family, but will herself eat in a different room. This does not mean she eats alone. If there are other brides in the family, they work and eat together, often accompanied by the family's unmarried daughters, and possibly by the mother-in-law as well. Young children eat with the women and these meals can be quite hectic, between feeding small children, and jumping up to serve the men.

The meal is served on a low round table or tray (four or five inches above the floor). Everyone manages to fit around the low table. Each person takes some flat bread, small bits of which can be used to pinch up mouthfuls of food out of the communal bowls and platters. Fingers, spoons and forks are also used to eat from these bowls. A typical meal consists of bread, pilaf or rice, yogurt soup with garlic and rice, cracked wheat or cucumber, and a stew of tomatoes, peppers, eggplant, onions, squash, and occasionally mutton or goat meat, depending upon the family's wealth. When a person has had enough to eat, he will leave the table and wash his hands and face and rinse his mouth. The young women of the household bring the water and pour it over the diner's hands into a small basin while he washes them. The young women then serve tea and sugar, in small tea glasses, while the men and older women lounge against the bolsters. A good host does not finish eating until after his guests have finished and left the table. To do so would be to suggest that the guest is eating too much. Rather, a guest is repeatedly admonished to eat more, and assured that there is plenty more of everything in the kitchen, even if it means someone else goes without. A good guest knows how much is enough. If the guest does not accept his host's generosity this may insult the host by implying that his food or hospitality is not good enough. When everyone has finished eating, washed his hands and been served tea, the young women clean and remove the table or tray, finish their own meal, and wash the dishes.

At night the women pull out the wool-filled mattresses, quilts and pillows which are stacked in a pile during the day. Each married couple will sleep in their own room with their unmarried children. The oldest couple and their children sleep in the room with the stove. If there are not enough rooms for each couple, the youngest couple will sleep in the kitchen or storeroom, wherever they can find privacy. The mattresses are laid out next to one another in a row. In the summer when the Kurds sleep on the roofs, each couple and their unmarried children sleep a little removed from the others. Screens may be put up to offer more privacy, or stacks of firewood or dried dung may separate the nuclear families sleeping on the roof.

In the morning the women prepare, serve, and wash up after a breakfast of tea, bread, yogurt, feta cheese, and perhaps olives, sliced tomatoes or cucumber, boiled eggs or honey. They then stack the bedding and, if they have one, go to their vegetable garden to weed and water. There is a system of ditches which flow from a stream or spring to the garden plots of all the households of the village. Each household has an allotted plot and day or time when the women of the household may open the ditch leading to their plot and irrigate their garden. The oldest woman of the household makes all the decisions regarding her garden. Much of the work is done by the younger women of the family. Women often grow tomatoes, red and green peppers, cucumbers, squash, eggplant, green beans, and melons in their gardens. In the winter when the animals are kept indoors, the women will give them food and water and milk them twice a day. In the summer the animals are herded out to graze in the cool of the night by a man or young boy. In the late morning they are brought back to be given water and milked by the women. Usually the mother-in-law will do the milking, and she controls whatever proceeds there are from the sale of the valuable butter. The daughters and daughters-in-law help by giving the animals water, holding the animal being milked, and keeping the animals which have been milked separate from those who have not. Some women train the sheep to wait their turn in line with only a little prodding.

Kurdish women do not go to the mosques, but pray five times a day in the privacy of their homes. Unless they are pregnant or nursing, they fast—as do the men—from sunrise to sunset every day during the month of Ramadan, and participate in the feasting that follows. On the holiday of Bairam, they do not accompany the men to the mosque, but help butcher the sheep which the men slaughter as a sacrifice to God. They prepare the meals and partici-pate in the visiting and feasting. Some women make the pilgrimage to Mecca, accompanied by their husbands, sons, or brothers.

A Kurdish woman's most important role is to bear and raise children. Upon the birth of a child, the mother is given gifts of gold coins or jewelry by her husband's family. Since daughters marry and leave the family, sons are important because they will support their parents in old age. A man's prestige is greater if he has many sons, for he may call upon their physical strength in a dispute or feud. If a woman bears only daughters her husband holds her responsible for his lack of sons. A woman who has many sons is beyond reproach. However, a woman also needs daughters to help with household tasks and tend younger brothers and sisters. While a man might be proud of his sons, he may dote on his daughters.

Kurdish women play an important role in the lives of their families, and are generally granted a good deal of respect and inde-pendence. While a young woman is expected to be submissive, this expectation lessens as she has children of her own. Middle aged and elderly women are quick to express their opinions, to disagree, or to scold their husbands. They may be considerate of their hus-band's feelings and not scold when his father, elder brothers or friends are present, but they manage to make their feelings known. Even among young women, the submissive respectful behavior shown to strangers and elders is quite different from the indepen-dence, strong will and sense of fun which are apparent in other set-tings. Although Kurdish women do wear headscarves, they have never been veiled.

Having seen how Kurdish women spend their time, you may be wondering where the men are and what they are doing. From the time a boy is seven or eight he begins to be included into the world of the men. First he will be expected to run errands for his grandmother, mother, aunts and sisters, and to help fetch water or run errands. As he gets older his errands take him further from home—from taking messages to other households, to making purchases in the stores or bazaars of nearby towns. When he is not in school, he may help his father and older brothers or sit quietly with them in someone's home, or at the tea houses. Since women do not travel or shop alone, older boys and young men do most of the shopping for their mothers, and sisters. When a woman wants to travel to a town or city, she asks her younger brother or son to accompany her. The men represent their families in every way, from owning property, to making a living, from participating in local and tribal politics, mosques and religious brotherhoods, to understanding national and international politics.

Traditionally, when the nomadic tribe owned its territory, it also "owned" the villagers who worked the fields in a kind of feudal system. These villagers, though not originally from the tribe, were incorporated into it in a subservient capacity. As a result of the drawing up and closing of borders across the Kurdish mountains, and of state policies aimed at settling the nomadic tribes, the Kurds were gradually forced to settle in permanent villages. The governments knew that a nomadic tribe is much more difficult to control than settled villagers, since they can pack up their possessions, round up their livestock, and "disappear" into the mountains on short notice. Settled villagers, on the other hand, risk the destruction of their crops and homes if they leave their villages. Although a few tribes continue to live a nomadic life, almost all Kurds are now settled.

When the various states began land reforms, the *aghas* were registered as the owners of the tribal lands and villages. The *aghas* may not have been aware at the time of the totally arbitrary power this registration gave them over tribal lands. They were merely fulfilling their role as leader and negotiator between the tribe and the government. The tribal members were reluctant to be registered individually because they associated registration by the state with taxation or conscription into the military. Therefore, much of the once communally owned tribal land is now the private property of the *aghas* and their heirs. Many of these land-owning *aghas* have moved to towns and cities so that they can live an easier and more sophisticated lifestyle and their children can be better educated. The villagers pay the landowners a percentage of the proceeds from their livestock and crops in exchange for use of village land and pasturage. Usually the landowners get fifty percent of the proceeds, although in some cases they take as much as two thirds to three quarters of the villager's income. When an *agha* owns an entire village, he owns everything in it, including the spring, the houses, the garden area, the fields and the pasturage. The villagers may live in the houses, till the land, and use the communal areas only as long as they work for the *agha*. In a village which is owned by several families, each family owns its own house, stable, fields and plot in the vegetable garden. The spring or well, and the pasturage are owned communally by all the landowning families.

In the villages, men are responsible for planting and harvesting the crops—other than the vegetable gardens—and making decisions regarding the sale and slaughter of animals. They also clip the sheep's wool in the spring. Depending upon the local conditions, most families grow wheat and/or barley for their family's consumption and for their livestock to eat in the winter. Excess grain will be sold for profit to merchants in nearby towns (5–50 miles away). Other crops grown for sale to the local merchants are tobacco, sunflowers, cotton, and melons. Raising and selling livestock is an important source of income, as is the sale of their wool, hides and butter. Much of the labor involved in planting and harvesting has been taken over by the tractor. This has left the men with more time on their hands, and a loss of income for those who own neither land nor tractor. Men will discuss the weather with their brothers and sons, and plan the best time to sow and harvest. If a villager owns a tractor he will plan when he will need it and then arrange with others to sow or harvest their fields for a fee or a portion of the harvest. In the case of more labor-intensive crops, a landowner or tenant may hire additional labor from the ranks of the under-employed.

Among the Kurds there are also occupations based on religious status. The *mullahs,* or priests, who reside in towns and larger villages provide religious instruction to the boys of the village, and lead religious ceremonies at the mosques. These days, whatever prestige or respect they are shown is based not so much on their status as mullah as on their wisdom and the integrity they show in their daily lives.[10]

Even among the Kurds there are *seyyids,* who claim to be directly descended from the Prophet through his son-in-law, Ali. These people are often poor and support themselves by moving from village to village selling religious amulets, acting as soothsayers, or merely claiming the right to financial support due to their descent. They are not shown much respect unless they also happen to be wealthy and powerful. In this case, their descent increases the prestige they have acquired by other means.[11]

The *shaikhs*, on the other hand are accorded both power and prestige based upon their status as leaders of the religious brotherhoods (sufi or dervish orders). The Qadiri and the Nagshi-bandi brotherhoods are the only such orders in Kurdistan. A *shaikh* gains his title after receiving religious instruction and being recognized by another shaikh. Shaikhly status is often handed down from father to son. A shaikh gains prestige and power through his ability to perform miracles—proof that he is indeed one of God's favored ones. Even after a powerful shaikh has died, his power is believed to continue to emanate from his tomb. People travel to the tomb to pray for miracles. The shaikh's descendants tend the shrine and organize pilgrimages, which may provide a substantial income. The Qadiri and Nagshibandi brotherhoods attract followers from many different Kurdish tribes. As the only form of organization (greater than the tribes) which was independent from the government, the brotherhoods served an important function. Because a shaikh had followers from many tribes, he was an ideal person to help mediate tribal disputes after the collapse of the emirates. Thus, in addition to religious power, shaikhs could gain substantial power as political leaders.[12]

The Kurdish "Tale of Suto and Tato" tells of a shaikh's attempt to profit from a dispute between rival aghas. Suto, agha of the Duskani tribe, had attacked and destroyed a fort belonging to Tato, agha of the Rekani tribe. Shaikh Muhammad Sadiq was "a great vulture" eager to get his hands on the Rekani lands. Tato was advised by someone in league with the Shaikh to seek the Shaikh's protection. The Shaikh offered to buy the fort and rebuild it for Tato, supply him with twenty men and a hundred rifles and a special order from the Ottoman government for his protection, in exchange for a tenth of the Rekani harvests every year. Tato agreed and the fort was rebuilt bigger and stronger than before. Suto realized that once complete, the fort and the protection of the Shaikh would give Tato enough power to entrap Suto and the Duskani tribe. He led his men in a dawn attack on the fort when Tato and his men were elsewhere. All but seven of the twenty of the Shaikh's men were killed. The Shaikh obtained government permission to protect Tato's village and install armed men at the fort. He then sent 400 of his followers—100 each from four different tribes—to the fort. The idea was to attack the Duskani villages. If the Duskani fought, they would find themselves at war with all four tribes. Suto understood this, so he fled with his men from the first village before it was attacked, and Tato's men burned it to the ground in revenge for the first attack on the fort. Suto felt his only option was to attempt to pacify the Shaikh. A meeting was arranged at the tomb of Shaikh Sadiq's grandfather where Suto agreed to pay 1,300 lira in blood money to the Shaikh for his men who were killed in the attack on the fort. By entering the dispute between the two aghas, Shaikh Sadiq gained ten percent of the future harvests from the Rekani lands, 1,300 liras from Suto, and increased prestige from his role as mediator and protector.[13]

Many landless Kurds have migrated to towns and cities, both near and far, to work as wage laborers in order to support their families. Unemployment—and underemployment—are a fact of life for many Kurds. The Kurds are increasingly aware of the importance of education in obtaining a better lifestyle for their children, and literacy rates are rising. Unfortunately, most Kurdish children are at a disadvantage when they begin schooling because they are taught in a foreign language; either Turkish, Arabic, or Persian, depending upon the country in which they live. One Turkish teacher informed me that his Kurdish students—who made up at least half the class—did much more poorly in all their subjects than did the Turkish students. When I asked him why he thought this was the case, he replied that they must be less intelligent. In addition to having to overcome the negative prejudices of their teachers, and the language problems, Kurdish children are confronted with government versions of their history. In Turkey they are taught that their ancestors were in fact ethnically Turkish, and that the language that they speak is an inferior dialect of Turkish. In fact, Turkish is not an Indo-European language, let alone related to Kurdish. To succeed in school, Kurdish children must be both extremely bright and diligent. Some families in Turkey, especially those in large cities, speak Turkish, rather than Kurdish, to their children, in the hopes that they will be better equipped to succeed in Turkish schools. Some parents have expressed their distress that their children do not speak Kurdish, but ask, "What else could we do?" Young adults who were raised speaking Turkish and who have become politically active have confided that they are ashamed not to speak Kurdish. Some of them have arranged to learn Kurdish as adults.

Kurdish men spend their abundant free time visiting or sitting in teahouses discussing local events and politics. Traditionally the agha maintained a guesthouse where visitors to the village were guaranteed hospitality. By accepting a man's hospitality, the visitor places himself in a subservient position under the protection of the host. The host thus gains prestige, but must protect his guest at all costs. Travellers from afar continue to be greatly valued as a source of news from the world beyond the village. As host the agha was able to control the villagers' access to information of the world at large. In the evenings the men would gather at the guesthouse to drink tea and discuss what news they had.

Troubadours travelled from place to place and were assured of a generous welcome at the guesthouses. They were skilled at singing and storytelling and were greatly appreciated. They recounted Kurdish legends and sang ballads and epic tales of courageous warriors and true love. Many of these epic poems were composed by Kurdish poets during the rule of the emirs. Some date back as early as the eleventh century, while tales of fairly recent battles were also elaborated as they were retold. The Tale of Suto and Tato, for example, is based on actual events which occurred around the turn of the century. Radio and television have since replaced the Kurdish troubadours, but an effort is underway to write down as many of the Kurdish tales as possible. Kurdish authors and poets continue to write of the Kurdish experience and study their literature in an effort to expand upon it and further develop the Kurdish language. Much of this activity is carried out in exile, since it is not tolerated by most of the governments which control Kurdistan. The greatest problems the Kurds have in developing a common literature are due to the differences in dialect and the fact that different countries use different alphabets. A modified Latin alphabet is used in Turkey. The arabic alphabet is used in Iran, Iraq and Syria, and the Cyrillic alphabet is used in the republics of the former Soviet Union. A Turkish Kurd who speaks Kurmanji must therefore learn the Arabic alphabet and comprehend Sorani before he is able to read the Kurdish literature written and published in Iraq, unless it has first been translated.

When the agha moved into the cities, the guesthouses were closed since no one else had the means to provide such hospitality. They have been replaced by teahouses which sell tea by the glass and provide a place for men to meet and visit with one another. Time spent in this way is not wasted. Visiting in homes or in teahouses is an important source of knowledge about how the world works, especially to a population with low rates of literacy. A man may gain advice from his cronies regarding how to get somewhere by bus; which local merchant is more honest, or can be haggled down to the best prices; how much of a bribe to pay to avoid a traffic citation; how to avoid being called for military service, etc. The government controls and censors the media and the Kurds view themselves as being at war with the government. Teahouses thus provide a place to meet and share information or interpretations about what is really happening; whether it is safe to travel to a neighboring district, or how to respond to local events. In Turkey, where the government denies the existence of Kurds, the exchange of knowledge about what it means to be a Kurd is not only political, but also illegal. Discussions between men are the basis for obtaining news of political activities and crackdowns. When all Kurdish organizations and historical, literary or political publications are banned, this kind of information can only be passed on by word of mouth or smuggled between friends.

> I think you will find, no matter which Kurds you talk to, that we all agree on one thing [the desire for some degree of Kurdish autonomy] even if we don't all agree on how we should accomplish it (A Kurdish man, in the late 1980s).

The right to live their lives by following their own cultural values and norms is behind the Kurdish desire for autonomy. It means having the right to make their own laws, to speak and write their own language, and to educate their children in their language, about their own history. It means having the right to develop and pass on Kurdish literary traditions, and to use and develop their land and its resources for the benefit of its inhabitants. The right to a full Kurdish culture is what the Kurds have fought for and been denied since the beginning of the 20th century. Although tribal leaders and shaikhs led many of the early revolts and rebellions, the Kurds have developed modern political parties. These parties provide a means of organizing greater numbers of Kurdish nationalists than could be brought together under a tribal system. Not all religious and tribal leaders were at odds with the younger, often more radical members of the political parties. The history of the Mahabad Republic demonstrates how traditional leaders and nationalist party members were able to work together toward a common goal. It also illustrates the way foreign governments have encouraged and funded Kurdish rebellions for their own purposes.

In 1941 the Soviets, British and Americans occupied Iran. The Soviets controlled and were anxious to annex portions of northern

Iran. They encouraged the Kurds and Azerbaijanis to demand local autonomy and provided financial support and military supplies to the Komala (The Society for the Rebirth of Kurdistan). With the help of Mullah Mustafa Barzani, a powerful tribal leader from Iraqi Kurdistan, the Kurds were able to gain control over the city of Mahabad and its environs. They established the first de facto Kurdish republic in January of 1946. It was governed by the Kurdish Democratic Party of Iran, which was made up of the members of the Komala, as well as a group of young Kurdish communists. This party was led by Qazi Mohammad, a Kurdish religious leader who had agreed to work with the Soviets. The "Mahabad Republic" was, however, short-lived. When the Soviet Union reached an agreement with the Shah of Iran, and no longer needed internal pressure exerted on the Shah, it withdrew its support of the Kurds. In December 1946, the Shah's forces, with the help of Kurds loyal to the government (in part because they were uneasy about communism), easily defeated and crushed the Kurdish forces. After the Mahabad Republic's defeat, the Shah prohibited the teaching of Kurdish and closed the printing press. Qazi Mohammed was executed and Barzani and his men found refuge in the Soviet Union. Kurdish books were burned, and weapons confiscated throughout the area.[14]

Government policies toward the Kurdish minorities have been the most repressive in the countries in which the Kurds make up a substantial proportion of the population: Iran, Iraq and Turkey. Turkey's ethnic policy was conceived by Kemal Ataturk, founder of the Turkish nation-state. He declared "Happy is he who can call himself a Turk." His policy was based on the assertion that all citizens of Turkey are ethnic Turks. The ten to twenty million Kurds, most of whom live in eastern Turkey, are officially referred to as "mountain Turks." The government's policy has taken the concept of assimilation to an extreme. To acknowledge the existence of Kurds in Turkey is illegal. Speaking, writing, or singing in Kurdish has been strictly forbidden until a recent (1991) law allowed the use of spoken Kurdish in private settings only. Children are taught in Turkish and punished if caught speaking Kurdish at school, even during recess. One young man told of how, as a child, he and his classmates were forced by their teacher to swear on the Koran that they would never speak a word of Kurdish. He and his classmates were terrified that they would forget and accidentally say something in Kurdish and be blinded by God as punishment. Upon graduation, these children made a pact to all speak Kurdish at the same time, so that if they were in fact blinded, they would all be in it together. Imagine their joy when they realized they could still see! This experience ultimately contributed to his ethnic pride and recognition of the power of language.

In 1924 all Kurdish schools, associations, publications, and religious brotherhoods were banned by the Turkish government.[15] The government response to Kurdish uprisings in the 1920s was mass executions, the burning of entire villages, and the death of tens or hundreds of thousands of peasants. Law No. 1,850, passed in 1930, made clear the government's attitude toward the rebellious Kurds. It proclaimed that murders and other actions against the Kurds would not be considered crimes.[16]

In addition, a 1932 law legalized the total evacuation of Kurds from some areas of Kurdistan to central Anatolia.[17] The idea was to move them to ethnically Turkish areas where they would be forced to assimilate. Turks were encouraged to move into eastern Turkey so that the Kurds would not be a majority and thus would have no basis for self-rule. The cost and logistics of moving so many people prevented the Turkish government from completing the evacuation of the entire Kurdish population. Nonetheless, hundreds of thousands of Kurds were forced from their villages to be resettled in central Anatolia. After such massacres and deportations, the Kurdish population no longer viewed rebellion as an option.

After World War II, when the Turkish political system was liberalized and a multiparty system allowed, Kurdish intellectuals began to work within the system. The 1961 Constitution granted freedom of the press, of expression and of association, but Kurdish associations and published or stated views in sympathy with Kurds have seldom been tolerated by the various Turkish regimes; countless Kurds have been—and continue to be—imprisoned and tortured for such activities. Many Kurds view the numerous military bases in eastern Turkey as a form of "colonial occupation" and fear and animosity is great between the local population and the Turkish soldiers stationed there. The young urbanized and politically active Kurds have tended to espouse leftist ideologies in part because eastern Turkey is substantially poorer and less developed than other areas of Turkey. The Kurdish activists have therefore often found themselves in opposition to the traditional Kurdish leaders who are the large landowners. Ironically, the severe retaliation meted out by the Turkish military in response to leftist-nationalist attacks have actually expanded the ranks of these parties.

The Iraqi and Iranian governments were more tolerant of Kurdish culture, but refused to grant local self-rule or equal access to the amenities doled out by the central governments. The Kurds of Iraq have resorted to armed resistance as a means of establishing Kurdish control over the Kurdish districts and of providing an incentive to the governments to negotiate with the Kurds. The Iraqi Kurds have occasionally been able to insist upon demands of local autonomy. In 1970, for example, the Iraqi government agreed to allow the use of Kurdish as the language of instruction in schools run by and for the Kurds. A university in the Kurdish region offered courses in Kurdish studies, and Kurdish literature has prospered in Iraq relative to the other countries. However, problems occurred before the agreement was fully implemented. Like the Turks in the 30's, the Iraqi government forced tens of thousands of Kurdish civilians out of their homes. It was an attempt to obtain control over the Kurdish population and deprive them of the basis for any demands for autonomous regions, especially in the oil and mineral-rich Kurdish districts. The Kurdish guerilla soldiers (*pesh merga*—literally, "one who looks Death in the eye") attempted to prevent the "Arabization" of Iraqi Kurdistan. They did not attempt to fully engage the Iraqi military, but merely to protect the civilian population. The rugged terrain, support from the local population, and off and on offers of aid from various countries interested in regional politics made it possible for the Kurdish guerilla soldiers in Iraq to sustain the kind of armed resistance and cultural freedom that was not possible in Turkey in the 1930s.[18]

After the fall of the Mahabad Republic, the Kurds of Iran were not allowed to express their Kurdish identity. The Kurds have a saying: "The enemy of my enemy is my friend." During the Iranian Revolution of 1979, most of the Kurds worked to overthrow the Shah in the hopes of establishing a government sensitive to Kurdish demands for regional self-rule. Once the revolution was accomplished, however, the Kurds learned that their place in the Islamic Republic was as fellow Muslims. They found themselves under the centralized control of the Islamic Revolutionary Council. Any demands for recognition of specific ethnic rights as Kurds were considered irrelevant and/or in conflict with the concept of an Islamic brotherhood.[19] Eventually many of the Kurds of Iran followed the example set by the Iraqi Kurds; alternating negotiation with the government with fighting to extend control of Kurdish territory.

During the Iran-Iraq war which began in 1980, the Kurds on both sides of the border took advantage of the opportunity to revolt against their respective governments and attempted to extend Kurdish control over all Kurdish districts. The government of Iran provided financial support and arms to the Kurds in Iraq, while the Kurds of Iran received similar support from the Iraqi government. Near the end of the war, each government turned its attention to punishing its own rebellious Kurds. The Iraqi military dropped bombs containing mustard gas on its own citizens, among other places, in the Kurdish city of Halabja in 1988. An estimated 6350 Kurds, many of them women and children, were killed.[20] In response, an estimated 60,000 Kurds fled to Turkey and as many more crossed into Iran, while well over a thousand civilians were killed en route.[21] An estimated 3159 Kurdish villages were systematically bulldozed to the ground in the "free fire zones" declared by Saddam Hussein.[22] According to Kurdish reports, 500,000 inhabitants were forcibly resettled in the uninhabitable desert regions of southern and western Iraq.[23]

The arrival of the Iraqi refugees caused a dilemma for the Turkish government. It could not refuse them entry without risking serious political repercussions from NATO allies and the European Community, which was considering Turkey's request for membership. However, the Turkish government preferred to avoid an influx of Kurdish nationalists from Iraq who might stir up the Kurdish population in eastern Turkey. It set up tent camps and invited foreign journalists to see how well it cared for the Iraqi Kurds. It refused offers by foreign aid agencies such as Save the Children to intervene. Instead, it suggested monetary aid be sent for the Turkish government to use as it saw fit. It refused to acknowledge that some of these Kurds had suffered from chemical gas attacks. As international interest waned, the Turkish government sent 20,000 refugees across the border to Iran, and sent the remaining refugees to live in three settlements in the cities of Diyarbekir, Mush and Mardin.[24] All three settlements were surrounded by barbed wire and guarded to keep the Iraqi Kurds isolated from the local Kurdish population.

The Turkish Kurds viewed the Iraqi Kurds as "true Kurds" because they had been allowed a degree of cultural freedom denied to the Turkish Kurds. They still wore traditional Kurdish clothes, had retained tribal structure to a greater extent, had established well organized political parties, and had been able to write and study the Kurdish language, and further develop Kurdish literature. Most of all, the Turkish Kurds admired the military feats of the Kurds from Iraq. Among the Turkish Kurds, young men began wearing baggy pants in similar shades to those worn by the Kurdish guerilla soldiers from Iraq. While Turkish Kurds reported feeling a great pride in and concern for the refugees, they felt frustrated by their inability to help them. A small number of refugees were allowed out of the camps each day to go to the cities on errands. Local Kurds spoke of their fear that a good number of the distinctively dressed refugees were actually agents for M.I.T. (the Turkish secret police). Since it was still illegal to speak Kurdish and the Iraqi Kurds did not speak Turkish, the more daring local Kurds mumbled a few words of Kurdish to the refugees, and offered to buy—at generous prices—whatever items the refugees' wives were able to fashion for sale, or even items of clothing worn by the refugees. They reported it was illegal to give aid to refugees, and were fearful that any such attempt could land them in jail. In the summer young refugee children were given blocks of ice from the freezers of sympathetic urban women. The children took some of this ice to the camps, and used some to earn a small income. They walked the streets selling glasses of ice water to thirsty townspeople. There were reports that some refugees died from cold, malnutrition and disease that autumn and winter. In 1993, the refugees are reportedly supporting themselves as street vendors, selling everything from toys to music cassettes, to cloth and clothes.

Their experiences with the Iraqi Kurds had a profound effect on the Kurds of Turkey. Although the predominantly Kurdish districts continued to be under martial law, the local population became more daring. Large public demonstrations were held, beginning in autumn of 1989. By 1991, thousands of protesters turned out for demonstrations celebrating Newroz in cities throughout Turkey. Newroz is the Kurdish new year celebration which takes place on March 21. It is a celebration of the return of light in the spring and commemorates the people's rebellion against a cruel and unjust king. The Kurds consider Newroz to be their national holiday. They find it perfectly suited as a day on which to demonstrate against the government.

After the Gulf War, when the U.S.-led forces routed the Iraqi army, President Bush called on the people of Iraq to revolt against Saddam Hussein. The Kurdish guerilla soldiers of northern Iraq were quick to establish control of virtually all of Iraqi Kurdistan, including the oil-rich district of Kirkuk. When Saddam Hussein's forces responded with force and President Bush refused to intervene, hundreds of thousands of Kurds fled into Iran and to the Turkish border. In Iran the refugees were aided by the government and by civilians, especially Iranian Kurds. The Turkish government refused to allow the refugees into Turkey, claiming there were too many of them for Turkey to handle. In response, the United Nations security council passed a resolution to allow international foreign aid into a "safe haven" area which was protected from Iraqi forces by international coalition forces.[25] The Kurds within these protected areas were encouraged to hold elections and set up a system of self-government. Many of the refugees returned to their homes in Kurdish controlled areas. All the while, negotiations were carried out between Saddam Hussein and the Kurdistan Front, who were unable to reach any agreement. The coalition forces extended their presence in the safe haven. After they withdrew completely in July 1991, the threat of troops stationed nearby in Turkey has been effective in protecting the Iraqi Kurds from further attack by Iraqi government forces. What will happen to the Iraqi Kurds when the United Nations withdraws its support remains to be seen.

As we have seen, many aspects of Kurdish culture have developed within the context of state-level political organization. As pastoral nomads with a fierce fighting tradition, the Kurds were able to maintain some degree of independence from the Ottoman Empire. Inhabiting the rugged terrain at the edge of two powerful empires helped make this possible. This theme of manipulating oppositions between neighboring states, and crossing the borders to escape pursuit by government forces has continued from the time of the Ottoman Empire to the present. With the incorporation of the Kurds into distinct nation-states, Kurdish ethnic identity developed in response to the various minority policies. In Turkey every aspect of Kurdish culture took on political meaning in response to the policy of acculturation. Speaking the language, singing Kurdish songs, wearing Kurdish clothes, even saying "I am a Kurd!" all became statements of opposition to the government. Iraqi and Iranian Kurds continued the theme of fierce battle to control Kurdish territory, coupled with negotiation with the government and foreign allies. Being a Kurd in Iraq is to "look Death in the eye" in order to assert Kurdish cultural and political independence. Kurds have asked, "How do you tell if someone is a Kurd?" The answer they give is "He looks straight ahead, and never diverts his eyes." In other words, a "true" Kurd will look even Death in the eye rather than look away.

It is easy to see how the men engage in political activity, but the women also play a vital role. Their most important role is to bear and raise Kurdish children. The men may speak of raising future guerilla soldiers, but the women are aware of the complexity of their role. Regardless of their ethnic pride, they want their children to be safe. They teach their children Kurdish ways; speak to them in Kurdish, and sing them Kurdish lullabies. The men then inspire their children to be proud of these emotional bonds that they developed in early childhood, and to be brave in proclaiming their Kurdishness. One man asked his child "Are you a Turk or a Kurd?" and praised her lavishly when she said she was a Kurd. In a different situation, a mother smiled as her three year old sang a Kurdish song. She was proud of her child but asked, "What can I do? The secret police have spies in the village. What would they do if they heard?" She proceeded to tell of the Kurdish music tape given to her husband by his relatives. She told of how she destroyed and disposed of it out of fear for her family. These two incidents exemplify the Kurds' continuing dilemma.

NOTES

1. Nader Entessar, *Kurdish Ethnonationalism* (Boulder, Colo.: Lynne Rienner Publishers, 1992), p. 3.

2. Kendal, "The Kurds in the Soviet Union," in Gerard Chaliand ed., *People Without A Country: The Kurds and Kurdistan* (London: Zed Press, 1980), p. 220.

3. M. M. Van Bruinessen, *Agha, Shaikh and State: On the Social and Political Organization of Kurdistan* (Rijswik: Endoprint/secondprint, 1978), pp. 20–22.

4. Kendal, "Kurdistan in Turkey" in Gerard Chaliand ed., *People Without A Country: The Kurds and Kurdistan* (London: Zed Press, 1980), p. 51.

5. Entessar, p. 3.

6. David McDowall, *The Kurds: A Nation Denied* (London: Minority Rights Publications, 1992), pp. 26–28.

7. Kendal, "The Kurds under the Ottoman Empire" in Gerard Chaliand, ed., *People Without A Country: The Kurds and Kurdistan* (London: Zed Press, 1980), pp. 34–37.

8. For a discussion of the Treaty of Sevres and why it was never rati-fied, see Kendal, "The Kurds under the Ottoman Empire" In Gerard Chaliand ed., *People Without a Country: The Kurds and Kurdistan* (London: Zed Press, 1980), pp. 34–44.

9. Ibid., pp. 41–44.

10. Van Bruinessen, *Agha, Shaikh and State*, pp. 257–58.

11. Ibid., pp. 254–55.

12. Ibid., pp. 410–12.

13. Major E.B. Soane and B. Nikitin, (collectors and translators), *The Tale of Suto and Tato* (London: Kurdologia Publications No. 7, 1988).

14. McDowall, p. 69.

15. Kendal, "Kurdistan in Turkey" in Gerard Chaliand ed., *People Without A Country: The Kurds and Kurdistan*, pp. 62–63.

16. Ibid., p. 65.

17. McDowall, *The Kurds: A Nation Denied* p. 38.

18. Ismet Sheriff Vanly, "Kurdistan in Iraq" in Gerard Chaliand ed., *People Without A Country: The Kurds and Kurdistan* (London: Zed Press, 1980), pp. 163–82.

19. Entessar, pp. 29–41.

20. Jalal Talabani, "Iraq's Colonial War in Kurdistan: 'A Special File'" *The Kurdish Culture Bulletin*, vol. 1, no. 1 (1988), p. 87.

21. McDowall, pp. 109–11.

22. Talabani, p. 88.

23. McDowall, p. 108.

24. Ibid., p. 49.

25. Entessar, pp. 153–54.

SUGGESTED READINGS

Barth, Fredrik. *Principles of Social Organization in Southern Kurdistan.* (Oslo: 1953). One of the early ethnographies of the Kurds, based on a short stay among Iraqi Kurds, this deals with the way *aghas* used hospitality to gain or maintain political power and prestige.

Chaliand, Gerard, ed. *People Without A Country: The Kurds and*

Kurdistan (London: Zed Press 1980). A collection of articles giving an historical overview of the Kurds' situation under each of the governments which have ruled over them.

Hansen, Henny Harald. *The Kurdish Woman's Life* (Copenhagen: Nationalmuseets skrifter 1961). An ethnographic description of the lives of Kurdish women, based on fieldwork among Iraqi Kurds.

Kahn, Margaret. *Children of the Jinn: In search of the Kurds and their Country* (New York: Seaview Books 1980). An interesting account of the author's experience as a guest among Kurdish women in Iran.

Leach, E.R. *Social and Economic Organization of the Rowanduz Kurds. Monographs in Social Anthropology no. 3.* (London: School of Economics and Political Science 1940). An early anthropological study among the Rowanduz Kurds of Iraq.

NANDI:
FROM CATTLE-KEEPERS TO CASH-CROP FARMERS

Regina Smith Oboler

As one travels northwest from Nairobi, Kenya, through lush farmland dotted with herds of dairy cattle, the terrain slopes gradually upward to the edge of the Great Rift Valley. Here the view stretches off seemingly to the ends of the earth. Winding down to the valley floor, the road continues across arid plains and finally descends toward Lake Nakuru—pink around the edge with thousands of flamingoes—and Nakuru town. Climbing the other side of the Rift Valley, the road levels off slightly but keeps ascending through the Tinderet Forest, crossing the equator near Timboroa Summit at an altitude of over 10,000 feet. Here begins a gradual descent across the Uasin Gishu Plateau—bleak, windy, chilly, and often overcast—to the town of Eldoret, and the home territory of the Nandi. The road into Nandi District descends gently from an altitude of over 7000 feet through rolling grasslands, crossing marshes filled with crested cranes before reaching Kapsabet, the District Center.

It is lush and green here, unlike the arid plains of the Rift Valley. It rains every month. During the main dry season in January and February it doesn't rain daily; as much as two weeks can pass with no rain. During the height of the rainy season in July, it can stay overcast and drizzly for days at a time. During most of the year, the day dawns bright and sunny, but rain clouds roll in predictably during the mid-afternoon. After a downpour, it clears again for the last few hours of daylight.

South and west of Kapsabet, the countryside becomes broken into more distinct and frequent hills and valleys with rocky out-croppings, until one reaches the Mau Escarpment in the west and the Southern Nandi Escarpment in the south. The edge of the Southern Escarpment, between 5500 and 6000 feet in altitude, over-looks another part of the Great Rift Valley. One can stand on the edge and look out at a part of Lake Victoria and sugar plantations on the surrounding plains more than a thousand feet below.

It's hard not to be affected by the grandeur of the physical environment, and to expect that the inhabitants will match it. And the Nandi are impressive: physically tall and fit, dignified in demeanor, though friendly, exuding self-confidence and fierce pride in their warrior heritage. The international track and field community knows these people very well, since they produce a disproportionate number of world-class distance runners, the best known of whom is Kipchoge ("Kip") Keino.

East Africa is known for aggressive cattle raiding. A popular myth among the Nandi is also found among the Maasai and other traditional pastoralist warrior peoples: "At the beginning of the world, God created cattle and gave them to our people. However, as time went on, many cattle wandered into the wrong hands. Though it is a serious crime to steal a cow from one of our own people, raiding others for cattle is simply restoring them to the ownership that God intended." Modern East African countries no longer permit cattle raids, but as a symbol this ethos is still alive. A young man, leaving home in 1976 on a track scholarship to an American university, was presented a spear and shield by his father's older brother and told: "In the past our young men raided with spears and shields; today you raid with pens and papers, but with the same goal—to bring wealth to our people."

The Nandi were among the most feared warriors of East Africa during the nineteenth century. "Nandi" is said to be a name of recent origin derived from the Swahili word for "cormorant", *mnandi*. This fish-eating, diving bird was a metaphor for Nandi warriors to the Swahili inland traders (East African coastal people of mixed African and Arab ancestry): like the cormorant, Nandi swept down from the heights to strike suddenly at their prey, the peoples of the plains. The Nandi came forcefully to British attention in the late 1800s as the bane of attempts to lay rail and telegraph lines; warriors repeatedly swooped down the Escarpment to steal iron and wires. The Nandi became famous among African peoples for the tenacity of their resistance to British rule; they were finally subdued only after a massive "punitive expedition" against them in 1905.

ECONOMY

Cattle have been central to Nandi life and economy for as long as anyone remembers. Fresh and preserved milk (*mursik*) were dietary staples. Nandi slaughtered sheep and goats, particularly on special occasions, but like other African pastoralists, they rarely slaughtered cattle. They added animal protein to their diet by bleeding cattle and mixing the blood with milk. This was done by tying a strap around the animal's neck so a large vein stood out, shooting an arrow into it so that it didn't go all the way through, then withdrawing the arrow and allowing the blood to flow into a container. The animal was damaged little, and could "give blood" again in a month to six weeks. This practice has now been all but abandoned. With limited pasture, people keep only plow oxen and dairy cattle, and cannot afford to weaken animals whose productivity has clear economic value.

However, the traditional economy did not depend only on cattle. Because of rich topsoil and plentiful rainfall, Nandi District is excellent farmland and the Nandi have always been farmers. Before the colonial period, the staple crop was eleusine, or finger millet, cooked into a hard porridge and eaten with a variety of green leafy vegetables. Crops were cultivated near homesteads, and most cattle were taken to graze in distant pastures by the neighborhood young men. It is said that during grain shortfalls women took sheep and goats to the lowland villages of neighboring ethnic groups to trade for grain. To what extent the Nandi consciously *chose* to concentrate on herding instead of producing grain is debatable.

During the colonial era, hybrid maize, which produces well at high altitudes and with heavy rainfall, replaced eleusine as the staple. Eleusine is still grown for dietary variety and as a component of local beer. Because the colonial government believed privatization of resources was the best route to economic development, land was divided into individual holdings with private titles beginning in 1954. Today Nandi live on small individual farms (averaging about twenty acres in the northern part of the district). Each family grows crops and grazes cattle on its own land. Most families produce a surplus of maize for the market, and tea is also a common cash crop.

Cattle continue to be important in the modern economy. The Nandi have an incredibly rich vocabulary describing cattle—anatomy, physical features, variations in color, and so on. Much conversation time was devoted to cows and their merits. This is still a popular topic, but the emphasis now is different. People no longer try to maximize the size of their herds; instead, they try to maximize milk production. Kenya Cooperative Creameries, the government sponsored dairy, buys milk daily and processes it into a wide variety of products including ultra-pasturized "shelf-milk" and tinned butter and cheese. These products are exported to other African countries. Most Nandi families' major source of income is production and sale of maize, milk, and tea in varying combinations. Few traditional zebu cattle remain in Nandi; they have been replaced by "upgraded" cattle, a mix of traditional and European strains valued for resistance to disease, or Holstein-Freisian dairy cattle, valued for high milk production. Bulls have largely been replaced by artificial insemination. In 1976–1977 the government Veterinary Service agent who drove around the countryside in a yellow VW Beetle offering insemination from an array of purebred varieties was known as the "bull-man."

FIELD SITUATION

I first arrived in Nandi in 1976 as a young doctoral candidate in anthropology, armed with research fellowships from the National Science Foundation, the National Institute of Mental Health, and the Woodrow Wilson Foundation. My husband Leon, then a graduate student in film and photography, accompanied me. Our goal was to study social change and gender roles. As a student, I had spent years preparing to do research. On one level, I was elated that the time had finally come, that I had passed my doctoral exams, that I had succeeded in snagging several sources of research funding, that after a long struggle with Kenyan government bureaucracies over research clearance, I had finally received it. On another level, I was terrified. That there were no longer any ordinary obstacles meant that there were no longer any excuses. What was left to do was to get in there, find a place to live, adjust to lack of heat and running water and the presence of daily rain, learn to communicate with these people in their own language, make friends, and learn everything it was possible to learn about their lives and their culture—all in eighteen months or so. How could anyone possibly do it? Yet I knew that my professors had all managed somehow. My major professor had been younger than I, and a single woman among a "stone age" people in Highland New Guinea who had barely been contacted by outsiders. I would be in a setting where almost every community contained a handful of English-speakers (English was the language of high school education), where there were stores with batteries for my tape recorder and radio, where not far from whatever area I ended up in there was a district center with electricity and running water—and I had Leon for company and moral support. With such luxurious field-work conditions, only a real wimp would complain!

We chose as our research site a sublocation north and slightly west of Kapsabet, on the edge of a forest. This was a recently settled area, typical of other Nandi communities in many ways, slightly different in some. Household heads were younger on average than elsewhere, and as a group they had a notably forward-looking attitude. Several men worked hard to get us to settle in their community. Why? I'm not sure I ever totally understood. Pride in community and the wish to publicize it played a part, as did curiosity about the new and exotic (us). They also asked us to teach in their self-help secondary school, since the students' English would profit by having native speakers as teachers. For us, it was a perfect way to pay back the community for its help.

One day in June of 1976 we moved into a round, mud-walled, thatched house in a family compound near the sublocation "center" (a group of shops and a tree where old men heard legal cases). It was a very small house—we later built a bigger one—and half the neighborhood turned out to watch us move in. They marvelled at the incredible collection of stuff "Chumbek" (Europeans) always bring with them. We thought we were travelling light, but between trunks full of clothes and office supplies, tables, typewriter, books, paper, stove, lanterns, and more, it was a squeeze. Fortunately, a traditional Nandi house has a storage loft, or "tabut" (for drying firewood), just under the thatched roof, above head level. We planned to buy a four-foot wide mattress in Nairobi and have a bed built to fit it. However, a Nandi friend convinced us that this extravagance would be seen as another bit of white people's insanity, and take up too much floor space. So the two of us ended up sleeping for eighteen months in a three-foot wide bed—a real hardship only at the end of our stay, when I was seven months pregnant.

Our host family was headed by Jacob (a pseudonym, as are all names used here for Africans), an enterprising young man about six years older than my husband. Jacob seemed never to sit still. He was famous in the community for his boundless energy—always dashing from place to place, involved in dozens of schemes and projects. One of his money-making projects was buying surplus cattle and driving them through the forest to sell to butchers in neighboring Trans-Nzoia District. Through enterprise and thrift,

Jacob had saved money and acquired any land that became available for sale near his original small holding, so that when we arrived he was one of the larger land-holders in the area. We interacted with the family and the community as if Leon were Jacob's younger brother, though we weren't formally adopted. That first day, after we unloaded the furniture, Jacob took Leon off to get acquainted, while Rael (Rachel), his wife, helped me organize our domestic life. She was younger than Jacob, about my age, a large, pleasant, extroverted woman with a ready smile and a directive, no-nonsense, take-charge manner. In another cultural setting, Rael might have been a politician—but among the Nandi this is an almost exclusively male role. The public demeanor of many Nandi women is subdued and submissive, but while Rael chatted easily and got along with everybody, I hardly ever saw her behave submissively except to Jacob, her father, and some of the older men. Though Rael spoke Swahili, she insisted from the first that I speak Nandi as much as possible. Much of my knowledge of the subtleties of Nandi culture came from the hours I spent in her smoky kitchen shed gossiping with local women.

A Nandi compound is a collection of houses, some close together, some further apart, that face each other across an open space and/or are connected by a network of pathways. The house belonging to Jacob, Rael, and their children, with their kitchen shed and granary, was the center of our compound. About twenty to thirty yards to one side of their house stood the house of Jacob's widowed mother. Our house faced "Kogo's" (grandma's) house across a wide pasture. Ultimately we had two houses, one split in half to accomodate our two field assistants, recent school-leavers from other communities. Behind Jacob's house was a maize field; at the far end of that was the house of Jacob's sister Marta, who was permanently separated from her husband. From Marta's, a path led to the home of one of the men who convinced us to settle in the community. The nearest neighbor on the other side was about thirty yards from our house, across a fence. The main road formed the third boundary; the nearest neighbors on the fourth side were on the next ridge, a fifteen-minute walk down a hill, across the river, and up the other side.

GENDER: EARLY LEARNING EXPERIENCES

The group of men who first recruited us to the community became Leon's "age-mates" and close associates. The first day we settled in, they came in the late afternoon to invite him to go to the river to bathe. A huge group of neighborhood boys trooped along after them (I assumed just for the novelty of seeing what a *chumbindet*, or white man, looked like naked). The next day I heard from Rael that Leon had neighborhood approval on two important counts: that he was circumcised (the mark of male adulthood among the Nandi, who practice adolescent circumcision); and that he didn't shiver in the cold water. Throughout the day, other women congratulated me on my husband's ability to tolerate cold water. I tried to remain sanguine, though the reaction inside my own mind was, "Say *what!?*" I dutifully wrote it down in my field notes, figuring that eventually it might make sense.

In time, I pieced together that the house and hearth are women's domain; the shade tree where gatherings take place (*kok*) is men's domain; it's effeminate to hang around the hearth too much; it's manly (in a climate where it rains a lot and due to the altitude can get quite cold) not to mind exposure to the elements; therefore, real men don't shiver. This sequence of associations seems bizarre at first, but upon reflection it is no more so than our own cultural notions of what is or is not suitable for "real men." The Nandi believe a woman can make her husband weak-willed and subject to her control by feeding him polluting bodily substances (*kerek*, discussed later) or ground-up grass crabs. Inability to stand cold and frequent shivering are the outward signs of such poisoning.

The day after we moved in, I also got to bathe in the river and do laundry along with Rael and her friends. There was a spot at the river where a waist-deep pool of water collected. Rocks ringed this pool, shielding it from the view of anybody on the pathway, and this was the community bathing place. There was a signalling system (hanging clothes on the outer edge of the rocks) and an elaborate system of rules designed to protect everyone's modesty. However, the Nandi definition of whose modesty needs protecting from whom—in other words, which categories of people may be

unclothed in front of one another—differs markedly from our
Euro-American expectations. Married women bathe together; children bathe with them. Unmarried, uninitiated women are permitted to bathe together with young men of the warrior age-set or
with married women. Young people of both sexes do not undress
in front of men of their fathers' age-set—and there are still more
complications. I, along with the other married women, was expected to undress without compunction in front of anyone defined as a
"child." The problem was that boys are "children" as long as they
remain uncircumcised, which can be as old as sixteen or eighteen.
In practice, older boys generally joined the young, unmarried men,
but that first day one of the "children" present was Rael's thirteen-
year-old son who was taller than I. It was difficult for me to take
my clothes off in the presence of this strapping youth, but it was
excellent practice in cultural relativism. "Relax," I kept telling
myself. "It's no big deal. It doesn't mean the same thing here as it
would at home. The other women aren't bothered. . ."

Another shock about gender norms—though one we had
already dealt with during our stay in Nairobi—was the expectation
of intimate touching between members of the same gender. Shortly
after our arrival in Nairobi, a Kenyan couple from our research
institute invited us to dinner. Over drinks, I sat with Georgia on
one bench, and Leon sat with John on the other. "Have another
drink," Georgia said brightly as she draped her arm around my
shoulders, stroking my arm, and leaning close across me to fill my
glass. On the other side of the table, I noted that John's hand was
on Leon's thigh as he inquired about his favorite authors. On the
North American continent, we'd be enacting a swingers' seduction
scene—but in Kenya, this body language has no such meaning. In
fact, the ideas that connect touching and sexuality are almost the
opposite of Euro-American norms. A naive American visitor to
Nairobi could easily assume that it's a gay paradise on the basis of
numerous same-sex couples strolling the sidewalks hand-in-hand.
This would be totally wrong. The Kenyan attitude toward homo-
sexuality is less tolerant than North Americans'. Holding hands or
touching intimately in public is a way of declaring the *absence* of
any possibility of a sexual relationship. If people are sexually interested in each other, they will refrain from touching. Husbands and
wives are never seen touching in public. This restraint in touching
each other was one of the most difficult things for us to get used to
in the field situation—much more difficult than walking hand-in-
hand with our same-sex friends.

The public dominance of husband over wife and the wife's overt submissiveness were more difficult to get used to, especially for me. One shows one's husband "respect," and never corrects, contradicts, shows anger, argues with him, or tells him what to do. One is also expected never to complain or say anything negative about a husband to anyone else, unless there is a very strong grievance. Husbands are also supposed to "respect" and refrain from complaining about their wives, but they are freer to contradict them, order them around, and even shout at them if there is provocation. As we became more intimately acquainted with several couples, we could see that behind the scenes their relationships were not as inegalitarian as this public façade made it seem. At any rate, I had difficulty keeping the public façade in place with never a crack, and I wondered if Leon's cronies secretly pitied him for being married to such a shrew. Since I intended to study gender roles, it was lucky that some of the cultural differences that initially presented themselves most forcefully concerned gender. But there was still much to learn.

MALE AND FEMALE IN
NANDI CULTURE

Toward the end of our fieldwork, when I became pregnant with our first child, I confided to Rael that I was really hoping for a girl. "No, Gina!" she exclaimed. "Don't tell anybody that! It's an insult to your husband. For him, you must hope for a boy, even though there's always a special love between mothers and daughters." As in so many world cultures, males in Nandi are the preferred sex at birth. However, the preference is only slight. The ideal family includes sons and daughters. Sons continue the line of descent, but the bridewealth received when daughters are married enables their brothers to marry in turn.

Clearly, parents have different expectations of sons and daughters. Girls wear dresses; boys dress in shirts and shorts. Both sexes have major work responsibilities, but the tasks they are usually assigned are different. Girls are expected to care for younger children and help with weeding fields and domestic chores, such as fetching water and firewood. Boys herd cattle and help with plowing, and perform miscellaneous errands and tasks. Boys' chores take them further from the compound and give them more scope for independent action. Boys *may* care for children, and girls *may* herd cattle, if no child of the ideal age and sex is available. However, families try to arrange things so that a child of the appropriate sex is available, and this in part accounts for the widespread custom of fostering.

Every household needs a *cheplakwet* (child nurse) and a *mestowot* (herdboy). So essential are these roles that a newly married couple not living in an extended family will "borrow" children from other relatives or friends to fill them. Many Nandi adults I interviewed spent time as foster children. Some must have had positive experiences, but most children seem quite distressed at being taken away from their mothers and familiar surroundings. This is reflected in their evaluation of the experience; "cruel uncles" figure in many life histories and in folklore. The fostering family is responsible for feeding and clothing the child, and in the modern setting for paying school fees.

Until recently, boys were much more likely than girls to attend school. A daughter leaves her family for another at marriage; a son remains and the family benefits from any increased earning potential he gains through education. In 1976, surveying 241 adults, I found that most men (72 percent) had completed more than the equivalent of 4th grade, most women (63 percent) had completed only fourth grade or less, and 24 percent of men, but only 11 percent of women, had attended high school. Nowadays, with primary education free, boys and girls are educated at the primary level in equal numbers. Boys are still more likely to pursue secondary school and higher education, though the gender gap in education is narrowing.

Though Nandi mothers denied that male and female babies are inherently different at birth, substantial adult gender differences in basic character traits are acknowledged. Men are said to have greater physical endurance; to be *korom*, "fierce" (courageous in confronting enemies or wild animals—women must also be courageous and stoic in childbirth and in coping with injury or grief); to be more intelligent, foresightful, and decisive; to be more inclined than women to forgive without holding a grudge. Women are seen as more empathic than men, more capable of feeling "pity" (*rirgei*, "cry together"). These differences are believed to be learned, but are also thought to be set in place and reinforced by initiation.

Adolescent initiation, especially of boys, is one of the most central Nandi institutions. Boys and girls are initiated between the ages of twelve and eighteen, most often fourteen or fifteen for girls and fifteen or sixteen for boys. The central feature of the process is male circumcision or female clitoridectomy. The mere thought of such operations makes my American students gasp and shudder. Yes, they are extremely painful, and they are meant to be. The initiates are expected to be brave, quiet, and unemotional throughout. Initiation is thought of consciously as a test of the courage and toughness needed for warfare (though it is now a thing of the past) or childbirth.

It's worth digressing for a moment to discuss the issue of clitoridectomy, genital surgery involving the excision of all or part of the clitoris, and sometimes part of the external labia as well. This is a customary operation in many Subsaharan African societies, not to be confused with "infibulation" (practiced in northern Sudan), the partial sewing shut of the vaginal opening. Clitoridectomy has been in the news in the last several years, with concerned Westerners increasingly urging the UN to pressure its African member states to ban what is viewed as a "barbaric, primitive" custom hazardous to women's health that denies them sexual pleasure. (It is argued that women are kept sexually faithful to unloving husbands by being kept from experiencing orgasm.) Certainly, there is partial truth in this criticism; deaths from infection and hemorrhage have occurred. I would point out, however, that these potential complications are also present for male circumcision, without producing any comparable international outcry. Initially, I struggled to keep my cultural relativism about me while confronting a people who, I was sure, robbed women of their sexuality. However, as I talked with women about the subject I discovered that they didn't see it this way. Nandi women, even those with sexual experience before and after clitoridectomy, insisted that their sexual pleasure was unimpaired, and acted amused at my belief that the quality of their sex lives should be affected. Since orgasmic response in women increases with age, perhaps these women have the clitoris removed before they are really aware of what they will be missing. However, there is another feasible interpretation.

Though I don't mean to be an apologist for clitoridectomy, I think that Western critics should consider the possibility that African women know what they are talking about and whether (because of "phantom limb phenomenon" or some other mechanism) it may be that women are *not* robbed of pleasure. Physiological research is needed before we can conclude anything. In many societies with clitoridectomy, wives' sexual infidelity is common. So clitoridectomy does not prevent adultery, contrary to the Western interpretation. The importance of abolishing clitoridectomy should be decided by African feminists (they have mostly not seen it as their highest priority). In any case, the ritual that includes clitoridectomy is usually an important focus of women's solidarity that may not be replaced easily.

Clitoridectomy has been illegal in Kenya for several years. Prior to this, Christian missionaries had been preaching against the practice for many years with some success. At the time I was in the field in 1976, about 20 percent of women in their twenties and thirties, primarily those with secondary education, but also some with higher levels of primary education, had refused to have the operation. Some women who had been traditionally initiated told me that they didn't see that they had gained anything much from it and wouldn't choose it again if they had the choice.

Girls' initiation takes place individually or in groups of two to four, in the family compound. The girls are outfitted in a standard costume for the occasion: a red skirt, men's white dress shirt, tie, a tall helmet, crossed bandoliers trimmed with colobus monkey fur and beads, knee socks, and athletic shoes. Many of these elements are associated either with the traditional dress of warriors, or with contemporary roles (e.g., the military, athletics, business) associated with men. Though women direct the ceremony, costuming is in the hands of male specialists. (Gender role reversals are seen in both female and male initiation. They include aspects of initiates' dress, men carrying water for the women, and, during girls' initiation, women attacking men physically with sticks.)

The ritual begins in the late afternoon. The girls dance through the night, accompanied by a group of younger girls. Guests visit throughout the night, and a crowd assembles in the morning, after dawn. The initiates distribute small gifts (candy, cigarettes, and so on) to the guests, and then a group of initiated women moves away from the main crowd and forms a circle in which the operation is performed. If the girl shows courage, the older women break from the circle and dash toward the crowd, whooping and ululating, to congratulate the male members of the families and drape them with *sinendet*, a ritually important plant. Singing, dancing, and celebrating continue all day. The initiates are secluded in neighboring compounds for several weeks, and are not to be seen again until their marriages are arranged.

Male circumcision is an important mark of both adult status and ethnic identity. Nandi ridicule ethnic groups whose men are uncircumcised. Male initiation is a community-wide event with larger numbers of initiates (ten to fifteen) than in female initiation. Men of the next older age-set supervise the process, which in many ways resembles fraternity pledging. Beginning in the morning, the boys have their heads shaved, are forced to behave submissively, are harangued and verbally abused, are made to perform "women's work" such as carrying water and firewood, and to sing and dance before the assembled crowd. At intervals, they are taken into a secluded grove for "secret instruction."

As sunset approaches the boys appear for the last time, and women friends and family members tie scarves around their necks as tokens of their moral support, since women may not be present at the actual circumcision. During the night the boys undergo minor tortures and physical hazing, building up to the operation itself in the pre-dawn hour. The women of their families sit up all night waiting around bonfires in the public ceremonial space. Just before dawn, some of the circumcision "instructors" reappear to return the headscarves and drape the women in *sinendet*. At a ceremony I attended, some women refused to accept the tokens until they were assured that their sons had been as brave as they could possibly have been. Moments later, as the first rays of the sun appeared above the horizon, all those assembled dropped to their knees facing it and sang a traditional Nandi hymn. The boys—now young men—remain together in seclusion until their wounds have healed, receiving instruction in traditional lore.

For young men, initiation marks the onset of a period of social freedom and intense sexual activity. Traditionally, this would also have been a time of high risk-taking as the new warriors went out on cattle raids to prove their mettle and began to amass their own herds. Today, very often, they are students, and otherwise exempt from adult responsibilities. In the late nineteenth century, the young men of each neighborhood slept in a communal barracks, often accompanied by their lovers, girls not yet old enough for initiation. These couples were free to engage in all forms of sex-play except actual penetration without any social stigma—girls were expected to be technically virgin at the time of their initiation. At present, young men have their own huts in their parents' compounds, and there is no disapproval of young uninitiated women spending nights in their boyfriends' huts.

SOCIAL AND POLITICAL ORGANIZATION

For men, initiation marks the entry into one of seven age-sets (*ibinda*, pl. *ibinwek*). The names of the age-sets are always the same, and rotate through time: Kaplelach, Kipkoimet, Sawe, Chuma, Maina, Nyongi, and Kimnyigei. At any time there are four sets of elders, the "senior warriors", the initiates, and a set of boys. When all in the oldest age-set have died, its name comes back into use as the name of the set of the new initiates.

All men who are circumcised within a certain period of time belong to the same age-set. Since age at circumcision varies, at the margins of age-sets there may be some overlap of ages, with the oldest members of a junior set being older than the youngest members of the next senior set. The age-set members move as a unit through the life-cycle (like "The Class of 1998" moving from freshmen to sophomores, juniors, and seniors). During the 1800s there was a huge centralized ritual in which every Nandi man moved on to the next status: initiates became senior warriors, senior warriors became elders, senior elders "retired" from active life, and a new age-set began for boys about to be initiated. Immediately afterwards, the new warriors would launch a series of raids as a way of proving themselves.

The colonial government banned this event, fearing it would lead to military uprisings, and after independence it never made a comeback. Informal discussions among elders of different locales now produce consensus on which age-set is being initiated.

There is a strong sense of solidarity within age-sets, and a tendency for the members to act as a unit in taking on activities such as community improvement projects. The idea of unity is especially strong among those men who were initiated together in the same ceremony (called a *mat*, or "fire"). They are likely to have strong bonds of friendship for their whole lives, and provide mutual aid and support. I once went with a young Nandi man to visit another young man. When we arrived he was not at home, and his door was closed. My friend walked in, and decided since his shirt was dirty to trade it for a clean one he found inside. I expressed surprise, but he responded, "Why should I not take anything I need? He's my age-mate. I am free to take whatever he has." It is said that in the past it was common and condoned for a man to have sex with his age-mate's wife.

Relations among members of different age-sets are controlled by definite rules of etiquette. Men of younger sets defer to men of older sets. Sons should not belong to the age-set adjacent to that of their father, but to the next lower one. Familiarity between members of these age-sets is avoided. A man may not marry his age-mate's daughter, nor a woman her father's age-mate.

There are no age-sets for women, and no one I interviewed remembered hearing that they had ever existed, though they exist or are reported to have existed among several peoples related to the Nandi. Groups of women around the same age are often referred to as "Wives of . . ." with the name of a men's age-set.

The Nandi have extended families and clans with animal totems. Descent or membership in a family or clan is traced patrilineally (through males only). The clans' only function is the regulation of marriage. Certain clans do not marry members of certain other clans, though ritual elders told me that the pattern of marriage rules is continually shifting, depending on what inter-clan marriages have been successful in the recent past. The kin term system is basically the Omaha type common in patrilineal societies: the term "father" is used for all men of the same generation within a person's own descent group, the term for "sibling" for patrilineal relatives of one's own generation, and one's mother's patrilineal kinsmen of all generations are called by a single term. One of the most interesting aspects of Nandi terminology is the rich vocabulary for different kinds of relatives by marriage, since relationships with close in-laws are much more important than distant "blood" relationships.

Marital residence is patrilocal; that is, a bride moves in with her husband's family. Communities are not, however, based on kinship. Traditionally, families could move into any locality where they would be sponsored by people already living there—relatives, in-laws, age-mates, or others. Now with private land-ownership, people move into communities where they can buy land.

Traditionally, the local community (koret), consisting of several hundred people, was the most important unit of day-to-day life, the site of ceremonial and economic cooperation and dispute settlement. The term for the community's council of elders, kokwet, is used for both the council and the territorial unit, which might be called a "neighborhood." In the modern political scheme, several such units make up a sublocation, with a government-appointed subchief. Sublocations combine to form locations, each with a chief. The unit immediately larger than the kokwet was the *pororiet*, called a "regimental area" because its warriors formed a single fighting unit. The pororiet council, which made decisions about matters of concern to the local communities, such as warfare, circumcision, and planting, was made up of representatives from each kokwet council, and two representatives each from the warriors and the Orkoiyot.[1]

The Orkoiyot was a religious/political figure—a kind of chief, though his power was more ritual than political. This hereditary office created some political centralization for all the Nandi for a short time, probably no longer than from a bit after mid-nineteenth century to the British Conquest. The main function of the Orkoiyot was to coordinate military activities and sanction cattle raids. Warriors planning a raid would ask the Orkoiyot (who was believed to forsee the future) to predict its outcome. They would stage the raid only if he predicted success, and thank him with a gift of captured cattle. In Nandi tradition the family of the Orkoiyot descended from powerful Maasai *ilaibonik* (ritual experts with paranormal powers), who immigrated to Nandi and were absorbed into the Talai clan. However, the Maasai also believe that their ilaibonik came from elsewhere, perhaps from Nandi, so the Nandi story may not be based on fact.

Prior to the emergence of the Orkoiyot as a political figure, the term *orkoiyot* was used to denote any man thought to have paranormal powers including the ability to foretell the future, to see things happening at a distance, to disappear and reappear somewhere else, and to control the weather and the health and fertility of humans and animals. The ability was thought to run in families and to be patrilineally inherited by men only. The institution of the Chief Orkoiyot was based on this model writ large. The *orkoiik* (plural of orkoiyot) of the Talai clan were believed to be more powerful than others, and people feared them because of the harm they could do to those who resisted their will. Talai men often had several wives because of the practice of "naming wives." A Talai stated his desire to marry a certain woman, with the implied threat to curse any other man who might try to win her. This abuse of power was resented by non-Talai. Other Nandi were not completely cowed, however, and there are stories of Orkoiik who displeased their constituencies being put to death—in one case, for example, an Orkoiyot erroneously predicted success for a raid in which many Nandi lives were lost.

Most Nandi still believe to some extent in the power of the Talai. One young Talai man told me that though his father and grandfather definitely could use Talai powers, he couldn't because of his Western education. In another case, a girl broke up with her Talai boyfriend, and he threatened (not jokingly) to curse other men she might take an interest in. Another highly educated man told an anecdote about his sister, who married into the Talai. She was astounded and upset one day when she couldn't find her first son, an infant not yet crawling. Her mother-in-law said, "Didn't you know? That's what Talai babies do—come and go as they please." Non-Talai are ambivalent in their feelings about the Talai. On the one hand, there is still some resentment over their past abuse of power. On the other, the Talai Orkoiyot who rallied the Nandi to resist the British is viewed as a glorious historical figure, and his descendants and those of other famous orkoiik bask in reflected glory.

RELIGION

There were a variety of minor supernatural beings in traditional Nandi cosmology, but most worship focussed on a single deity called Asis or Cheptalel (and other names). Nandi believed that ancestral spirits continued to exist after death, but they were relatively unimportant in human affairs.

Missionaries have long been active in Nandi District. Since the Nandi were monotheists for all practical purposes, it was not difficult for them to assimilate Christianity into their beliefs. "Jehovah" is equivalent to Asis; that God had a son was news, but not hard to accept. More difficult to accept were teachings concerning sexuality, polygyny, initiation, and similar issues. Most Nandi Christians are Roman Catholics, though many are also adherents of the Africa Inland Church. The Africa Inland Mission, with ties to Baptists and Methodists, translated the Bible into Nandi in 1925. Some Nandi are Anglicans and Seventh Day Adventists. Nandi are less likely than neighboring ethnic groups to join African independent churches. In 1977, over 60 percent of household heads in the community I lived in were at least nominal Christians. Most Nandi continue to believe that certain people can "bewitch" others, primarily through envy.

MARRIAGE

For women, marriage took place shortly after initiation and for the most part still does. The average age at marriage for women in my census was 17.8. Young men, following initiation, spent a period of about twelve to fifteen years as warriors, and did not marry until most of this time had elapsed. Today, with peace, men's average age at marriage is younger, in the early 20s.

Ideally, a girl in seclusion following initiation waits for people to come seeking her as a bride on behalf of a young man. This is known as coming for "engagement" (koito). This group, the "engagement party," contains both women and men, including the prospective groom's parents, uncles, aunts, and older siblings, and close friends and relatives, at least some of whom know both families well. On the second visit, the girl's family makes sure to also have relatives and friends assembled, and the two groups get down to negotiating details of the proposal. There is no formal marriage contract, but information on such matters as how many cattle the groom has or stands to inherit, where the couple will live, and so on, is sought. The exact amount (which varies only slightly) of the bridewealth to be paid, in cattle, sheep and goats, and money, is also negotiated. Women in the engagement parties negotiate almost as actively as the men.

Ultimately, the bride must observe the prospective groom from behind a screen, and it is the responsibility of the father's sister to ensure that she finds the man acceptable. If she really dislikes him, she can hold out against the arrangement; however, girls are sometimes pressured into accepting less than ideal matches. In reality, when a girl is initiated her marriage may already be arranged, at least informally (after talks between the two mothers). Romantically involved couples can arrange in this way to be married, and this is becoming more popular.

Marriages between people whose families live in the same community are common. Sisters, in particular, try to marry men who live near each other, so that they will be able easily to turn to each other for assistance. There is a term, lemenyi, for men married to sisters, and this relationship is supposed to be close and support-ive. Friends and age-mates sometimes try to arrange to marry sisters, and thus become lemenyi.

Nandi men and women expect that the husband will be the dominant partner. In public, wives behave submissively toward husbands, though often private behavior is more egalitarian. Marriage is usually a fairly harmonious give-and-take, though even a wife who has a lot of influence with her husband will ask his permission to do anything out of the ordinary. The husband has the right to punish the wife physically for "misbehavior," in particular for public disrespect. A Nandi college student told me that he did not like this aspect of his culture, but admitted that he might have to buy into it. "It depends on what *she* does. If she does certain things, I will have to beat her or people will lose respect for me." Both men and women spend more social time with same-sex friends than with their spouses, but socializing as couples is becoming more common among younger, educated people.

The payment of bridewealth by the groom's to the bride's family is the central act that creates a marriage among East African pastoralists. Nandi bridewealth is lower than most, at five to seven cattle, one or a few sheep and goats, varying amounts of cowrie shells (an item sometimes omitted now), and cash generally equal to the value of a cow. When families negotiate bridewealth, specific animals are indicated by name, and attention is paid to the history of their social exchange. It is important to include at least one cow from the bridewealth given for the groom's father's sister, or its progeny. If the groom's full sister is married, an animal received as her bride-wealth is given. At the wedding feast, the animals are displayed so that the bride's brothers can come later to take them away.

The cattle given as bridewealth for a daughter should be used for the marriages of, or inherited by, *only* her full brothers. Each of a man's wives is the founder of a separate genealogical unit called a "house", and holds cattle separately from any other wives. At her marriage, a woman is given some of her husband's cattle to serve as the basis of her "house-property" herd. This herd also includes animals her relatives give her as wedding gifts, and grows through natural increase, further allocations from her husband, the addition of cattle she can sometimes acquire herself, and bridewealth given for daughters. In any decisions concerning house-property cattle, a wife must consult with her husband; he also is not supposed to sell, give away, or do anything with them without consulting with her.

A husband, however, usually has cattle that have not been allotted to the house of any of his wives, and these are his to do with as he pleases. While husbands therefore have greater property rights than wives, they do not have complete control of family property. Nandi women told me that wives have the right to go to any lengths to prevent their husbands from taking their house-property cattle. In one instance, the wife took her complaint to the community elders and stopped the sale of her cow.[2] In some other African "house-property" systems, husbands have greater freedom to dispose of their wives' cattle.[3]

Cattle that husbands inherited were traditionally allocated as house-property in equal numbers to all wives. Today, this norm has been extended to forms of property such as land and money. Cattle gained in raids belonged to the husband, and this has been extended to cover cattle a man buys with money gained through wage labor. Many families sell low-milk-producing African cattle from the house-property herd and use the proceeds *plus* the wage-labor earnings to replace them with European dairy breeds. It is not always clear what rights each partner has in the new animals, and this has the potential to create conflict between spouses.

As in most African societies, marrying more than one wife was a mark of status for a Nandi man. Many men now claim that as Christians they have no intention of marrying second wives. Analysis of census data shows, however, that with age controlled, Christians are only slightly less likely to be polygynists than Nandi traditionalists. With private land ownership, it is becoming difficult for a man to provide adequate land inheritance for the family of more than one wife. Seventeen percent of married men in my census were polygynists. (For Nandi District as a whole, the figure could be closer to 25 percent.) Wives have no right to object to their husbands' marrying other wives, and some desire it. As in other societies, relations among co-wives may be friendly, neutral, or hostile, depending on individual personalities. I have observed physical battles between co-wives, and I have also seen them spring to one another's defense in conflicts with their mutual husband. Nandi folk-wisdom says that jealousy between co-wives is inevitable, and that their husband should arrange, if possible, for them to live far apart.

Traditionally, a marriage was not considered irrevocable until after the birth of the first child. After that point, divorce was commonly considered to be impossible. There was a divorce procedure, but no one could give any hypothetical circumstances under which it might be used. A Nandi woman, once married, is forever the wife of the man who first married her, and all children she bears are considered his children, even if she has not seen him for years. A widow is not free to remarry; if she has further children, the father is considered to be her original husband, and it is his property that her sons inherit. A young widow is expected to practice the levirate, cohabiting with a kinsman of her husband, who begets children regarded as those of her dead husband. Though this is the "respectable" thing to do, it is not required. A widow might, rather, take lovers of her own choice. Not being able to divorce an unbearable husband or legitimately remarry seems like a great infringement of a woman's freedom. However, the other side of the situation is that once-in-a-lifetime marriage gives her and her children exceptionally strong rights in her husband's property.

The Nandi also practice woman-woman marriage. Such marriages are about 3 percent of all marriages, and this incidence does not seem to be declining. Though each married woman holds a separate fund of property and is expected to become the founder of a "house," only sons, never daughters, may inherit property. If the house has no male heir, its property goes to sons of co-wives of the husband's brother, but this is a very distasteful alternative. What to do? The Nandi solution is for the heirless woman to become the "female husband" to a younger woman, and "father" to her children; the sons of the younger woman become the heirs of the house. Once when I asked a man something about his father he told me, "The woman who married my mother was my father. She acted just like any other father." (Note that the father-child relationship is normally distant.) The culture insists that the female husband becomes a man. She must discontinue sexual relations with men. Though she has no sexual relationship with her wife, she has all the other rights of a husband. Her wife should cook for her and do all the domestic work. Outside the home, there is considerable ambiguity about whether female husbands in fact act like men in ways they claim are permitted to them, such as participating in political meetings and attending male initiation. Some female husbands did make a point of frequenting the "men's side" in the local beer hall (there are no longer beer halls since sale of African-style beer is now illegal.) It might be more accurate to see female husbands as occupying an ambiguous gender status, while they and others go to great rhetorical lengths to argue that they are in fact men.

Another alternative when there is no heir for house property is for a daughter of the house to "marry the center-post." She thus becomes like a daughter-in-law rather than a daughter. She remains at home and takes lovers, and her sons are the heirs.

Childbirth usually takes place at home, attended by local midwives, though some women now go to the hospital in the District Center. Women in labor are expected to be very stoic. I watched a young woman give birth without even a whimper, though pain was etched clearly on her face. In another instance, a woman behaved in a cowardly way during labor, and this became the subject of amused gossip and a lot of teasing for a long time afterward. Childbirth is "women's business," and men are expected to stay away from the house at this time, waiting nearby with other men for news of the birth. In the nineteenth and early twentieth centuries, it is said, the father would not resume living in the house for months, and would not touch the child or have sex with the mother again until the child was weaned and could walk. Fathers thus had very little intimate contact with young children; older children were expected to treat their fathers with respectful formality. The father-child relationship was important, but not warm and close. With regard to cross-cultural variation in men's participation in child-rearing, the Nandi were probably toward the extreme non-participation end of the spectrum.

Part of the reason for this distance between fathers and children was the belief in *kerek*, a mystical substance that was thought to emanate from infants and nursing women and was ritually polluting to men. Informants gave me contradictory information about sources of the pollution: the child's urine or feces, or the mother's milk. In any case, close contact with either the mother or the child could make the father (and perhaps other men) lose skill with weapons, become weak-willed and indecisive, and shiver in the cold. Wives could cook for their husbands while nursing only after going through a lengthy process of ritual washing with river sand and cow-dung, and returning home without touching their bodies or clothes; the *cheplakwet* (child nurse) held the baby until after the mother cooked. If an unweaned child touched an object in the house, it was traded to a childless neighbor for a similar object. A favorite anecdote of old women was how their husbands used to spy on them to make sure they were thorough enough in their ritual washing. Some people now claim that all this was merely superstition, not real; others argue that kerek, though real, became a matter of less concern with the introduction of soap, which dissipates it very effectively. In any case, men now rarely hesitate about having contact with children, and most people say this is a positive change. It is also true that births are now spaced much more closely and families are larger; men's fear of kerek was probably a mechanism that helped to keep the birth rate down, even though the Nandi ideal was always to have as many children as possible.

DIVISION OF LABOR

All family members have a part in the process of production. Men clear ground for planting and initially break it, in the past with iron-bladed hoes, today with an ox-drawn plow. It takes a team of two men to plow, one to drive the oxen with a whip, and one to hold the plow. The only instance of a woman plowing that I ever saw was Rael helping a man she hired to plow a field for vegetables she was growing to sell. Most people rent a tractor for a second round of plowing, and this is a source of cash for households in the community that own tractors (five in 1977). All ages and sexes plant and harvest, usually in cooperative work groups larger than one household. Cultivation during the growing cycle is done by both sexes, and women spend slightly more time at agricultural activities than do men. Cattle herding is mostly done by children, but women (more than men) also participate. Women and children do most of the milking.

Most men try to find some sort of full-time or part-time employment, but jobs are not plentiful in rural areas. Many men not formally employed, however, engage in some kind of entrepreneurial activity: agricultural contract labor for large land-holders, cattle trading, charcoal making, dredging sand from rivers to sell for making concrete, and so on. There are also some skilled artisans with shops in the local center, for example, a tailor and a bicycle repairman. Only a few women engage in such activities or have jobs. Profit from the sale of cash crops—maize, tea, and milk—goes to male household heads, who are supposed to use it for the benefit of the household. Women often grow vegetables for sale, or sell chickens and eggs. Women are said to "own" chickens (sometimes called "the cattle of women"), vegetables, and the afternoon milk, which is for family consumption. (Morning milk, which belongs to men, is marketed through the Kenya Co-operative Creameries.) Women's biggest source of cash in 1976–1977 was brewing and selling maize beer. In the 1980s a ban on selling beer cut off this income source.

CHANGES

Each return to Nandi sees more changes: individualized kerosene-powered water pumps, generators, an occasional television, new roads, telephone service in rural village post offices, even the possibility of rural electrification in the not-too-distant future. Changes on the social level occur too, as greater educational opportunities bring new ideas. Which are "good" and which "bad" depends on one's personal perspective. Increasing incorporation into the cash economy has brought material wealth to many Nandi, especially as the Nandi are land-wealthy by rural Kenyan standards and live in an agriculturally rich area. The corollary, however, is a growing gap between rich and poor, as some prosper more than others. Improved medical technology has lowered infant mortality—something women often mention as an improvement over the "old days." But less infant death means population growth and increasing land shortage (so far less acute in Nandi than in many other areas). In terms of gender, the idea of companionate marriage has taken hold among the educated elite, but women may be losing the right to independent control of property. Nevertheless, some things will not change. I expect that the land will always be beautiful, and the people always warm, friendly, and proud of their distinct Nandi heritage.

NOTES

1. G.W.B. Huntingford, *The Nandi of Kenya: Tribal Control in a Pastoral Society* (London: Routledge & Kegan Paul, 1953), pp. 34–35.
2. R.S. Oboler, *Women, Power, and Economic Change: The Nandi of Kenya* (Stanford, CA: Stanford University Press, 1985), p. 120.

3. Thomas Hakansson, "Family Structure, Bridewealth and Environment in Eastern Africa: A Comparative Study of House Property Systems," *Ethnology* 28 (1989): 117–134.

SUGGESTED READINGS

Krige, Eileen Jensen. "Woman Marriage with Special Reference to the Lovedu: Its Significance for the Definition of Marriage." *Africa* 44 (1974): 11–36. Good account of a South African society with a different kind of woman-woman marriage.

Obbo, Christine. "Dominant Male Ideology and Female Options: Three East African Societies." *Africa* 46 (1976): 371–384. Describes some ways women use traditional norms and institutions, including woman-woman marriage, to gain autonomy.

Oboler, Regina Smith. "Is the Female Husband a Man?: Woman/Woman Marriage Among the Nandi of Kenya." *Ethnology* 19 (1980): 69–88. A more thorough description of the Nandi institution.

____. "Nandi Widows," in Betty Potash, ed. *Widows in African Societies.* Stanford, Calif.: Stanford U. Press, 1986, pp. 66–83. More on Nandi widows' status. The book also includes good articles on widows in other African societies.

Orchardson, Ian. *The Kipsigis.* Nairobi: E. African Literature Bureau, 1961. A good, short ethnography of a society related to the Nandi and very similar in many ways.

ROTUMA:
INTERPRETING A WEDDING

Alan Howard and Jan Rensel

In most societies there are one or two activities that express, in highly condensed ways, what life is all about for its members. In Bali it is the cockfight,[1] among the Australian Aborigines the corroboree, in Brazil there is carnival. One might make a case for the Super Bowl in the United States. On Rotuma, a small isolated island in the South Pacific, weddings express, in practice and symbolically, the deepest values of the culture. In the bringing together of a young man and young woman, in the work that goes into preparing the wedding feast, in the participation of chiefs both as paragons of virtue and targets of humor, in the displays of food and fine white mats, and in the sequence of ceremonial rites performed, Rotumans communicate to one another what they care about most: kinship and community, fertility of the people and land, the political balance between chiefs and commoners, and perpetuation of Rotuman custom. After providing a brief description of Rotuma and its people, we narrate an account of a wedding in which we participated. We then interpret key features of the wedding, showing how they express, in various ways, core Rotuman values.

THE ISLAND AND ITS PEOPLE

Rotuma is situated approximately three hundred miles north of Fiji, on the western fringe of Polynesia. The island is volcanic in origin, forming a land area of about seventeen square miles, with the highest craters rising to eight hundred feet above sea level. From the air, Rotuma appears a dark green jewel framed by a white garland of breaking surf in the midst of the vast blue ocean. On closer inspection one sees a far greater array of colors and hues; the dark green of coconut trees that cover much of the island are complemented by the softer tints of breadfruit trees, banana plants, and taro and yam gardens. The white sand beaches on parts of the coast are offset by black lava rocks from ancient eruptions. Tropical flowers and vines add even more variety to a kaleidoscopic landscape of living things. The island is nearly as beautiful up close as it is from afar, and one can understand why some early visitors confused it with paradise. But after one experiences the sometimes overpowering heat and humidity—Rotuma is only 12 degrees from the equator and has an average 140 inches of rain per year—and the ubiquitous flies and mosquitoes, illusions of paradise are likely to evaporate.

The island is divided into two parts joined by an isthmus of sand, forming a configuration about eight miles long and at its widest three miles across, with its lengthwise axis running due east and west. A packed sand road, reinforced in places with concrete strips, circles the perimeter of the eastern segment of the island and extends to coastal plains west of the isthmus. Villages and hamlets are scattered along the road, with occasional stretches of bushland in between. The interior of the island is heavily cultivated with gardens of taro, yams, cassava, bananas, pineapples, watermelons, and other food crops. A few people plant vanilla, cocoa, or kava as commercial crops as well. Kava is a plant of the pepper family, the roots of which are used to make a drink with mild narcotic properties; it is an essential part of Rotuman ceremonies at which chiefs and dignitaries are honored. Fruit trees abound: mango, papaya, orange. Rotuman oranges—wonderfully sweet and juicy—are justifiably famous in that part of the Pacific. Cattle and goats are tethered to coconut trees adjacent to plantations, and pigs are kept in stone walled enclosures.

Linguists have long debated the place of the Rotuman language in the Austronesian family. Although sharing a significant portion of vocabulary with Tongan and Samoan, Rotuman has some unique characteristics that set it apart from others in the vicinity. The current view is that an earlier form of the language was closely related to ancestral languages in western Fiji,[2] but that invasions from Tonga and Samoa resulted in a good deal of borrowing and innovation. The product is a language that is unintelligible to speakers of other Pacific tongues.

Politically Rotuma has been governed as part of Fiji for over one hundred years. When the paramount chiefs of Rotuma's seven districts ceded the island to Great Britain in 1881, for administrative convenience the British decided to incorporate it into the Crown Colony of Fiji, some three hundred miles away. When Fiji was granted independence in 1970, the Rotuman people decided to remain a part of Fiji. They also decided to stay with Fiji, though not without controversy, following two military coups in 1987.

The total number of Rotumans enumerated in the 1986 census of Fiji was 8652, of whom only 2588 were resident on the home island. The remainder live mostly in Fiji's urban centers, where they are conspicuously successful in professions, government service, and private industry. Travel back and forth between Fiji and Rotuma is facilitated by weekly flights and cargo vessels that take passengers. A substantial number of Rotumans have also migrated to Australia and New Zealand, and they, too, make return visits on occasion. In addition to keeping in touch by mail and radio-telephone, Rotumans living in Fiji and abroad host visitors from the island and send remittances, household appliances and other manufactured goods back home to enhance their kinsmen's standard of living.[3] For their part, those remaining on Rotuma frequently send gifts of produce, prepared foods and Rotuman handicrafts to their relatives living away.

Culturally, Rotuma clearly falls within the Polynesian orbit. Titled chiefs are important to the social and political life of the island, and Rotuman values and custom show strong resemblances to other cultures of western Polynesia (especially Tonga, Samoa, Futuna, and Uvea). At the heart of the kinship system is the concept of *kainaga*, which in its broadest sense refers to all one's "blood" relations, that is, anyone who is descended from a common ancestor. In its restricted usage, kainaga refers to common rights in a specific named house-site. Rotumans say that each person ideally belongs to eight kainaga, corresponding to their great-grandparents' homes. At life-crisis ceremonies such as first birthdays, weddings, and funerals, relevant house-sites are gathering places where members congregate to prepare food and materials for the event. They then go as a group to make their presentations.

Also important for life-crisis events is the institution of name giving. Prior to the birth of a child, someone with a special relationship to one or both parents requests that the baby be named after him or her. Name givers may or may not be close relatives, but when accepted a special bond is formed between them and the newborn child. Name givers are expected to bestow special gifts on birthdays, Christmas, and other occasions, and to champion the causes of their namesakes. At weddings they play a special role, as we shall see.

PRELUDE TO A WEDDING

As recently as 1960, when Alan first began research on Rotuma, marriages were often arranged by parents without their children's direct involvement. Sometimes bride and groom met for the first time on their wedding day. Arrangements for such a marriage were formal and complex. They began with representatives of the young man seeking approval from the young woman's parents for the match. If her parents agreed, a more formal delegation was formed to approach the chief of the woman's district. In Rotuman, this event is called *süf hani*. The gravity of the proposal would be enhanced by each side's asking titled men, perhaps even their district chief, to represent them. To emphasize the seriousness of the request the young man's representatives would bring a gift of a whole pig cooked in an earthen oven and a small kava plant.

In turn, the young woman's kinsmen would feed the young man's representatives. The pros and cons of the prospective match would be discussed, and if agreed upon, preparations would begin for the next stage, *fai ran ta,* a ceremony at which the wedding date was set.

The following field notes, obtained by Alan from a participant in an arranged marriage in 1960, provides a sense of what these negotiations were like. The groom, Aisea, was a school teacher from the district of Malhaha; the bride, Ieli, was the granddaughter of Tokaniua, the paramount chief of Oinafa district. Aisea met Ieli during the Christmas "play" season[4] and decided he wanted to marry her. He went to Tokaniua and told him of his intentions.[5] Tokaniua was reluctant because of Aisea's reputation for drinking, but said he would accept if Aisea would change his ways. Aisea promised that he would.

When he left Oinafa, Aisea went back to his home in Malhaha and early the next morning told his father the news. Immediately Aisea's father went to the Chief of Malhaha (also named Aisea; we will refer to him as Chief Aisea) and informed him. This was necessary because Ieli, being a district chief's granddaughter, should be asked for by someone of chiefly rank. Chief Aisea decided on the best time to go süf hani to ask formally for Ieli's hand.

Süf hani: Asking for a
Young Woman's Hand in Marriage

All the sub-chiefs in Malhaha were called on to join the delegation. The only person of rank to stay behind was Aisea's brother, who remained to supervise the preparation of food for the delegation, who would have to be fed upon their return. In addition to Chief Aisea and five sub-chiefs, Aisea's namesake and one other untitled man joined the delegation; the latter was selected by Chief Aisea to carry the kava plant.

In keeping with Rotuman custom, the delegation left early in the morning. The district messenger from Malhaha had been sent earlier to Oinafa to inform Chief Tokaniua of the date and time of the delegation's arrival. (Each district has a formal position of messenger, responsible for communicating the paramount chief's desires and intentions vis-à-vis other districts.) When the süf hani delegation reached Oinafa they were greeted at the chief's house by Tokaniua himself. This was a sign of acceptance. If Tokaniua had not been there to offer them greetings, this would have been a bad sign—a note of disapproval. Even if a marriage does not directly involve the chief's family, if the bride and groom are from different districts, proper custom requires the chief of the young woman's district to receive the süf hani delegation, provided the union is agreeable to her family.

After the delegation was greeted by Tokaniua they were asked into the house and sat down. Already seated and waiting were Ieli's namesake and members of her kainaga. Tokaniua opened the meeting by welcoming the delegation and thanking them for coming. Then, the oldest member of the groom's delegation, a man in his eighties by the name of Hanfakaga, began to talk and came straight to the point. He took the initiative because he was related to Tokaniua and therefore less restrained by barriers of respect. Hanfakaga talked very humbly about Aisea. His job was made more difficult by Aisea's reputation for drinking, but in any case humility is called for by custom.

The interaction between the two groups was essentially democratic, with each person speaking in turn. Generally the young man's delegation "talks down" his desirability as a husband and apologizes for his faults, while it is up to the young woman's side, provided they are disposed toward acceptance, to emphasize his good points. Eventually, after each person on both sides had their say, Tokaniua gave an official acceptance on Ieli's behalf. If a verdict is in doubt the young woman's representatives may go into private conference in order to reach a decision, but the final answer can only be properly given by the chief. During all this time Ieli was not present, nor did she have any official say in the scheduling or form of the wedding.

Tokaniua then advised the Malhaha delegation to tell Aisea to come to Oinafa the next the day so that the chief could talk to him and Ieli together, to advise them and instruct Aisea when to go to the government station to post their marital banns (usually the day after such a meeting). He also gave the delegation a date for their next meeting, the fai ran ta, when the wedding date would be arranged. The date for the fai ran ta is discussed along with the other business of süf hani, but the final decision is made by the young woman's side and announced by the chief. After concluding their official business, tea and biscuits were served to all who were present, following which the Malhaha delegation returned home to inform Aisea and the rest of his kainaga of the good news.

Fai ran ta: Appointing the Day

The same people who went on the süf hani formed Aisea's delegation for the fai ran ta expedition. One of the members provided the following account:

> When we left Malhaha we had to take a kava plant. A special person, Kaitu'u, chosen by Chief Aisea, took the kava. [He was the same man appointed to take the kava for the süf hani.] Arriving at Oinafa at seven in the morning, we were welcomed at the chief's house by Chief Tokaniua and Ritia, Ieli's mother [the daughter of Tokaniua.] When we entered the house, some of Ieli's kainaga were already there waiting. We shook hands with them and sat down on some *apei* [fine white mats] that had been spread out for us. The first thing they did was serve us with a coconut each. We had to wait until Chief Aisea began to drink and then we each could drink. That is the Rotuman way.

After we finished drinking, Tokaniua gave the first speech. He's the one to date the wedding. He gave the date for the wedding as February 20th, 1960. He asked us what we thought about it. Chief Aisea gave a speech and said that anything that Tokaniua and his kainaga think best is all right with us.

It didn't matter that we came early. We had to wait for all Ieli's kainaga to come before the meeting took place. Tokaniua gave his speech announcing the date before the "meeting" took place, that is, before all the kainaga had arrived. He should really have waited until all the kainaga were assembled before giving his speech. After they all arrived, Tokaniua told them he had already informed Aisea's contingent of the date set for the wedding. We had nothing further to say, simply to thank Tokaniua and Ieli's kainaga. Chief Aisea gave that speech. Then they thanked us. First Tokaniua gave a speech of thanks for Ieli's side and next Fakraufon, the Chief of Noatau, who is one of Ieli's relatives. They told us everything was all right.

After that they prepared breakfast. First the higher ranking chiefs from both sides ate breakfast together; the lesser ranking chiefs ate at a second sitting with other members of Ieli's kainaga. Right after breakfast we shook hands with all the members of the Ieli's party and left. Ieli was not present at the meeting. We left at 10:00 A.M. When we arrived back at Malhaha (10:30), Aisea's father welcomed us and we entered the house and sat down on the regular floor mats. They prepared a breakfast for us—coffee, cocoa, bread, biscuits, butter and jam—the same things we had in Oinafa. When we were eating Chief Aisea gave a speech telling Aisea's father and his family the date of the wedding. Only Aisea's family (including Aisea) were there. Aisea's father then gave a speech of thanks. After breakfast we left.

Soon after the date of the wedding had been set, each side would hold a meeting to decide who would be responsible for providing the various items such as pigs, apei, mosquito netting and bedding for the couple's bed, the bridal purse, and other paraphernalia required at a proper wedding. Usually relatives and friends would volunteer, but the man and woman designated to take charge of the preparations might assign specific tasks.

MAIKA AND SUSIE'S WEDDING

Although in many respects life on Rotuma has not changed radically since 1960, some things have.[6] For one, arranged marriages of the type described above have all but disappeared. More open courtship is tolerated and youths are given more freedom in choosing their spouses. They also play a more active role in planning their weddings. Nevertheless, the form of weddings has not changed significantly, and Rotuman rituals are still performed in conjunction with church and civil ceremonies.

The wedding we shall describe took place in the village of Lopta, district of Oinafa on July 21, 1989. The groom, Maika, was from nearby Oinafa village. He was a policeman in the Fiji constabulary, assigned to duty at the government station on Rotuma. The bride, Susie, whose parental home is in Lopta, was employed at the Rotuman branch of the National Bank of Fiji, also situated at the government station. Maika was twenty-six years old and had been previously married and divorced. Susie was twenty-four and had never been married.

Fao Te: The Day Before

The day prior to a wedding is set aside for preparations. A number of house-sites on the groom's side and bride's side are designated gathering places where kinsmen, friends, and neighbors bring their donations of food, mats, and other materials central to the wedding. Each grouping is referred to as a *sal hapa*, a 'part' of the bride or groom's kainaga. Although in theory there should be eight sal hapa on each side, in practice convenience and social relationships often change this. Almost all Rotumans are related to one another, some in multiple ways, so people can usually choose among several sal hapa. The choices they make are an indication of social solidarity, of who is getting along with whom at the moment.

Since we were living in the groom's village we participated in one of his side's seven sal hapa. In fact six of the seven sal hapa were located in our village, the other was from the neighboring district of Noatau. Food and mats at each sal hapa location had been accumulating for several days previously. On this day, they would be taken to the groom's home, or to be more precise, the groom's father's home. The groom's father, Sautiak, is a greatly respected sub-chief, second in rank only to the paramount chief of the district.

From early in the morning we watched as pickup trucks full of food—taro, yams, squealing pigs and noisy chickens—headed for Sautiak's place. At around 9:00 A.M. our sal hapa organized and made its way across the village to the gathering throng. The women carried mats in procession; those carrying apei headed the line, those with common mats followed. In deference to our curiosity over everything taking place, Jan was asked to head the parade and was given a quick lesson in etiquette concerning the proper way to carry a fine mat. Some excerpts from her diary give the flavor of the occasion.

> When we got there we went in the front door and into the sitting room. Two or three women were in there—I recognized Manava sitting in the doorway. [Manava played the role of designated elder and announced each white mat brought indoors.] We all put our mats down and sat around and said a few words. Then Vera and another woman took the mats into the bedroom and the rest of us went out to the verandah where they were serving bread and tea. . . . I was trying to find Alan with the camera because another group was arriving with mats, followed by men with taro (carrying it in bunches with stalks and leaves upright). Marieta was calling out nonsense like "Here we come," and afterwards she explained that she'd done it to liven things up—"What is this, a wedding or a funeral?"
>
> I decided to ask Harieta how she was related (which sal hapa) and found out that more people can come than just sal hapa—Sautiak made an open invitation to everyone. . . . People were clustered in groups from Sautiak's house toward the beach, on mats, under trees, playing checkers and cards, talking, eating. The young men were singeing the hair off two pigs and then gutting them, preparing them for the next earthen oven. The smoke smelled awful.

Much of the day was spent preparing food for the wedding feast. A large number of pigs and several cows were slaughtered and cooked in earthen ovens, fashioned by digging large holes in the sandy soil, placing kindling wood inside, covering them with lava rocks and lighting a fire. When the coals are red hot, whole pigs (gutted and cleaned), sections of beef, chickens, and tubers of various kinds were wrapped in leaves and placed inside. The contents were then covered with leaves, burlap bags and finally with earth. This is how the ceremonial food is prepared; it is allowed to cook from a few hours to overnight, depending on its size.

Preparing ceremonial food is the work of young men, and they were busy throughout the day. The young women spent much of their time setting out lighter food for the people who had gathered—tinned corned beef and tinned fish, tea, and biscuits. Cooked taro and yams were also served by the women. The work, and the festivities, lasted into the night.

Let us return to Jan's journal, amplified by our field notes, for an account of the wedding day:

> We woke early, dressed in our wedding clothes, ate breakfast at 6:30 and Tarterani drove us to Lopta at 7:00 A.M. People had already gathered, the band was playing and the female clown was at work. [At large, proper, Rotuman weddings the bride's side designates a woman to act as hostess and clown; she is formally in charge of the wedding, and is given a great deal of license to joke, mock, tease, and generally raise havoc. Her antics are a major source of amusement for everyone in attendance.] She was taunting people, especially the chiefs, and making them dance. She soon seized on Alan and me since we were going back and forth taking pictures. She snagged me and gestured for me to sit down on her chair. I did but then patted my lap for her to sit down. But she gestured for me to get up, and *she* sat down and I sat on her lap and then swung around and put my arms around her neck and laid my head on her chest. She got up, holding me, then sat down and I got up and left. A little later she ordered Alan to come to her and he ran to her with his arms open and sat/sprawled on her lap so they both nearly fell over. She pretty much left us alone after that but blew us kisses and announced that she wanted to take Alan home with her.
>
> Semesi [a cousin of Susie's, at whose house the wedding feast was held] came up to us, saying he felt a little sick. He asked Alan to videotape the events of the day with his, Semesi's, camera. So I got charge of the still camera and photographed the clown and others dancing as we waited for the groom's side to arrive. (They were held up by a contingent from Faguta who were supposed to come to Oinafa for break-

fast at 5:00 A.M. but didn't arrive till seven. We saw them as we left Oinafa. They had mats with matching yarn decorations—hot pink.) I sat with my friend Nina on the steps to the house, behind the *päega* [ceremonial seat made from a pile of common mats topped with a fine white mat and a colorful piece of cloth] where Susie was sitting. Nina advised some men who were hanging a white mat above the päega as protection against bugs dropping. But I spent most of the day running from side to side taking pictures.

[In Rotuman custom, the bride initially takes her place on a päega provided by her relatives. Then, prior to the formal arrival of the groom's procession, his side brings mats to form another päega on top of hers, but a fine mat provided by the bride's side is always placed on top of the pile.]

We saw the groom's side assembling down the hill and walked down to greet them. After talking with various people for a while we went back up to the house to await their formal arrival. They finally came up the hill at about 9:30, led by Maika, who, because he is from a chiefly family, did not need an *'a su* to represent/precede him [At a proper wedding, the groom's procession must be led by someone from a high-ranking family; usually the district chief selects a close female relative to be *'a su*]. Maika and his best man wore their Royal Fiji Police uniforms.

Qwenda, the district chief's unmarried nineteen year-old granddaughter, led the women bearing mats. So many mats were brought by the groom's side that there weren't enough women to carry them. I saw three or four men helping out. Then came the men with baskets of cooked food, pigs and cow, and finally the kava and sugar cane. All the food was set down across the road from the *ri hapa*, a temporary shelter built for the occasion to shield the day's dignitaries from sun and rain. (The only problem was that there was so much food it extended into the road, and every now and then a car or the bus had to get through!) A portion of the food they brought was already cooked and ready to serve; another portion was uncooked. The pile of uncooked taro, leaves and all, was covered with mats after it was laid out, along with a live, tied-up pig. The whole thing was topped by a fine white mat. [This food represents the groom's own garden, even though all the produce may have been donated by his relatives.]

When the groom's party got close they stopped and assumed a crouching position. A repesentative for the group then called out the traditional greeting, which was responded to by a representative from the bride's side. Maika then moved forward and took his place beside Susie. This was followed by speeches of greeting. A couple of other women from the groom's party unrolled bolts of cloth and hung them around the perimeter of the shelter. As soon as Maika sat down, members of his party came to congratulate the couple, one by one. Each would kneel or crouch in front of the päega to shake Maika's hand and kiss Susie's cheek, sometimes pressing an envelope into his hand or tucking a five or ten dollar note into her clothing.

As soon as things settled down, Fakrau brought a change of clothes (osi) and presented them on behalf of the groom's side to Susie, who quickly and unobtrusively changed on the spot.[7] (Later on, before going to church, Susie went inside the house to change to her wedding gown and veil.) After this, Fakrau draped and tied traditional Rotuman garlands (tefui) around Susie's and Maika's necks, then doused them with perfume. Concurrently, several young women from the groom's side moved about on their knees, dousing the chiefs, and others under the shelter, with perfume or sprinkling them with sweet-smelling powder (Johnson's Baby Powder is a favorite). After Fakrau had finished, a woman from the bride's side presented Maika and Susie with garlands and perfumed them.

As the time for the [Methodist] church service approached, Susie's uncle, Mekatoa, apologized that the church would be too small for everyone to attend the service. About 11:00 A.M. Sautiak's flatbed truck drove up to take the chiefs to the church. Alan and I realized that we should go too, since we were the designated photographers, and scurried to get on. Unfortunately it had rained a bit and although they put a mat down (the clown had called for the mat and had added in English, "Please," to the amusement of the crowd), it still puddled. Both Chief Maraf's wife Feagai and I got our dresses wet and dirty.

At the church we were asked to sit up with the chiefs from the groom's side, but in front of them (in deference to our roles as photographers). Our pews were on the right hand side of the church facing across to another set of pews where the chiefs from the bride's side sat. While we waited for the bride to arrive some of the congregation sang. Maika and his best man sat waiting. When Susie came in (veiled) everyone rose.

There were prayers, the service, vows, exchange of rings, a brief kiss and speeches by the various chiefs. Some of them talked about Susie's and Maika's life histories. I nearly fell asleep during Reverend Erone's sermon because it was so hot—I'd forgotten to bring a fan. At the end of the service, Alan climbed out the window so he could videotape the couple coming out of the church. I followed the couple and the District Officer, whom I bumped as we got out and missed getting a shot of the wedding party before they dissolved into a reception line. We rode back to the house, this time in the front of a truck. Tokaniua[8] brought the couple back to the house in his car, which was decorated with leaves, flowers, and ribbons.

Both sides presented mats to make a new päega in front of the one on which the couple already sat. Then the couple moved forward and sat on the new päega, and soon afterwards they had the hair snipping ceremony. Susie's namesake came with a pair of scissors trimmed with colorful ribbons and passed them over her head. Maika did not participate in this ceremony, in which his namesake would have passed scissors over his head. Nor did he participate fully in the following ceremony, called *fau*, in which the bride and groom are wrapped in white mats. [This ceremony is performed only at big weddings, and only when the bride is young and virginal. Only fine white mats are used to wrap the bride, and the groom if he participates.]

Susie was wrapped in three or four or large fine mats. Then groups of young men carried both of them (Susie and Maika), with much joking and laughter, from the bride's side to the groom's side of the shelter. Maika's white mat was simply tied with a sash and carried over, along with Susie's '*at fara*, which was tied with a blue ribbon. [The 'at fara is a small woven purse made specially for the bride. Although people now put money in it, in olden times it held a small container of coconut oil, a supply of turmeric powder and a piece of soft native cloth to hang at the end of the bridal bed. We were told that the oil was for lubrication, the turmeric for medicine/antiseptic, and the cloth to clean up with following intercourse. Elisapeti Inia, a knowledgeable elder, told us that 'at fara translates as "to beg soul", and explained that the man begs for the woman's soul and she gives it to him in intercourse.] The 'at fara is carried by a representative of the highest ranking person from the groom's side, in this case the district chief's granddaughter, Qwenda. After the fau ceremony,

Qwenda carried the 'at fara back to the central päega, preceding the couple and carrying it over her head for all to see.

Soon after this each side brought out the fine white mats for display—about thirteen from each side, not counting the ones used for the päega and for the fau ceremony. Then the kava ceremony was held and dinner was served to the honored guests, including us. We sat next to Kafoa, the catechist, and were served by Fanifau. It was very hot and I thought longingly of Fiji beer and ate only two bites of beef, a little taro, half a banana and two globs of Rotuman pudding (made by baking a pounded starchy root, such as taro or yam, or banana, mixed with coconut cream and sugar). When we finally got home in the early evening we were so tired we could barely talk.

For most people the highlight of the wedding day is the feast, which begins with the ceremonial presentation of food and kava. When all the contributions of food (in coconut-leaf baskets) and kava roots are assembled in front of the shelter, the men squat and a spokesman announces quantities of pigs, cows, chickens and baskets of taro, yams, etc. It is customary to greatly exaggerate the numbers involved, perhaps to enhance the prestige of the occasion.

After this announcement, food is distributed according to ceremonial protocol. Chiefs on Rotuma eat off low tables called 'umefe (at feasts, everyone including chiefs sit cross-legged on the ground to eat). In times past there were carved wooden bowls unique to each chief. 'Umefe were symbolic of the chief's title. Even today, taking a chiefly title is referred to as "turning the 'umefe up," and relinquishing a title as "turning the 'umefe down." At contemporary feasts, low wooden tables have taken the place of these traditional food bowls. The tables are initially placed upside down. Only when food is about to be served are they turned upright. The designated elder calls out the names of persons in rank order, and the young men bring baskets of food to each table in turn. The first presentation of food is to the a'su, and includes the best selections. The newlyweds are served next, then the chiefs. Visiting dignitaries are fit into the order depending on their status; a high ranking church official is likely to be served before the chiefs, a lesser dignitary after them. Each table has a young woman in attendance. She lays a covering of banana leaves on the table, takes the food out of the basket, unwraps it, cuts or breaks it up into manageable chunks, and arranges them on the table. If something is missing, or if more food is needed, she calls to the young men who are distributing the food and they do their best to accommodate her.

Once the food has been distributed, the kava ceremony begins. Each bundle of kava roots has a spokesman who recites a short ceremonial speech relating heroic deeds, often in obscure language not understood by the audience. Once this part of the ritual is concluded, kava bowls are brought forward, attended by three young women each. One mixes the previously pulverized kava with water and strains it through a clean cloth, the second assists by pouring fresh water and filling cups, and the third acts as cup bearer. When the kava is ready a designated elder announces the persons to whom each cup of kava is to be served. The order of serving reflects relative rank and is crucial; mistakes are likely to be deemed intentional insults by those who are passed over and in the past were grounds for war.

Following a Christian prayer said by a minister or priest, the meal starts when the a'su begins to eat. The attendants fan the tables with woven pandanus fans to keep the pesky flies off the food. Everyone eats with their hands, although knives are usually provided to cut up larger chunks of meat or starchy roots. Commoners eat away from the shelter, wherever a level patch of ground can be used. A "table" is prepared by laying down rows of banana leaves, upon which the food is set by the young men, but there are no attendants and all must fan the flies for themselves. During the meal speeches are made by chiefs from both the bride, and groom's side, thanking everyone for their work and cooperation, and reminding the newlyweds of all the labor that has been expended on their behalf. It is a way of impressing upon them the seriousness of the commitment they have made to one another.

The feast concludes the formal rituals, but people may stay on for some time afterwards. Entertainment is always provided. In the past, the people from one village, or even a whole district, would be asked well in advance to prepare traditional Rotuman group dances. The songs accompanying such dances were composed for the occasion; they centered on the bride and groom and their families and praised the location of the wedding and associated chiefs and dignitaries. The dance group would bring some fine white mats to the wedding and would be given some in return, as a show of appreciation.[9] Nowadays it is more common to invite one of several local bands to play instead. Bands usually consist of four or five men, playing guitars and electronic keyboards with amplifiers.

They, too, may compose songs to honor the occasion, but for the most part they play modern Polynesian-style music with Rotuman, English, or Fijian lyrics. Dancing to the music—in a kind of adapted disco style—is one of two main forms of entertainment throughout the day.

The other main form of entertainment is provided by the female clown. On the wedding day she generally dresses in flashy clothes and carries a stick, with which she mock-threatens people, or taps them to dance or do various chores. In her role as clown she is permitted to act in an outrageous fashion, such as ordering chiefs to dance, kneel and otherwise humiliate themselves—actions that invert the usual social order. In turn, people tease her, and taunt her with insults that she quickly returns.

On the day of Susie and Maika's wedding, the clown was especially active. Her name was (perhaps fittingly, perhaps ironically) Kava, and she had been chosen, according to custom, by Susie's parents. Among the observations we made of interaction between Kava and the crowd on the wedding day were the following:

> 1) Kava danced almost every dance throughout the day, mostly in a humorous fashion, involving exaggerated motions, often having sexual overtones (though nothing explicit). She sometimes danced on her own, and sometimes grabbed one of the chiefs or other dignitaries and danced in a silly way with them.

> 2) People in the crowd teased Kava about being dirty and black (neither of which was really the case). One of our friends commented, after Alan's encounter with her (which involved a fair amount of physical contact) that it would require bathing in hot water that night to wash off the dirt; he jokingly promised to bring some Detol (disinfectant).

> 3) At one point a man handed Kava the jawbone of a pig. Apparently this was in reference to a standing joke between him and Kava. The story is that he had some time previously suggested to Kava that she get false teeth to replace her front ones, which had been extracted. Kava's response was, "Are you going to give them to me?" The man answered, "Yes." Apparently this developed into a standing joke, so that when the two met Kava would ask if he had the false teeth and he would answer, "No," or "Not yet." When he handed Kava the pig jaw at the wedding he apparently said, "Here's your teeth." She laughed and played with putting the jawbone up to her mouth, pretending to open and close it like false teeth, much to the crowd's amusement.

4) The wedding site was transected by the road, which was Kava's main "stage." She created several amusing incidents with passing traffic. When a bus came by she stopped it imperially and bellied up to it, as if it had hit her, and recoiled as though injured. She bantered with the driver for a few moments, then let him go on.

5) Dr. Panapasa [Chief Medical Officer on the island] at one point drove up in the Medical Department's vehicle and pulled right up to Kava. He then got out of the car and grabbed her arm, pulling her to the passenger's side and pretended to push her in. He joked that he would take her to the hospital, or to a pig sty. She resisted and adopted a mock begging mode, falling to her knees and pleading not to be taken away. Dr. Panapasa relented and finally got into the car and backed away.

The Day After

By custom, a married couple initially establishes residence with the bride's family, although practical considerations may dictate otherwise (in this case Maika and Susie took a cottage at the Government Station where both of them worked). In order to affirm their commitment to the groom's family, however, a day or two after the wedding the couple go ceremonially to his parents' home, along with a contingent of her relatives and friends. Formerly this took place the day after the marriage was consumated; a piece of white bark with the bride's hymenal blood was featured as proof that she was a virgin.

At the groom's home the couple are fed and entertained, and another marital bed is prepared for them. They generally stay for a few days before returning to the bride's family home. In this instance, Maika and Susie came to Sautiak's home in Oinafa on the day after the wedding. Jan's diary captures the mood of the gathering.

At about 5:00 P.M. we walked over to Sautiak's and were invited to sit under the canopy they had strung up in front of the house. The band was playing and people were dancing. After one dance, people (Vai, Mekatoa) started asking me to dance, and I asked Maika and Reverend Erone—it was fun. At six they announced dinner and we all shifted around;

Susie and Maika and their päega were moved forward, her relations on the left, his (including us) on the right. Her relatives and the couple, being treated as the honored guests, were served on 'umefe; the rest of us just ate on banana leaves. We were served taro, pork, tinned corned beef, Rotuman pudding, and sugar cane. Tokaniua's wife cut me some nice pieces of pork off a big hunk they gave us and I actually found it quite tasty and still hot. I ate quite a bit (for me, especially compared to yesterday) and caught the eyes of a number of women, including Fanifau, looking on approvingly. Then we wanted to wash our hands so went in the side door to the kitchen. Inside, Torike told us to go have a look at the bridal bed made of mats—lovely with a ribboned mosquito net above. She pointed to a pile of mats in the living room, including five fine white mats which, she said, were *not* used in the wedding presentations.

We came out and sat down again. The non-chiefs from the bride's side were eating on banana leaves out on the grass; after they finished the groom's side was fed. Maika's close relatives were served last, and his parents told us later that they did not eat at all. Throughout the feasting people were making speeches, praising the couple, acknowledging the abundance of good will, and thanking all those who contributed. Alan made a speech praising both sides for creating such a grand event, and for contributing to the perpetuation of Rotuma custom.

The band started to play again and the dancing resumed. I danced with Tokaniua, Dr. Panapasa, Reverend Erone and some little boys! They started asking me after I saw [three-year old] Isimeli dancing with a group of small children. I went over and asked him to dance with me, making the gracious gesture I'd seen others making before the bride and groom—bowing and holding hands out, with palms up. He took me quite seriously and we danced. Alan said Maika and Susie loved it. After that the children surged up at each song, to ask people to dance; the little girls asked the little boys, and the little boys asked me, Susie, and Qwenda. Sometimes the whole group of children surged toward the couple and seemed to be inviting them en masse.

The adult dancing continued without incident, although there seemed to be a competition between the sides with regard to who could be more outrageous. The Lopta people, including Farpapau [a schoolteacher], Mekatoa [Susie's uncle] and Kava [who was still playing the clown, although here in an unofficial capacity] would dance in silly or provocative ways, and Sautiak [Maika's father], Kaurasi and Vera [Maika's aunts] responded in kind. Farpapau was crawling between men's legs and rolling on the ground (carefully clutching her sarong). Mekatoa got me on a chain dance and clutched me tightly from behind, making faces and lifting me up.

There was lots of play around the couple's päega—people taking the bride or groom's places pretending to be the ones who had just gotten married (and by implication would occupy the bridal bed that night). It ended up with Alan and Kava rolling on the floor behind the päega. She had her legs wrapped around him from behind, and when he tried to get away she would let him get part way up, then draw him back down. People roared with laughter at the suggestive display, and someone came up and threw a mat over them, as if to afford them privacy. Someone else brought over an empty plastic bucket, which also set Kava off. She put it on her head like a hat. Then a woman came over and took it from Kava; she motioned as if the bucket were full of water and doused Alan and Kava with it, as if to cool their uncontrollable ardor.

After that, Tokaniua came over to make sure we understood it was all in fun. Of course we did. We danced until our feet and knees hurt [much of the dancing is in the Rarotongan fashion, requiring bent knees. It was wonderful—all together, old and young, dancing and sweating. The band had some trouble with static in their speakers but it didn't matter. Sometimes people even danced without music. They kept saying, "Too bad tomorrow is Sunday" [when such activity is prohibited on the Methodist side of the island.] After dinner Mekatoa said that the Lopta people would stay for three or four dances only. About an hour and a half later he said they would stay for only two or three more, but we went on until nearly midnight [when the Sunday taboo on partying begins]. When Alan and I left people thanked us profusely for participating so actively. At home we showered, took Nuprin for our aching knees, and fell into bed.

Susie and Maika stayed for two days at Maika's home, then were ceremonially returned to Susie's home in Lopta. Again a ritual presentation of pigs and mats was required. That day Jan's diary includes the following entry.

Tarterani dropped us off in Lopta and left, later bringing Qwenda and some of the Malhaha High School kids. We waited till everyone was assembled, then proceeded up the hill with mats (I carried one) and the ceremonial food. We deposited the mats in front of Susie and Maika and later someone cleared them away (there was one fine white mat, five or six Fijian-syle ordinary mats and five or six large Rotuman ordinary mats.

The band was playing between speeches, although there was sometimes a long time between songs and the dancing didn't get off the ground. One of the speeches was about both sides winning through the wedding. That was a nice ending to the mock competition that characterized much of the dancing.

The clown was still active and at one point danced with an Indian man who feigned pregnancy, making all sorts of lewd gestures; at another she was the pregnant one; and later she dressed in jeans, black tee shirt and black plastic sleeveless raincoat with a baseball cap and swimming goggles. She also wore a belt of Fijian one dollar bills.

A group of men from the groom's side also made a valiant and sustained effort to get things moving—and the young men, who according to Joe [Qwenda's brother] had been drinking beer and rum, eventually showed up and joined in. The clown played with them, then jokingly told the bride's side that she liked the groom's side better.

Like everyone else, Alan and I were tired and it was hot so eventually we just sat. When dinner was to be served, one of the men gestured for Alan to go sit with the chiefs and honored guests. I just kept sitting with the women. Just before serving began Vamarasi took my hand and led me up to sit next to Alan. Then as the food was being set out, Reverend Erone told Alan to take Maika's place on the päega. Alan asked, "Why me?" and Erone said, "Because all the young boys are too scared." He said it was Rotuman custom for someone to relieve the bride or groom if they get too tired. Then he told me to go too. Maika seemed quite ready to be relieved of the spotlight, but Susie just shifted to one side. At first I was embarrassed to be sitting so high, especially when I realized the best food had been put in front of us. At one point a little girl (a niece of Susie's?) came and asked for some pork from her. The piece in front of her had been pretty well picked over whereas the one in front of me (originally served to her) was barely touched. I picked it up and put it in front of Susie. I just knew that etiquette wouldn't allow anyone to take it away from us even though we were "usurpers." The old lady who sat behind us kept fanning us as the honor of the päega required and I heard her say something to Alan about me having a good head and knowing how to behave properly *fak Rotuma* [according to Rotuman custom]. That was gratifying.

We talked with Susie a little bit and found she was going to work the next day. Then we left immediately after eating as it was all breaking up and a group were taking the couple to their home in Ahau.

INTERPRETATION

Before we begin to examine the events described above for their cultural meanings there is one point we would like to make: there is no such thing as a "typical" wedding, in Rotuma or elsewhere. To describe an event as "typical" is to decontextualize it, to treat it as if it were unconnected to other events. In fact all such events are embedded in particular histories that color them and give specific meanings to their unfolding. In the case of Susie and Maika's wedding, a number of historical factors were involved. To begin with, the wedding was the culmination of a healing process between Lopta and Oinafa villages following some serious disputes. At the heart of the disputes was disagreement over visits by tourist ships, which discharged visitors on the beach at Oinafa.[10] The people of Lopta disapproved of the tourist incursions, which disproportionately benefitted residents of Oinafa village, and withdrew their cooperation from district activities. Maika's father, Sautiak, was one of the main advocates (and beneficiaries) of tourist visits; Susie's uncle, Mekatoa, led the Lopta resistence. Hard feelings prevailed for more than two years, so there were profound tensions in the air prior to the wedding. However, it was clear that everyone welcomed the opportunity for reconciliation—in fact, opposition to tourist visits had toned down quite a bit following the initial furor. Speeches at the wedding focused heavily on the importance of cooperation and on laying old grievances aside. At one point during the proceedings, Mekatoa, who was in the position of host, declared the formal rules of protocol, that act to keep the bride's and groom's parties separated inoperative, since "we are all one family." As confirmation, the feast was served without the usual formalities.

Other factors contributing to the specific form of this wedding were Maika's status and the particular site at which it was held. As a member of a chiefly kainaga, Maika's parents chose not to have him represented by an 'a su selected by the district chief. This was a matter of choice, and constituted a political statement of sorts by his immediate family. The fact that Maika had been married before also was relevant, since it rendered two of the rituals irrelevant: the symbolic haircutting, and the wrapping in mats. These rituals are reserved for individuals who are in transition between unmarried youth to married adult, and since Maika had already been through them once they were inappropriate for him.

The choice of Semesi's house as location for the wedding also affected events. Had his house been nearer to the church, for example, vehicles would not have been needed to transport people back and forth, and the fact that the road transected the site affected arrangements in several ways. In fact choices must be made in connection with any wedding, giving each its unique flavor.

A Note on the Process of Interpretation

As should be evident by now, Rotuman weddings, like ceremonies everywhere, are rich in symbolism. Interpreting the meaning of these symbols is no easy task and is fraught with pitfalls. One can, of course, ask people involved what the various symbols mean, and receive some perfectly reasonable answers. For example, Rotumans will readily tell you that the importance of the 'a su is to elevate the event to a chiefly plane, taking it out of the realm of the ordinary. But ritual symbolism is largely unconscious, or at least unarticulated; it is therefore left to the ethnographer to make sense of it. Doing so requires a great deal of cultural knowledge: a familiarity with history, myths, language, and patterns of behavior. The task is made more difficult by the fact that key cultural symbols are polysemic; that is, they condense meanings from many different aspects of experience. They are also multivocal, suggesting different things to different people. Thus, the cross, for Christians, stands for a wide variety of beliefs, values, and institutions. It condenses an enormous array of historical and cultural meaning.

Another complication is the fact that rituals originating in one historical context are often perpetuated into another, changing the meaning of some symbols and robbing others of their initial significance. On Rotuma, most of the non-Christian wedding rituals had their origins in rites associated with ancestral spirits and Polynesian gods. Conversion to Christianity has certainly altered their significance in many important respects. Nevertheless, we believe that they remain meaningful, and that their current meanings resonate with their pre-Christian precursors. To put this differently, we believe that some of the most important values in pre-Christian Rotuman society remain vibrant today, and that holdover symbols and rites still signify those values, although their specific associations may differ. For these reasons we shall not try to interpet the wedding described above ritual by ritual, symbol by symbol. Rather, we shall proceed by articulating core values, then show how various aspects of the wedding reflect them. Fortunately in this instance we have an extraordinary resource to draw upon—the work of Vilsoni Hereniko, a Rotuman playwright-scholar who has recently completed a study of the role of the female clown at Rotuman weddings.[11] In the course of his analysis, Hereniko offers compelling explanations for much of the symbolism we witnessed; we make liberal use of his insights in our analysis.

Value 1: Kinship and Community

As are most Pacific societies, Rotuma is organized primarily on the basis of kinship relations. In any village most people are related to each other, sometimes in multiple ways. Chiefs are chosen on the basis of their kin connections to ancestral titleholders. Kinship considerations therefore serve to organize interhousehold cooperation, productive labor, and political activity. Reaffirming kin connections through exchanges of food and labor is central to being considered a person of good character. The fisherman coming back from an expedition is likely to share his catch with his neighbors/kinsmen; the woman who makes banana jam sends jars to selected households. If someone needs their house repaired, or help preparing for a family event, they can generally count on their village mates for assistance. When times are good and relationships strong, people look for things to do for one another; they use any excuse to hold an event that will bring people together, no matter how much work is involved.

Weddings are prime events for celebrating kinship relations and community cooperation. A wedding the size of Maika and

Susie's, involving around five hundred people, requires a great deal of effort and interaction. The men must spend much time in their gardens producing and harvesting taro, yams, and, if in season, pineapples and watermelon. In preparation for the wedding they gather pigs, and perhaps a cow or two, to be slaughtered and cooked in earthen ovens. The women plait mats, which is also labor intensive. To make an apei takes a skilled woman a month or so of steady work. All of this effort, and the products that result from it, are donated to the wedding. The total value of donations adds up to thousands of dollars (a fine white mat has a sale value of up to 400 Fijian dollars, or about US $268; a pig from 25 to 100 Fijian dollars depending on size; a cow around 400 Fijian dollars). Thus the formal presentations of food and mats at a wedding are announcements to the whole community of the work that has been done on behalf of the bride and groom. It is as if each mat unfolded and each basket of food presented symbolizes the willingness of the presenters to labor on behalf of those being honored. The speeches at a wedding focus on thanking all those who contributed, and impressing on the bride and groom the magnitude of effort expended on their behalf. The implication, of course, is that the couple are beholden to a great many people and owe it to them to make their marriage successful and fruitful.

Much of the time prior to the wedding is spent working with kin and neighbors on the preparations. The choice of with whom to work affirms certain relationships and possibly slights others. Which sal hapa one chooses to join—people usually have a number of kainaga with whom they could affiliate—is a statement about one's sense of closeness to various relatives. Working together, and especially sharing food at meals, signifies the very essence of kinship for Rotumans. Sharing in the preparation of the wedding, and participating together in the wedding feast, symbolizes the new relationship between the families of bride and groom, as much as the marriage itself.

The central role of namesakes in the wedding can also be seen as a way of impressing upon everyone that there is more involved in a marriage than simply joining two individuals, or two families. In a very important respect namesakes represent broader kin rights and responsibilities—the fact that parents are not the only ones with a stake in the fate of individuals. By acting as surrogate parents in this context namesakes thus render the occasion communal rather than familial in orientation.

The female clown can be understood in this light as well. She is technically in charge of the wedding, given that authority by the leading chief from the bride's side. The event is thus taken out of parental or familial control and transformed into one put on by the chiefs and wider community. As mistress of ceremonies she is responsible for facilitating interaction between the two sides, and for creating a jocular environment where all can enjoy themselves. By serving as a focus of attention, she relieves the bride and groom of the intensive scrutiny they might otherwise receive and involves a greater segment of the community in the activities of the day.

Value 2: Fertility of People and Land

The dominant theme in pre-Christian Rotuman religious rituals, and in supporting myths,[12] was securing from the gods and ancestral spirits abundance here on earth. Rites focused on insuring fertility of the land and perpetuating the kainaga through the fertility of its people. The major religious figure in early Rotuma was the *sau*, an office occupied for periods ranging from six months (one ritual cycle) to several years. Men were chosen as sau by the leading chief on the island to represent the well-being of Rotuma. When not participating in specific rites the sau did little but sit and eat. Districts took turns hosting him, and each was obliged to feed him to satiation. It seems that the sau was seen as a temporary incarnation of the gods. To feed him was to feed the gods, in return for which they were expected to bring prosperity.

Ceremonial feasts were dedicated to the gods and involved sacrifices to them. Sacrifice is a way of feeding gods, of infusing them with life. The ultimate sacrifice, of course, is a human life. There is no evidence that Rotumans ever engaged in human sacrifice, but their myths make it clear that pigs are a substitute for human beings. (Reversing this equation, pre-Christian Fijians referred to humans eaten at cannibal feasts as "long pig.") It is not fortuitous, therefore, that pigs must be cooked whole for a ceremonial feast, for they would lose their essential quality as sacrificial animals if cut into pieces prior to cooking. In contrast to pigs, cows, which were introduced by Europeans, are not considered sacrificial animals and are butchered prior to cooking.

The formal presentations of food prior to the feast can be better understood in the light of this cultural concern for abundance. The food is assembled to public attention to its volume, and the ritual calling out of exaggerated quantities is a way of further increasing the magnitude of the display. It is a way of demonstrating to the community the beneficence of the gods (or contemporarily, the Christian God). The food display is followed by the kava ceremony, which in ancient Rotuma was a ritual form of communion, aimed at obtaining divine blessings. Kava was conceived as originating in the realm of the supernatural, and hence as a drink of the gods. The chanted recitation prior to its being served traditionally tells the story of its arrival in Rotuma. That the words of the chant are not understood by most people serves to further mystify kava, enhancing its ritual potency.[13] Finally, just prior to eating, Christian prayers are offered in thanks for the food to be eaten.

This central Rotuman concern for productivity of the land is matched by a concern for human fertility. Through the production of children families prosper. Barrenness is regarded as one of the worst misfortunes that can afflict a Rotuman couple; it is considered a sign of divine disfavor. In pre-contact Rotuma childbirth was dangerous for both mother and child, and with the coming of Europeans, introduced childhood diseases like measles and whooping cough took a terrible toll. This put an even greater premium on having children (and keeping them alive).

Many aspects of a wedding allude to the fact that the couple form a new breeding unit, one that can potentially contribute descendants to each of the kainaga represented (since they are all formed around ascendants of either the bride or groom). In many respects the bride and groom are treated like gods on their wedding day, perhaps because they are making a transition from a state of presumed barrenness to a state of presumed fecundity. Through marriage they are socially recognized as having the "god-given" capacity to create life. They are seated upon a fine white mat, itself a sacred symbol, and the shelter under which they sit with the chiefs is marked off as sacred by the rolls of cloth hung up by the groom's party following their arrival. (In earlier days fine mats were used.) Tiu Malo, a Rotuman who has written about marriage on the island, states that:

> This 'screening' of the *ri hapa* [shelter] symbolically creates a sacred atmosphere. The simple shed is now a temple, a holy place for the marriage rituals. Hence the *mafua* [spokes-

man] refers to entering the *su'ura* [king's house, that is, a sacred or taboo place].

Several of the rituals symbolize the change in status of the bride and groom. The public change of clothes is one instance. The fact that the bride and groom are both given clothes by the other side underscores the claim each side has over the couple's potential offspring. Clothes are perhaps the pre-eminent symbol of cultural conformity. To publicly don the clothes someone else has given you is to symbolize your acceptance of a new role, and in this instance, a new set of relationships.

Another instance is the hair-snipping ceremony, in which the groom's namesake symbolically cuts the bride's hair and vice versa. In ancient times youths grew a long lock of hair until they were married, so the ceremony was conducted in earnest. Cutting the hair signified a shift in status from that of youth, with minimal responsibilities to the community, to that of an adult. It also signified community recognition of the couple's reproductive capabilities. Today, since youths do not grow a long lock, cutting is only symbolic, but the implication is the same.

The ritual that most dramatically symbolizes the couple's new status as breeders is the *fau* ceremony, in which bride and groom are each wrapped in fine mats and bound with cloth. They are then carried from the bride's side of the shelter to the groom's side, where the cloth binding is removed and they are unwrapped. There is much evidence to suggest that the act of wrapping the couple symbolizes the binding of spiritual powers in the service of fertility. The carrying of the couple from the bride's side to the groom's side dramatizes the legitimate claims the groom's family has (in addition to the bride's family) to the offspring of the union.

It should now be clear why Maika did not actively participate in these rituals. Having been married before, he had already made the ritual transformation from youth to adult. His reproductive capabilities had already been ritually bound; all that was necessary now was to transfer his virility to the service of his new wife and her family. This was sufficiently symbolized in other ways (for example, the wedding vows in church).

Apei are key symbols in many of the wedding rituals. They are carried by the highest ranking women and formally unfolded for all to see. The bride and groom's seat is topped with an apei, and an apei is placed above them as "protection." The uncooked food brought by the groom's side is covered with mats topped by an apei. The bride and groom are wrapped in apei during the fau ceremony. Furthermore, apei are given in gratitude to chiefs and other participants, such as the female clown, who contribute to the success of an affair. The bride and groom's parents exchange mats, as do their namesakes. Ultimately, most of the apei presented at a wedding are redistributed among the main participants.

To understand the meaning of ritual transactions it is necessary to have a good sense of the importance of apei in Rotuman culture. One thing is clear—that apei are the most important traditional valuable. Apei are central to every ceremonial transaction, and are even used to influence political events. A request backed by the gift of an apei is nearly impossible to refuse, and an apei assures a plea for forgiveness will be accepted no matter how grevious the offense. Why should this be so?

Vilsoni Hereniko has argued persuasively that traditionally apei were conceived by Rotumans as "woven gods." He cites several lines of evidence to support his assertion: that in a popular Rotuman myth malicious spirits are domesticated by capturing them in woven nets; that in earlier times women who were commissioned by a chief to make apei were granted license to act outrageously, like unrestrained spirits, until the task was completed; that an apei must be consecrated with a sacrificial pig (thereby transferring the life force of the pig into the mat). To give an apei is therefore equivalent in Rotuman cultural logic to a gift of life. Since the gift of life ultimately comes from the gods, an apei is comparable to a god, and has divine associations.[14]

The importance of apei at weddings becomes clear in the light of Hereniko's analysis. They represent the binding of life forces, derived from the gods, in the service of human reproduction.

The clown's paraphernalia and behavior also underscore the importance of fertility and reproduction. The stick she wields is more than a useful prop for pointing and threatening people. It also reminds spectators of the digging stick that men use to plant taro and cassava in their gardens, and hence to the production of food. However its primary referent, according to Hereniko, is the male phallus and its procreative function in human propagation.[15] In addition, the clown's sexual banter and lascivious innuendoes draw attention to the theme of reproduction.

Value 3: Political Balance
Between Chiefsand Commoners

The role of chiefs in Rotuman weddings is central. Chiefs elevate the status of events in which they participate; they lend dignity to any proceedings. By representing the bride's and groom's parties they transform a family occasion into an affair of state, implicating all whom they represent. But they do more than this, for in pre-Christian Rotuma chiefs were conceived as sacred beings—as conduits to the gods. Although the ultimate source of prosperity was thought to reside with the gods (including distinguished ancestors), it was the responsibility of chiefs to act as intermediaries, to influence them to act benignly. Conceptually the distinction between gods and chiefs was somewhat blurred, in fact, since chiefs were thought to be transformed into gods following their deaths. The presence of chiefs at a wedding therefore sanctifies the event, increasing the likelihood that the couple will be blessed with good fortune.

Since this is the case, the behavior of the female clown is something of a puzzle, for she is granted license to badger the chiefs, to order them around, to make them the butt of jokes. How can this be reconciled with the notion of chiefs as sacred beings?

To paraphrase Hereniko's compelling explanation: Rotuman weddings, like plays in the western world, provide safe arenas in which forces potentially threatening to the well-being of society's members can be acted out, diffused, displaced, or resolved. Clowning, in the frame of a wedding, is an act of communication from the bottom up, from females to males, from the bride's kin to the groom's kin, and from commoners to chiefs.

The female clown at a Rotuman wedding communicates through inversion. Values of humility, respect and restraint—cornerstones of Rotuman society—are inverted and replaced by their antithesis in her antics. Paradoxically, the clown's violation of Rotuman values reinforces them at the same time. For example, by dethroning the chiefs, she draws attention to the importance of their normal role. For Rotuman society to function submission to authority is necessary. The clown temporarily displaces the chiefs and assumes their power in a parodied form. If everyone in the community can submit to a clown, then submission to chiefs should be second nature.

Furthermore, in a society where the chiefs are men, the public portrayal of authority in female hands invites laughter, particularly when the exercise of chiefly power is displayed in its extreme form. As the clown is female but behaves as male, both male and female attributes are indirectly communicated. The conjunction in one individual of male aggressiveness and a presumed female lack of control results in chaos. The destructive and chaotic world portrayed by the female clown is the antithesis of harmony, testimony to the impracticability of a world in which folly reigns. The model that the clown holds up for scrutiny is therefore to be rejected. Through inversion, the clown affirms the complementary but different natures of chiefs and commoners, of males and females.

There is another message in the clown's outrageous behavior. The wedding frame is an opportunity for chiefs to be made aware of what it is like to be ordered about. The clown holds up a mirror to the chiefs, showing them how they will appear if they get too pompous. Her actions graphically remind them that although they may have divine sanctification for their positions, they are still mere mortals who depend on their fellow beings for their privileged status. A Rotuman wedding is therefore an arena in which chiefs learn the importance of humility.[16]

Perpetuation of Rotuman Custom

Legally one can get married on Rotuma simply by getting a license at the Government Station and by having the district officer or a justice of the peace perform a civil ceremony. In fact, many couples do just that, or have a simple ceremony at home performed by their priest or minister. By doing so they avoid large expenses and increased obligations. Therefore, full-scale weddings, like Susie and Maika's, play a special role in perpetuating Rotuman culture and are valued accordingly.

As in most Polynesian societies many key features of the traditional culture were suppressed or abandoned following European intrusion. Methodist and Catholic missionaries attacked customs associated with the ancestral religion; government officials undermined the traditional roles played by chiefs; imported goods replaced those of indigenous manufacture. The world was turned upside down, and like colonized people everywhere, Rotumans

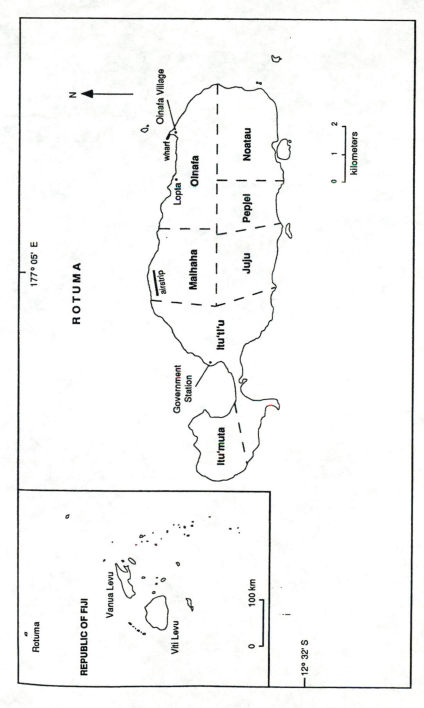

REPUBLIC OF FIJI

Rotuma

Vanua Levu

Viti Levu

12° 32' S

0   100 km

ROTUMA

177° 05' E

N

Itu'muta

Government
Station

Itu'ti'u

airstrip

Malhaha

Lopta

Oinafa

wharf

Oinafa Village

Pepjel

Juju

Noatau

0   1   2
kilometers

Adapted from maps drawn by Joan Lawrence.

faced a future that could have stripped them of their unique traditions. But despite pressures to desist—missionaries and colonial officials often chastized Rotumans for "wasting" so much food and money on "useless" ceremonies—the people on this small, isolated island have persisted in adhering to those customs they see as central to Rotuman identity. Even the most cosmopolitan Rotumans recognize the value of an apei, the importance of a pig cooked whole in an earthen oven, the significance of the kava ceremony. They may criticize individual chiefs, but they support the institution of chieftainship. They value these customs regardless of personal beliefs because the customs have come to symbolize their unique cultural heritage.

In a full-scale Rotuman wedding feast, all of these key Rotuman cultural symbols are highlighted. When Susie and Maika got married, therefore, they not only celebrated their union. They celebrated Rotuman culture as well. They provided a setting for the entire community to affirm everything that is essential to their identity as a people.

NOTES

1. Clifford Geertz, "Deep Play: Notes on the Balinese Cockfight." *Daedalus,* 101 (1972): 1–37.

2. Andrew Pawley, "New Evidence on the Position of Rotuman." *Working Papers in Linguistics,* No. 56, Department of Anthropology, University of Auckland, New Zealand, August 1979.

3. For an account of Rotuman migration and its consequences for life on the island, see Alan Howard and Jan Rensel, "Rotuma in the 1990s: From Hinterland to Neighbourhood," *Journal of the Polynesian Society* (in press).

4. For about six weeks during the holiday season Rotumans stop nearly all serious work and engage in a variety of leisure activities. In the past, it was a prime time for courtship and continues to be so today.

5. If he were following Rotuman custom strictly, he would have asked an elder to speak to the chief on his behalf.

6. For a general overview of changes, see Alan Howard, "Reflections on Change in Rotuma, 1959–1989," in Anselmo Fatiaki et al.,

Rotuma: Hanua Pumue (Precious Land), (Suva, Fiji: Institute of Pacific Studies, University of the South Pacific, 1991), pp. 227–254.

7. Both sides present the couple with new clothes at this point as well as later on in the ceremony. Formerly, weddings took place over many more days, and these gifts of new clothes would be donned each morning and afternoon. Today, the couple changes less frequently; in this case, Maika wore his policeman's uniform throughout the day's activities.

8. This is not the Tokaniua who had been Oinafa district chief in 1960 but a prominent sub-chief who later succeeded to the title.

9. Tiu Malo, "Rotuman Marriage." in Anselmo Fatiaki et al., *Rotuma: Hanua Pumue (Precious Land)* (Suva, Fiji: Institute of Pacific Studies, University of the South Pacific, 1991) p. 72.

10. See Alan Howard, "Dispute Management in Rotuma," *Journal of Anthropological Research,* 46 (1990): 263–292.

11. Vilsoni Hereniko, *Woven Gods: Female Clowns and Power in Rotuma.* (Honolulu, Hawaii: University Press of Hawaii, in press).

12. For interpretations of Rotuman myths along these lines, see Alan Howard, "History, Myth and Polynesian Chieftainship: The Case of Rotuman Kings," in Antony Hooper and Judith Huntsman, eds., *Transformations of Polynesian Culture* (Auckland: Polynesian Society, 1985), pp. 39–77 and Alan Howard, "Cannibal Chiefs and the Charter for Rebellion in Rotuman Myth," *Pacific Studies,* 10 (1986): 1–27.

13. Today most people do not know the traditional chants, and often substitute stories or recitations of their own. Even so, the words remain largely unintelligible, either because they are mumbled or because nonsense syllables are included. It appears that intelligibility would undermine the association of chanting with the mystified world of gods and spirits.

14. See Hereniko, *Woven Gods.*

15. Ibid.

16. Ibid.

SUGGESTED READINGS

Fatiaki, Anselmo, et al. *Rotuma: Hanua Pumue (Precious Land).* Suva, Fiji: Institute of Pacific Studies, University of the South Pacific,

1991. A collection of essays, mostly by Rotumans, on various aspects of their society and culture. Includes an essay by Tiu Malo on Rotuman marriage.

Gardiner, J. Stanley. "The Natives of Rotuma," *Journal of the Royal Anthropological Institute*, 27 (1898): 396–435, 457–524. A comprehensive account of Rotuman society in the nineteenth century.

Hereniko, Vilsoni. *Woven Gods: Female Clowns and Power in Rotuma*. Honolulu, Hawaii: University Press of Hawaii, in press. A masterful analysis by a Rotuman playwright, combining the intuitions of a cultural insider with the theoretical insights of a sophisticated scholar.

Howard, Alan. *Learning to Be Rotuma*. New York: Columbia University Teachers College Press, 1970. An account of Rotuman child-rearing practices and character development in the context of culture change. Includes an account of formal schooling on Rotuma and how it contrasts with indigenous socialization.

Howard, Alan. "History, Myth and Polynesian Chieftainship: The Case of Rotuman Kings." In Antony Hooper and Judith Huntsman, eds., *Transformations of Polynesian Culture*. Auckland: Polynesian Society, 1985, pp. 39–77. A symbolic analysis of Rotuman myths focusing on the sacred role of chiefs, fertility, and the relationship between humans and gods.

HAN:

PASTORALISTS AND FARMERS ON A CHINESE FRONTIER

Burton Pasternak

There developed a perpetual antagonism, which demanded a decisive choice of every people and state that in the course of history overlapped the Great Wall Frontier, whether its founders were Chinese or non-Chinese— the choice between agriculture of a notably intensive form and nomadism of an especially dispersed form. Of the repeated attempts to create societies or states that could integrate both orders not one succeeded.[1]

When Han farmers first crossed the Great Wall in search of a better life, they found a setting where the climate was unmerciful, the land unyielding, and the local inhabitants unfriendly. Many eventually gave up and went home; only those prepared to alter their behavior were able to remain. This chapter is about their adjustment on the grasslands, and about their response to a government which has, especially in recent years, taken strong measures to shape their lives. It is about how tradition, politics, and economy have interacted to define life on the Inner Mongolian frontier.

Whether they speak Mandarin or some other dialect, Han have a common history and tradition. They use the same written language, and share many goals and values. Their way of life is rooted in intensive farming. They transfer population pressure to land, applying ever more labor and attention to squeeze marginal increments out of limited space. Male-headed extended families (consisting of two or more married couples) provide the workers.

The history of Han expansion testifies to the success of their adaptation. But there have been limits, areas inhospitable to their way. It was at just such a frontier that they drew a line of stone, a Great Wall, to mark the end of the "civilized" world. It was a frontier beyond which they could not long survive as Han, or at least that is what many believed.

The Chinese state endorsed an ideology that encouraged homogeneity. Pressures to sameness increased in post-1949 China, as the communist state extended its apparatus downward to influence and control all aspects of life. Never before had government

185

so controlled where people lived, where they worked, what they might grow, what they could eat or buy, when they could marry, and even when and how many children they might have. People took their place in a hierarchy of groups. Throughout the country children learned Mandarin in school. Collectivization provided a common framework for the deployment of land and labor. By eliminating private property, regulating marriage, and stimulating class struggle within families, the state attempted to redirect orientations from family and locality to nation. Differences of wealth, life-style, and opportunity narrowed. People married, formed families, and even bore children in increasingly similar ways.

But older themes played on, along with their variations. In so vast and varied a country, with its multitude of climates, topographies, crops, and cultures, it could not have been otherwise. With the recent collapse of communes and restoration of family-based production, the potential for variation has increased.

We focus on Han adjustment on the Inner Mongolian frontier, but we are also interested in changes underway in rural China as it shifts from a socialist to a market economy. The world watches as the Chinese try another tack, and there is much at stake. If their efforts are successful, an elusive prosperity may come to China, and provide a model for others to modify and use. If the attempt fails, we may witness yet another monumental upheaval in China.

Our study is based on fieldwork in four communities conducted in collaboration with Janet Salaff, a sociologist at the University of Toronto, and Chinese colleagues from the Institute of Sociology at Peking University.[2] During the summers of 1988 and 1990, we crossed into northeastern Inner Mongolia. We visited two communities of people whose recent ancestors settled where they could use hoes, plows drawn by draft animals, and other familiar north Chinese tools and techniques. We then crossed the Great Chingan mountains to the west, entering vast grasslands that run to Outer Mongolia and Siberia, where we chose to study two communities of Han herdsmen. It is there that the homogenizing power of the Chinese state confronts a special challenge.

Did Han there become, over time, more like their Mongol neighbors than like Han who tilled fields at the fringes of the grassland? Or were pressures to uniformity so powerful that they overwhelmed differences of ethnicity and ecology? Our work will show how ecology and technology create diversity in China, how the nature of labor influences family formation and relations within families. It did so during the collective era and before, and now as the economy decentralizes and moves toward a market economy, we can expect even more varied local responses.

Farming and herding differ in fundamental ways. The nature of crucial resources and the timing and places of work determine the tasks assigned to women and men of different ages and influence the family structure and reproduction. Farmers can only work harder because they depend on an essentially unexpandable resource—land. Labor is intensive, but not uniform. Each phase of the farming cycle—preparation, planting, maintenance, harvest—calls for a special kind of effort, and there are marked peaks and troughs in demand. By farming near home, women can work alongside men, doing much the same tasks while still managing domestic chores.

The situation is different for pastoralists. Herds and flocks are expandable, and their managers may obtain great rewards. With sufficient grassland they can enlarge and diversify livestock, even cut hay for sale. The routine is more continuous and repetitive. Grazing, cutting hay, and most other pastoral work take place some distance from home. Women cannot do such work and at the same time milk the cows and run the household. The division of labor is thus sharper.

The ideal herdsman is an adult male. Strength and experience are important. Mistakes can menace generations of animals; therefore, youngsters contribute less than they do among the farmers, while old people have more to offer and remain selfsufficient longer. An elderly couple would have a hard time plowing, building mounds, or harvesting on their own, so at about age sixty-five farmers gradually retire. They do not become idle even then. Old women free younger ones for work outside by looking after home and grandchildren. The elderly of both sexes lend a hand in the fields and process harvested crops when labor is badly needed.

Farming and herding differently shape family structure, the relationships of women and men and their access to education, the ages at which people marry and bear children, and even the number of children they have. The contrasts predate the commune and have outlasted it. Collectivization changed the way property and labor were used, and the state extended its control deeper, but differences rooted in ecology and technology have always precluded uniformity. Below we explore these linkages in greater detail, tracing continuities and discontinuities. At the same time we will try to get some feel for important changes now taking place in rural China.

FROM COMMUNE TO FAMILY RESPONSIBILITY

After long discouraging private enterprise, the Chinese began to dismantle rural collectives in 1979. Communes had promised economic security and increased productivity through economies of scale, mechanization, and the deployment of mass labor. They would improve livelihoods and promote equality. But equality and production were in tension; the system designed to reduce disparities ultimately hampered development.

Collective life diluted risk, providing some protection against failure. But there was little incentive for hard work since everyone shared earnings. The disjointing of effort and reward weakened commitment. Large scale management was especially problematic in the herding area. When responsibility shifted from worker to worker, weakening the identification herdsmen had with particular animals, attention flagged and losses were considerable.

In the region we studied, abandonment of communes was complete by 1983. To encourage production with minimal state investment, the government now allocates land to individual families, encouraging them to adopt new ways to increase income. Many report increased activity and higher rural incomes, along with some negative changes. There is evidence that education, health care, and welfare, previously collective responsibilities, have weakened. There are questions about whether, as they move toward a market economy, the Chinese will be able to reconcile their longstanding commitment to equality with their desire for increased production. Under the family "responsibility system" the collective slogan "everyone eating out of the same big pot," has given way to "some will get rich first." Emerging differences within and between communities arouse tension.

Some propose that production will decline as land divides into plots too small to support machines. Fragmentation could also disturb an already precarious balance between people and land. Reports suggest that the unleashing of "get rich quick" attitudes and uncertainties about the duration of family responsibility contracts are encouraging people to despoil land and water for immediate profits. Farmers cultivate fragile hillsides without returning nutrients. Herdsmen think only of animal numbers, disregarding the effects on pasture. With the abandonment of communes, it is hard to restrain these depredations or mobilize to improve the environment.

There are also questions about how these changes will affect women. In some places low labor productivity draws men to new opportunities elsewhere, leaving women, the old, and the young behind to work the land. Will the burdens of women now expand to include new and greater obligations, including those associated with handicrafts, husbandry, or other ventures additional to farming and family reproduction? Our four communities provide windows through which to explore these issues.

THE SETTING

Inner Mongolia provides an exceptional setting in which to explore the way ecology shapes labor and, through it, marriage and family structure. We compare two modes of production, pastoralism and cultivation, each with subvariants—pure farming versus mixed cultivation—dairying, limited versus extensive pastoralism. Our laboratory, Hulunbuir League in northeastern Inner Mongolia, borders Heilongjiang province to the east, the (former) Soviet Union to the northeast, and Mongolia to the northwest. To the north, in the foothills of the Great Chingan range, is an area rich in minerals and forest. East of the mountains people farm (mainly maize, soybeans, wheat, potatoes, and sugar beets), or combine cultivation with limited dairying. Lush grasslands west of the mountains support sedentary and nomadic pastoralism (cattle and sheep).

Seasons are extreme, the winters cold and long, summers cool and short. In January the temperature dips to -7.6 degrees Fahrenheit (-22 degrees Celsius) in the cultivating area and -18.4 degrees Fahrenheit (-28 degrees Celsius) on the grasslands. Because the frost-free period is less than 135 days, farmers produce only one crop. Large scale cutting during the first half of this century left few trees; the loss has permitted erosion in the cultivating regions and threatens desertification on the grasslands. Seasonal wind storms sweep through. Soils are sandy. Nature is capricious, periodically providing either too much or too little rain. Rivers and streams flood, destroying crops and eroding farmland.

The climate is a problem for herdsmen as well. Sudden changes can dramatically reduce animal numbers, denying their future contributions as well. Most dangerous are "white disasters," heavy or early snowstorms that threaten lambs and prevent sheep from pawing to grasses beneath. Then there are "black disasters," when snowfall is so light that there is little water for the animals and grasses are poor.

Inner Mongolia is one of China's poorest regions. In 1989, income per capita was only 478 RMB, compared to 602 RMB in rural China generally.[3] It was in part because of this that families in all of the sites we visited welcomed the shift to family production. Income has risen in recent years, but much of the region continues to be remote, undeveloped, and sparsely populated.

Although the 1990 census of Inner Mongolia indicated a large ethnic minority population, most of whom are Mongols, we focus on the Han. Their number has increased steadily to 80.6 percent of the population, 83.4 percent in Hulunbuir League. Centuries of cultural and political separation have left a legacy of ill will. A massive intrusion of Han after the turn of this century, and the associated displacement of pastoral peoples, magnified the problem. Conversion of grassland into farms in the earlier settled south ruined traditional grazing lands, prompting a pastoral retreat. Heavy-handed attempts to create a Chinese version of socialist uniformity during the Cultural Revolution brought the problem to a head, and distrust remains on both sides.

DOING FIELDWORK IN INNER MONGOLIA

Since 1979, the Chinese have permitted a limited number of foreigners to conduct local studies. There is an enduring distrust of foreigners in China, and to complicate matters we were working in a border region, where local sensitivities were particularly intense. Our colleagues from Beijing were concerned, especially during our second visit shortly after the Tiananmen massacre in 1989, about ongoing changes in China's distant heartland that might later color the political correctness of our visit.

If our hosts had to come to terms with our presence, we had to adjust as well. The pastoral sites were reminiscent of the early North American frontier. Problems of water, sanitation, climate, and isolation pose formidable challenges. They call for adjustments on the part of the local inhabitants as well as ourselves. Water was one problem, both too much and too little of it. There are no pipes or sewers. Earthen roads are muddy and, during the rainy season, many impassible. Paradoxically, water is also a precious commodity, particularly on the open grassland. In Great Pasture Town, one of our sites, water is carted from a central well and stored in large jars that are all too quickly emptied. Bathing is episodic, a big treat from a small pan. We also had to contend constantly with the fine, windblown earth that covered everything, including our computers.

Conveniences everywhere were simple or absent. In the towns, we made use of all too frequently overwhelmed public outhouses and backyard pits. On the open grassland there were no designated latrines at all. For Mongols it is no problem, they simply squat under their long robes. But for trousered visitors it is more complicated on unobstructed plain, lacking rock or tree, where one can see for miles.

On the grassland, yurt encampments are far apart. We split up and moved about by tractor, sometimes by horse-drawn cart. We consumed large quantities of milk-tea, wine, dried sheep's milk cheese, mutton fat, and noodles during our stay on the grassland. Eating the Mongol way took some getting used to. Meat is boiled in a large pot, after which pieces, especially the choice fatty parts, are pressed on guests. The parts are quite recognizable—rib cage, lower jaw, etc. In the farming villages, we had water and a more varied diet, including vegetables. On arrival in Middle Village, in our honor, a dog was killed for us to eat. That took some getting used to, especially since we had seen someone blow-torch its fur. It was disconcerting to see one of the cadres (administrative workers) assigned to manage our visit removing the caps of beer bottles with the pistol he carried "to defend us."

For local officials, hosting outsiders in an uncertain political climate introduced an element of troublesome unpredictability. The Soviet border was only an hour away. Who would be responsible if the Russians chose to assassinate us to create a rift? We were not there to study Han-Mongol relations, but what might we say about them later? Would we portray local folk as backward? What if we wrote uncomplimentary things, or published controversial materials or pictures? What if unsuspecting townsfolk revealed aspects of local life, or of recent history, that might upset officialdom above? Our second visits were at a time of even greater uncertainty. The wrenching disintegration of socialist states, including Mongolia just across the border, ethnic tensions in Tibet and the Soviet Union, and events in Tiananmen Square combined to deepen sensitivities.

I can convey some sense of this by describing an event that took place during our first days at one site. We believed our way had already been prepared, but during a welcome dinner provided by the local leadership we learned otherwise. Our host, called from the room, returned ashen faced and soon conveyed the reason for his somber mood to one of our Chinese colleagues. When, after dinner, our Chinese colleagues conferred without us, we anticipated a storm.

Clearances for our project should have passed down through three chains of command—government, Communist party, and security. The security clearance had gotten stuck somewhere. We had been walking about talking to people for two days without clearance! Local officials suggested we return to the League capital on the next train. It took some doing to persuade them to let us send a Chinese colleague to clear the administrative block. We were allowed twenty-four hours to resolve the matter, during which we foreigners would confine ourselves to our rooms.

After the matter was worked out, our embarrassed hosts reminded us that the Soviet border was only an hour away, and that the region is normally closed to foreigners. They assured us that even if a local person should go fishing along the Russian border and come back empty handed, there would be many questions to answer. We were foreigners wandering without notice into the local middle school and other places. We were taking photographs of homes, including some rather picturesque (in their view shabby) Russian homes, which might create the "wrong impression." We were far from Beijing, and news reached here slowly. It was not easy to know which way the winds were blowing at any particular time. Better that we limit our conversations and visits to persons and places agreed on in advance. Sensitive issues having to do with the Cultural Revolution, family planning, Han-Mongol relations, or corruption had to be avoided so as not to threaten our local hosts or our Chinese colleagues. Were we to write something unacceptable they would answer for it.

As a result, even where local people were eager to cooperate, it was not always possible to pursue issues our colleagues viewed as politically sensitive. Some people were eager to talk about birth control policies, but the simplest questions on these matters reminded our colleagues of American criticisms of their one child per family policy, so we had to pursue this topic in the most indirect fashion. We also had to stay clear of factional struggles and ethnic disputes, and deal with the manipulations of particular individuals. At one site, a young Mongol cadre new on the job suggested that his older colleagues might be harboring an American spy. To his mind I had all the requisites—a miniature radio, a computer, and a camera. It took a while and a few drinking bouts to ease his suspicions.

The restrictions, naturally frustrating, became less burdensome as time passed. At first, we were not to take pictures or casually visit people and, for our safety's sake (and theirs), we were not to swim in the river or ride horses. We were reminded not to cross certain bridges into townships for which we had no clearance. But once our presence was accepted and no longer a novelty, we wandered, visited, and photographed somewhat more freely.

FRONTIER FARMERS

Tranquillity Village and Middle Villages provide a baseline against which to measure changes that occurred when Han moved into areas less hospitable to cultivation. They were settled by parents or grandparents of the people we met, who came from impoverished regions across the line of stone to scratch some sort of living out of the dry, sandy earth. Life was hard, even during the era of collectives. As before, the commune depended heavily on the labor of everyone. But the scale of operation created serious problems here and in the pastoral communes. The collective consciousness that endless political campaigns had tried to evoke proved hard to sustain. Some people, content to live on collective allotments and vegetables grown on small private garden plots, put few hours and little energy into collective fields. Others had to work harder simply to maintain output and work-point value. Low productivity meant low work-point value, so even with hard work there was little difference between what top and bottom earners brought home.

Families no longer owned land or major implements, but the number of family workers still governed income. Families with several men earned most because cadres reserved the best-paying jobs for men. To make a decent living, however, everyone had to do something; if there were not enough men, women or youngsters or older persons could substitute. Indeed, people claim that women did more during the collective period than before.[4]

In theory, women doing the same "heavy" jobs as men could earn as many work-points, but in fact they earned less. The assumption was that women are "not strong enough" to do the heaviest work, and that they work "less well." Since the leadership defined women's tasks as "lighter," they were assigned fewer points. Women's work days were also shorter because they had unremunerated household tasks to do. The fact that women worked fewer hours for lower wages only reinforced the traditional notion that men are "more valuable."

Women often found themselves torn between farming and domestic work. A mother-in-law relieved a younger woman for work in the fields. Or a young mother might leave her infant in a nursery, in the care of older siblings, or even alone constrained on the family sleeping platform, a solution that sometimes had tragic consequences when unattended infants rolled off onto the floor. Because the women often worked far from home, nursing was inconvenient. A mother could not bring her infant to the fields, and having it brought when it cried or returning home to nurse it were impractical. This was a common problem without easy solution, and a significant problem as well since nursing frequency is an important determinant of fertility. It is well known that frequent and longer nursing lengthens birth intervals and therefore lowers fertility.

After her sons married, a woman gradually reduced her outside work, and remained at home more to care for grandchildren and manage lighter household chores. Her daughters-in-law replaced her in the fields. Even retired, men and women did light field tasks, especially during periods of high demand. They could plant potatoes, pull weeds, turn compost, and help process the harvest. Essential characteristics of collective labor use—intensive use of all workers, minimal use of machines, and the general substitutability of labor—are still salient. The types and amounts of labor needed have changed, but these general features have endured.

By 1979 communes were in serious trouble. People were not eager to work for low wages, and value of the work-point had fallen so low that many were in debt. Rumors of plans to replace the commune only increased uncertainty and worsened morale. Toward the end of 1982, the countryside shifted to a new system in which collective land was given to households under long term contract, the so-called "responsibility system." After years of collectivization, the family resumed its role as basic unit of production as well as consumption, but with an important difference. Land remained publicly owned; it still cannot be bought or sold and therefore cannot reconcentrate in fewer hands as in former times. Families may sink into poverty, but they cannot solve their problems by selling land.

Under the new system farmers contract to sell a certain amount of grain to the government at a set price. In return they enjoy the right to manage their land and dispose of the rest of their crop nearly as they choose. The average holding per person has remained the same since the system was put in place. In Tranquillity Village and Middle Villages it is just under six *mu*, including garden plots.[5] This is so little land that no family can get rich on production alone.

The intention was to assign land by contract for at least fifteen years to encourage improvement. But family division, population growth, and erosion created problems. In Tranquillity two further redistributions took place before the original contracts expired, which contributed to substantial peasant insecurity. Farmers who had worked hard, carefully rotating crops and applying compost and chemical fertilizers, lost plots they had struggled to improve. With tenure uncertain, many are reluctant to invest time and resources.

The new system has also altered labor needs. Households are thrown back on their own resources. The family determines what, when, how, and where to plant; how to allocate labor, what sidelines to undertake, and with whom to cooperate, if anyone. People are eager to supplement earnings from sidelines in Tranquillity, and by raising a few milk cows in Middle Village. The ability to diversify depends heavily on the amount of labor a family has.

Villagers occasionally repeat the old adage, "Boys are precious, girls useless," but it has little substance in these farming villages. Indeed, the restoration of family-based production, and the development of new sidelines, increased the variety and value of women's contribution. By age seventeen or eighteen, all teenagers have acquired basic farm skills. Even children under fourteen can help, which is why parents short on labor sometimes end a child's schooling early. Nearly all children finish elementary school now; formal schooling is no longer a privilege of the few or limited to boys. However, while fewer than 5 percent of boys and girls (ages ten to nineteen) have had no formal schooling, most go no further than primary school because additional education has little to offer youngsters destined to replace their parents.

It is not easy for a woman to combine domestic and outside work, especially if there are infants to care for. It is actually more important to have more than one woman in a household than more than one man. Women can make up for a shortage of men, but it is hard to make up for a lack of women. Women's work is held in lower esteem, so men avoid housework and are not trained for it. It is the multifaceted contribution of women that enables farmers to undertake sidelines without greatly cutting into farm work.

Since land cannot be enlarged and cultivation earnings are limited, sidelines provide an important supplement to income. In Tranquillity people gather and transport gravel, collect and sift construction sand, process grain, make potato noodles and bean curd, tend a few sheep, fish, and manage small grocery stores. Such sidelines contribute about 19 percent of village income. In Middle Village, which is further from substantial markets, these sidelines are less common (only 6 percent of income). Most families (89 percent) raise a few dairy cows (average of four) on limited grassland, and they provide 27 percent of village income. Dairying is a simple matter; there is no need to travel far, nor do men spend much time away cutting hay. Mostly they raise their animals in sheds, buying fodder from other places. Animals and stalls are close by, and so distract little from the fields.

Men tend sheds, women milk cows, and families often hire local cowboys to graze their cows. Because of the heavy demand for labor from farming, however, the division of labor by sex cannot be hard and fast. Women often work in the fields, and men occasionally help with the milking. When men are busy in the fields, women may help in the sheds. In Middle Village, as in Tranquillity, cultivation remains central.

INCOME AND ITS DISTRIBUTION

Motivation and income improved once the responsibility system was in place. The view that modernization requires a freeing of initiative replaced older egalitarian notions at the foundation of collectives. But in a society that struggled to eliminate extremes of wealth and misery, even a modest increase in inequality causes concern. It has not yet turned to outrage in the communities we visited only because, while differences have widened, most have seen improvement and few have become poorer.

In 1987, the mean net income per person was 594 RMB in Tranquillity, 712 RMB in Middle Village. In both just under 7 percent of households were below a "poverty line" officially defined as 200 RMB per person. Nineteen percent of households in Tranquillity, and 36 percent in Middle Village were "wealthy," earning over 800 RMB per person. The spread was about the same in both villages.[6] In general, families with more land enjoyed higher incomes. Grouping the communities, the "wealthy" farmed areas 40 percent larger than the "poor."[7] Although cultivated area declined slightly in recent years, production has risen, thanks mainly to greater use of compost and chemical fertilizer.

Land and labor are not the whole story. Much depends on what families do with their capital and labor. Seventy percent of Tranquillity villagers have some sort of nonagricultural sideline, which contributed 31 percent of income for the wealthy compared to only 10 percent among the poor. In Middle Village, dairying furnished 29 percent of income for the wealthy, but only 7 percent in poor households. Wages do not make a significant contribution to income (less than 5 percent) or to income disparity in either farming village. There are few jobs, and people who take them cannot easily manage farm work. Sidelines complement farming, starting and stopping in rhythm with peaks and slacks.

There is still little money for emergencies, let alone for saving or investment, and many costs are rising. It costs more to feed, dress, educate, and marry off children. At the same time, youngsters spend more time in school and contribute later. Further, many expenses once underwritten by the collective, like education and medical care, are now the family's burden. As incomes rise, people are tempted to acquire the consumer goods increasingly available. Thanks to dairying, many Middle Village homes are newer and of more substantial construction, but in both communities people spend more on housing.

Marriage is no longer so simple as during the more spartan years of Chinese communism. There has been a dramatic increase in cost, for bride as well as groom, especially since the shift to a privatized economy. Cadres tolerate greater display, and villagers spend more. In fact, getting children married is probably the heaviest burden any family must bear. Traditionally more costly for the groom, even the expense of marrying a daughter has increased, which is another indication of growing prosperity. It is interesting that some families are still content to accept compensation for a daughter's labor (bridewealth) without giving dowry in return; bridewealth without dowry is more common than the reverse, reflecting perhaps the importance of women's labor.

Children are costly even after marriage. At some point every family divides; sons move off to live on their own, taking a share of family assets. Ideally the share of each should be equivalent. Preparations have become more urgent in recent years because there is more to divide and because sons begin to live on their own sooner. On all fronts farmers work harder to achieve ever rising standards and expectations. No one would want to reverse that, but the situation does lead people to rethink older notions about marriage, family division, and family reproduction.

THE NEW HERDSMEN

In the farming area Mongols adopted the Han mode of farming and way of life. Because of their smaller numbers and the demands of cultivation, they live interspersed with the Han and have become culturally indistinguishable from them. Few can speak Mongol. They often intermarry and, like the Han, they favor early patrilocal marriage (bride joins her husband's family), two or three children, and "stem" families consisting of parents and one married son. As Han adapted to the grassland, they abandoned farming for a pastoral life, which now shapes what they do and value. They did not cease to be Han, however, and despite the homogenizing efforts of the state, they forged another kind of Han Chinese society.

In the pastoral region there are more Mongols and more marked cultural and political differences. Han and Mongols share public facilities and have many common interests, but at another level remain distinct subcommunities. We see this reflected in dress, speech, political competition, rarity of intermarriage, and occasional fights. More so than among the cultivators, people speak their own languages and marry their own kind. Their children go to separate schools where instruction is in their native tongues. Separate clinics treat according to distinct traditions.

There is an uneasy mix of traditions in Sandhill and Great Pasture. Mongols in town have homes like those of the Han, and like them grow vegetables in small gardens. They dress like Han, and most speak Mandarin in addition to their native tongue. Few Han speak Mongol, but they too eat beef and mutton rather than pork, drink milk-tea, and share a regional penchant for hard liquor. When they cut hay or graze animals on the open grassland they, too, live in yurts.

When Han first turned to pastoralism, dairying was more in keeping with their sedentary farming tradition. In Sandhill wages supplement dairying, and in Great Pasture many sell hay, raise sheep, or fish. Used to a more nomadic way, the Mongols have favored sheep. They rarely cut hay for sale and do not fish because these activities would interfere with shepherding. Just as cultivation forged similarities, so too has pastoralism encouraged convergence. Old specializations blur as Han add sheep and Mongols expand into dairying. Han shepherds add yurts, while Mongol dairymen acquire fixed residences in or near town, close to schools and milk collection stations. The size and structure of their families respond similarly to the needs of herding. Both marry later, are more often neolocal (couples live separately from kin), and have smaller, simpler families than Han and Mongol farmers. In these regards pastoral Han are more like Mongol herdsmen than like Han or Mongol farmers.

FROM COLLECTIVE TO
FAMILY HERDING

Here, too, collective management ultimately turned out to be problematic. There was little incentive to carefully tend livestock, and cadres could not effectively control how people did their work. They allocated more points for harder and longer tasks, but there was little reason to work hard because one earned a day's wages no matter how well one performed. The problem was exacerbated during the Cultural Revolution (1966–1976), when cadres assigned points according to days worked regardless of difficulty. Herdsmen then had every reason to avoid the hardest work. Many animals were lost, and livestock numbers expanded slowly if at all. Much labor was also unused because then, as now, women and youngsters did little on the open range.

There were attempts along the way to allocate each household a couple of cows to raise. Inevitably they fared better than those in collective herds, but the leadership worried about encouraging family-level management under a socialist regime, so none of the experiments lasted long. The frequent policy reversals left a legacy of uncertainty that also reduced the benefits.

When the family became the basic unit of accounting, administrative responsibilities passed from commune to township, and brigades became villages. Families drew lots for cows and sheep expecting that they would pay for them over time. Not many Han were interested in sheep, but everyone wanted cows, which do not require long periods on the move far from home. Most Sandhill and Great Pasture Han lent their sheep to Mongol shepherds in exchange for meat. Pasture and grassland remain publicly managed and commonly shared. In Great Pasture, where it is more abundant, herds are larger and people cut large quantities of hay. There, cadres assign cutting areas to families annually in terms of the number of animals they have.

While they lost a good deal of power with demise of the commune, cadres still make many important decisions. They allocate land for home construction, collect taxes and fees, count livestock, resolve arguments and disputes, and pay stipends to demobilized soldiers. They supply veterinary services, assign fishing rights, manage pasture, and regulate seasonal flock movements and grass-cutting. They underwrite the cost of artificial insemination, and offer incentives to encourage flock development. But because they no longer have direct control over livestock, they have lost crucial power since commune days.

FORMS OF PASTORALISM AND THE DIVISION OF LABOR

In Sandhill and Great Pasture the shift from farming is complete. Grassland is more abundant and herds larger than in Middle Village. In 1988, most Sandhillers (83 percent of households) had cows, an average of six. Three percent had more than fifteen. In Middle Village no family had a herd that large. Herds were larger still in Great Pasture. There, 98 percent of Han families had cows, an average of fifteen, and fully 51 percent had more than fifteen. There are also differences in the way livestock are managed. Dairying is more intensive in Sandhill, the goal is more to increase milk yields by selective breeding (artificial insemination) and use of costly feed supplements than to enlarge herds. Great Pasture's pasture supports a larger number and variety of animals, and herdsmen have adopted a more extensive strategy. They are more interested in increasing animal numbers than in applying costly technologies.

Pastoralism has demanded adjustment of the Han way. Livestock require constant attention. There are periods of greater demand, but they are not as well marked as among the farmers, and there are no slack periods. The distances herdsmen travel and the need for skilled, experienced labor underlie sharper differences in the tasks of women and men, young and old. Even in collectives the division of labor was very sharp. Teams of men pastured collective livestock, a smaller group of women earned points milking them. Other women and a few older men worked collective gardens during the short growing season. Some wove baskets at home, a brigade sideline. In Great Pasture men also dominated important supplementary activities—cutting hay and river fishing. Groups cut hay on distant pastures in summer. From spring through autumn others hauled boats to the nearby river, and in winter went ice-fishing. Construction and transportation, too, were men's work.

Men earned points at a variety of tasks year round, but women and older men were "half labor," and their work was more limited. They often remained at home. For most tasks cadres preferred men. Maturity, experience, strength, and endurance were crucial since harsh weather, mismanagement, wolves, and disease could quickly decimate herds and flocks. Herdsmen had to know what they were doing, be able to lift heavy animals and other objects, and be prepared to spend long periods away from home, often in severe weather. Youngsters lacked the necessary judgement, women were inexperienced and in any case had to remain close to home to run the household and care for children.

With the collective gone, families depend more heavily on their own resources, and for the full range of tasks. Especially in Great Pasture, where larger herds spend more time in open pastures, and where men put more into cutting hay or fishing, dairying takes so much time and energy that neither men nor women can easily take regular additional employment or undertake unrelated sidelines. And since men all do their work at about the same time, just as women all milk at the same time, exchanges of labor between sexes and between families are not easy to arrange.

Sheep are risky and most efficiently managed in sizeable flocks (over two hundred), so only people with experience and prepared to make a serious commitment find it worthwhile. Sheep need more substantial pasture and closer attention than cows; they must be moved often and watched constantly. Great Pasture Han were initially no more eager than Sandhillers to spend long periods on the open grasslands, so they, too, put the few sheep they obtained in the care of Mongol shepherds. But recently, as their selling price began to rise, a number of Han with sufficient family labor (men) have added sheep-herding to dairying.

Han shepherds have become the new nomads of China's northeastern frontier. Sheep, not assimilation to Mongol culture, encourage commonalities in behavior. Indeed, combining sheep and dairy cows from either direction requires substantial adjustment. Not only does the combination require lots of labor in different places at the same time, but patterns of living must change. Dairying is easier with sedentism, proximity to milk collection stations, while sheep pasture year round on open grassland, and move over substantial distances. Shepherds change the location of their yurts and flocks six times a year.

While Mongols still prefer life in yurts on the open range, Han shepherds come from a sedentary tradition and still rely more heavily on dairying. They must have men on the range year round, but they prefer to leave their families and cows in town. Mongols adapt in the other direction, as they expand their dairy herds, by compromising mobility. Their women, elderly, pre-schoolers, and cows move among seasonal encampments close to town even while the men graze sheep elsewhere. The encampments are close enough to milk-collection stations to market milk, but too far for children to attend school. Some, even those without dairy cows, find temporary housing in town until schooling ends, or send children to live with kin in town, or in the Mongol school dormitory.

Among the herdsmen, each sex has different work to do. Men work hardest in winter, when cows are penned much of the time. Women are busiest during the summer peak milking time. But compared to farmers, the tasks men and women do, and when they do them, change little during the year. Men have principal responsibility for work away from home, and for tasks that demand great strength. In Great Pasture, they hitch up tank carts and haul water from the community well each day. Only they have the strength to free fully laden carts stuck in the mud. They cut, haul, and pile hay. They shovel cow pens and feed livestock in winter. Pasturing sheep through the deep cold of winter imposes heavy demands, and only men fish in the nearby river. Women and men classify all these jobs as "heavy work," largely the domain of men.

Women do most of their work within compound gates. They care for children, build and maintain fires, clean, cook, wash, repair and refill the padding in winter clothing, sew clothes, make shoes, garden, and put up vegetables. They milk cows in the courtyard. Women also convert cow dung into cooking fuel, shaping it into disks that they turn and dry in the winter sun, then pile for storage. They also make mud bricks used to fix the house. They do all this with bare hands in bitter cold.

On occasion, when there are not enough men, women and young sons help shovel the pens or pile straw, but most consider such work too taxing for them on a regular basis. In fact, there are few tasks for which women and men readily replace each other. Local people explain that women are built differently, and they have more stamina. They can maintain long term, low levels of energy. Doing "lighter" work, women spread their energy evenly over time. They are capable of short bursts of intense power, but men are believed to be more so.

A woman may provide temporary relief by watching sheep in deep winter, but relying too heavily on her could be costly. There is little room for error, especially with sheep. We often heard comments like, "What would happen if there was a sudden storm and the sheep began to scatter? How could an inexperienced girl handle that?" In any case, a woman should not remain on the open grassland through winter they believe. When the weather turns cold, a brother or hired shepherd must replace her.

Because the lines are more clearly drawn than among the farmers, men show even less willingness to do "women's work." Once home, they "rest." They may occasionally milk cows, even do housework, but only when female labor is really short. And while women might appreciate having men do more around the house, they are also convinced that the division of labor is natural and reasonable. By bolstering traditional concepts, the pastoral regime sustains a self-fulfilling prophesy. Once culturally defined capabilities become the basis of task assignment, people considered wrong for certain jobs are not trained to do them.

The assignment of work by age is also different from that among farmers. Youngsters are too inexperienced to do much until about age fourteen, later than among the farmers. They lead calves to nearby pastures at daybreak, and carry milk cans to the collection station twice a day. Girls help with milking. In general, people under twenty do not fully participate in herding sheep or cows, milking, cutting grass, or fishing. Like women, they may fill in but cannot replace men.

Because they start working later, not because education has anything more to offer, children among the pastoralists go to school longer than among the farmers. More attend junior high, and the farmer-herdsmen difference is especially marked for girls. Among the farmers, girls receive the least schooling, but among the herders they are even better educated than males; more go to middle school. That is because they do little, and because milking takes place before or after school.

At the other end of life, retirement for pastoralists comes later than among cultivators. An elderly couple can actually make a living on their own until they are quite old. They can reduce the number of cows they manage, and thus the amount of pen cleaning and winter feeding they do. They may hire a cowherd to pasture their cows. Their children cut the hay they need, or they can trade grass cutting rights for hay.

In Great Pasture, where dairymen make every effort to increase the number of cows they tend, haying is a major source of income in its own right. Much of it is transported to other re-gions of China or exported to Japan. But cutting grass on that scale requires expensive machines and an ample supply of men prepared to spend several months at a time on distant grasslands. There must also be men at home to pasture cows and handle routine dairying tasks. Families with large herds but not enough men to cut grass and tend cows often hire someone to pasture their animals during the haying season. Women, even young children, clean pens and do "men's jobs" at such times. If herdsmen add haying, then, they cannot easily raise sheep, take jobs, or undertake other sidelines as well.

Because they make a better living than farmers, have a sharper division of labor, and work continuously with livestock, often in distant places, herdsmen have little time for regular jobs or sidelines in fixed locations. Instead, they concentrate on expanding their herds and flocks, altering their mix. It is difficult even to combine different pastoral activities—to cut large amounts of grass for sale, manage a flock of sheep, and tend a herd of dairy cows, for example.

INCOME AND INEQUALITY: HERDSMEN AND CULTIVATORS COMPARED

Herdsmen earn significantly more than farmers. Income decreases as we go from extensive pastoralism to pure cultivation. Tranquillity farmers earn the least notwithstanding their sidelines. Shed dairying provides greater advantage to Middle Villagers, and wages added to dairying yield still higher incomes in Sandhill. But Great Pasture households, with their extensive pastoralism and large scale haying, earn most. Their mean per capita income in 1987 was 1,156 RMB, compared to 811 RMB in Sandhill.

Privatization and diversification have increased income inequalities within and between communities. Great Pasture has the largest proportion of wealthy households and the widest income spread. Sandhill has the second largest proportion, and Tranquillity the lowest.[8] A good start in land or animals and abundant family labor are no guarantee of higher income. Household size and income are certainly related; larger families earn more, but only because more workers allow farmers to develop sidelines, and herdsmen to expand their herds, raise different sorts of animals, cut grass for sale, or fish. Only the number of *men* in a herding family is significantly related to income. That the number of *women* is also related to income among the farmers is further testimony to their more important and more varied role in the farming communities.

By allowing families to enlarge and diversify their enterprises, the new family responsibility system provided the basis for greater income inequality. Families that work harder, at a greater variety of tasks, see incomes rise. Inequality is on the increase, especially among the herdsmen, but there has also been a general rise in living standards. Contrary to direct predictions, there is no evidence yet of growing poverty in any of the sites we visited. This is especially clear if, in comparing communities, we keep in mind that income alone is not a sufficient indicator of wealth. It is especially imprecise for pastoralists because it does not consider capital assets (for example, savings, livestock, or machines). Animals are expendable as well as expandable capital; they represent wealth on the hoof.[9] The herdsman invests care, feed, and capital and, if all goes well, they multiply. Farmers also invest labor and capital, but their holdings do not grow.

Nor does income reveal differences in risk, or in ability to rebound from setbacks. Even herders with ample labor, livestock, and equipment experience difficult years. They may have to replace animals, or purchase and repair machines. As everywhere, marriages and funerals may produce negative incomes. Whereas even a small rise in expenses can throw a farm family into enduring debt from which it is difficult to recover, challenges for herdsmen are shorter term. They also adjust more easily to changes in labor availability. Land cannot be sold when labor is short and bought back later. But by adjusting the number and kinds of livestock they tend, herdsmen can make a living with few workers.

ECONOMY AND FAMILY

It was not necessary that every commune family handle the full range of tasks; work teams drew from many families. In the farming area, there were ample opportunities for all family members to earn points, and the more members a family had, the more it could earn. It was particularly desirable to have more than one woman, one to handle domestic chores while the other earned points. In that sense collectivization encouraged a continuation of early patrilocal marriage, delayed family division, and enlargement of the family to stem form.

In the pastoral area family labor was not fully used, and because the most remunerative jobs were assigned to men, having more than one in the household was useful. There was no great need for more than one woman. Because the herdsmen did not need to mobilize as much labor as the farmers, and because their women played a smaller role, they could marry later and live more often in simple neolocal households.

Families all have more to do on their own now, but the farmers have greater short-term requirements, and more reason to cooperate seasonally with others. Such arrangements seem to work well only where a small number of families is involved and relationships close enough to ensure reliability. Even so, people prefer to place primary reliance on the family, and therefore still favor early, patrilocal marriage, and stem families with one woman to work outside, and another inside the home.

Family division is a bigger setback for farmers because it removes labor and can especially leave women in a bind, saddling them with simultaneous obligations at home and in the fields.[10] Small holdings become smaller and more fragmented since parents give land to sons who establish their own families. It is not easy to recover what is lost, or continue profitable sidelines after family division. It is important to preserve at least the stem family (parents and one married son) since it provides security for the elderly. This is of special concern now that families limit childbearing, people live longer, and rural folk still do not enjoy the pensions of urban workers. Moreover, there are fewer public services since dissolution of the communes.

Herdsmen, too, prefer patrilocal marriage and stem families, but they more often depart from those traditional forms. Early marriage is less pressing for them because adding a daughter-in-law early is less important, while holding a son longer is more important. Still, family division is less of a setback. A son takes livestock when he leaves, but animals multiply in a way land cannot. For that reason, even though herdsmen marry somewhat later than farmers, they divide their families sooner thereafter, and more often live apart from kin (neolocally) when they marry.

In pre-Communist China, technological factors sometimes discouraged partition long enough to produce "joint" families, in which married brothers remained together. There is evidence, for example, that farming on the basis of rainfall rather than canals and cultivation of tobacco discouraged family division; the former because it put a premium on having a lot of men in the family, the latter because it increased the need for women. When families invested capital and labor in different enterprises, too, there were sound reasons to avoid partition.[11] By maintaining a single family, married brothers could economize labor and capital, shifting both from enterprise to enterprise to avoid hiring or borrowing. If they lived apart as separate households within a single property-owning family, they could avoid the strife that so often precipitated family division.

Under normal circumstances joint families were fragile and short-lived. Strife, especially among women, eventually triggered division. The custom of passing property from father to sons underlay conflicts between mother and daughter-in-law, and between sisters-in-law, all of whom depended on men for access to the family estate. A woman tried to exert some control first through her husband, and then through her sons. But sons' wives sought control through their husbands, trying to defend the interests of their conjugal units (husband, wife, and children if any) against those of other conjugal units within the larger family.

Once collectives took over productive resources and discouraged private enterprise, there was little reason to maintain joint families. In that sense, collectivization undermined some traditional sources of family complexity. Because policy now endorses family diversification, some predict an increase in the number of joint families, but for the present few resist inherent tendencies to divide. There are no technological reasons to discourage it, and family investment is likely to remain simple here because capital is scarce and markets distant and undeveloped. For cultivators and pastoralists alike, stem families suffice to diversify the household economy and integrate the elderly. It is also important to keep in mind that present families reflect earlier reproductive patterns capable of supplying personnel for large families. If strict family limitation continues, stem families are likely to remain the most complex form in which most people will have lived.

Because farmers need more women sooner, they have long married earlier than herdsmen, and are more likely to marry before legal ages. From 1950–1980 (when legal age was eighteen for women and twenty for men), 17 percent of farm men (sites combined), and 13 percent of the herdsmen married early. The difference was greater for women—22 percent of the farmers were early, only 8 percent of the herders. From 1981, when minimum ages were raised to twenty for women and twenty for men, 45 percent of the farm men married early, compared to 14 percent for herders. Thirty-nine percent of farm women wed early, but only 14 percent of the herders did.

Han prefer patrilocal marriage, a form of marriage which minimally produces stem families. However, marriage is more commonly patrilocal, and families more often stem, among the farmers. Herding households are simpler and smaller, only 4.5 persons compared to 4.9 for the farmers.

Older herdsmen are also more likely to live independently longer; 9.5 percent of pastoral households contain couples or individuals (mainly older people), compared to only 2.5 percent among the farmers. Whereas 61 percent of herding households contain people 65 or older, 84 percent of the farm households have them. Much of farm work would simply be too difficult for the elderly on their own. Without someone to share women's work, it would be particularly hard on a farm woman.

Pastoralists are also more likely to divide their families *at* marriage. Since they marry later, however, the event comes later, and despite that fact, they more readily recover. Farmers usually partition some time *after* marriage, and division reduces earnings all around. They therefore try to separate marriage and division, avoiding the latter as long as possible.

FAMILY REPRODUCTION

Throughout China the government has encouraged people to delay marriage and limit family size. Inner Mongolia has not escaped these efforts, although family planning has not been as strictly enforced as in interior China. Regulations should have levelled differences in age at marriage and number of children born, or at least altered behavior uniformly, but they have not. Parents continue to arrange marriages close to the legal thresholds, with little change in average age at marriage, although herdsmen still delay longer than farmers. Regulations limiting childbirth have had a greater impact on reproductive behavior, however. In all sites women have fewer children, but for all age groups farmers have more children than herdsmen. They exhibit higher fertility (measured by mean number of children born alive) despite *stricter* implementation of family planning regulations, and the difference predates family planning.

When infant and child mortality were high, many children increased the likelihood that enough would survive to assure care in old age. When collectives subsidized medical care and education, raising children cost less. Fewer children need be born now to be certain some will survive, but the cost of raising and marrying them have increased, especially among the herders. For these reasons couples, especially pastoral couples, are content to stop with two or three children, and would likely restrain childbearing beyond that even without state regulations. Indeed, family planning is probably tapping already-present inclinations to have fewer children. Had they been free to do so, women might have placed brakes on childbearing earlier. Present policy, propaganda, and enforcement empower them to do that.

While pastoralists and cultivators are no longer eager to have as many children as they can, neither are they prepared to stop with one. Herdsmen have more reason to avoid having many children, given their greater cost, longer school attendance, and later contribution, but even they have not embraced the one-child model urged by the state. During 1980–1988, when family planning regulations tightened, most children delivered were *not* firstborns (only 17 percent), although people did have fewer later children than during the preceding decade. Only 15 percent of births during 1980–88 was a fourth or later child compared to 56 percent during the previous decade. Many mothers still have a second child (and even additional children), and they have their second child sooner than the state would like. Despite a requirement that couples wait four years to conceive, only 6 percent of women between the ages of fifteen and twenty-nine and only 11 percent of those between thirty and thirty-four waited that long.

Childbearing exceeds state recommendations in all sites, but the farmers have more children than the pastoralists. Long-standing differences in reproductive behavior, rooted in ecology and economy, have carried forward to the present. While there is no significant difference in the average number of children born to Han and Mongol herdsmen, Han herders have fewer children than Han farmers. This suggests that differences in economy and ecology are more important than ethnicity in this regard.

Earlier marriage may contribute to higher fertility, but it cannot be the whole story since farmers aged forty and over had more children but did *not* marry earlier. Farm women in every age group had more children during the first ten years of marriage. Differences in infant mortality, morbidity, and frequency of intercourse could also affect birth spacing. Unfortunately, our data cannot tell us whether the farmers had higher mortality.

Goiter was once common in Tranquillity, but it would hardly have *raised* fertility and was no problem in Middle Village. Venereal disease, endemic among grassland Mongols during the late 1930s and 1940s, came under control in the early 1950s. It is not clear how affected the Han were, but there is some suggestion in the literature that they were less so. The effect may have been minimal in our villages, however, since we find no difference in Han and Mongol parities (births), and lower herdsmen fertility persisted even *after* venereal disease was eliminated on the grassland.

Nor are differences in frequency of sexual intercourse important. Herdsmen do periodically leave for months at a time, but they visit periodically. Moreover, shepherding and hay cutting on a large scale are recent while lower fertility is not. What then might account for the long-standing difference in fertility (average number of children born by mother's age)? In all likelihood differences in nursing behavior, in turn a product of dissimilarities in the division of labor, are the main cause. In a natural fertility context (where people make no conscious effort to limit conception or childbirth) the more frequently and longer a woman nurses, the longer are her intervals to next conception and birth and, consequently, the lower her fertility. Farm women nurse less often than pastoral women, who are always at home. Thus, farming may encourage higher fertility as well as larger and more complex families.

COWBOYS, CULTIVATORS, AND THE STATUS OF WOMEN

The communist emphasis on mass participation brought large numbers of women into the labor force, and some suggest that it enhanced their leverage at home. Indeed, the collective, too, benefited from their contribution. If women enhance their value and voice by adding to income, then farm women should certainly be advantaged, especially in the new economy. There were fewer ways for pastoral women to earn work-points during the collective era, and they still largely confine themselves to milking and tending the home. It is unlikely that non-pastoral sidelines will develop to involve them.

But the connection between work and status is not straight forward. For one thing, women do not control their work, product, or income. Further, for a woman's labor to be considered "important" it probably must be visible and clearly linked to her efforts. But even when women have worked outside, their earnings have usually been delivered to the family head. Neither among farmers nor herders do people consider women's work "important" in the sense of being central to the household economy. When asked to specify the "most important" pastoral work, women and men mentioned grass cutting, fishing, or cleaning stalls, not milking. Even farm women's labor is seen as "lighter" or "domestic," and therefore not real labor. With the collective gone, women who once brought in work-points now work *for the family*, work too easily thought of as subsidiary. It is far from certain, then, that the reforms of recent years will enhance the value, influence, or autonomy of women. But no one has yet systematically measured the effect of outside work, and the clues we have are ambiguous, even contradictory.

Since they bring wealth or property when they marry, for example, farm women should have more influence. Everyone born is entitled an allocation of land. Granted to a person, it actually becomes part of a family estate controlled almost invariably by a male. When she marries, a woman's land flows back into community reserve and her husband's family requests an assignment on her behalf. Farm women thus enjoy a right to property that pastoral women do not. The community assigns herding women no animals, pasture, or grassland when they are born or marry. If property confers status or influence, then, pastoral women would be disadvantaged. However, in the minds of farm family members even the land a woman brings with her is not identified with her. She does not decide what will be grown on it, who will use it, or how it will be planted. We cannot simply assume, then, that it necessarily elevates her position.

Structural differences might even tip the scales the other way, to enhance the position of herding women. Recall that cultivators more often marry patrilocally. A farm woman is more subject to her mother-in-law's judgements and moods. Since pastoralists more often marry neolocally and live in conjugal families, we might expect that herding women would enjoy a greater measure of autonomy. Consider, too, the fact that herding women go to school longer, work and marry later, and bear fewer children, and that many are better educated than their husbands. Is it not possible that these characteristics, which derive from their *lesser* contribution, confer a measure of influence or self-fulfillment?

In fact, the educational advantage of pastoral girls does not lead to a better job or a better life. Most follow in the steps of their mothers. Indeed, the lower education of farm women, their earlier marriages, and their higher parities reflect their importance to the domestic economy. Nonetheless, it is doubtful that the earlier and more substantial input of farm women give them any great bargaining power. It may only make their lives more difficult. Our unsystematic and limited observations in the field suggest that farm women do enjoy greater voice, but the matter is clearly complicated and deserving of further careful study.

NOTES

1. Owen Lattimore, *Inner Asian Frontiers of China* (Boston: Beacon Press, 1962), p. 39.
2. Although the findings presented here summarize the findings of a more detailed analysis of the data by Salaff and myself (Pasternak & Salaff 1993), I hasten to relieve her of responsibility for this summary of our common work. For a full analysis of our data see Burton Pasternak and Janet W. Salaff, *Cowboys & Cultivators: The Chinese of Inner Mongolia* (Boulder, Colo. Westview Press, 1993).

3. RMB or *renminbi* is a monetary unit equivalent to .172 US dollars as of December 1992.

4. During the Great Leap Forward (1958–1960), the leadership collectivized many domestic burdens in an unusual effort to draw women into the fields. For a brief (and unsuccessful) period of several months, even food preparation and child care were done in common.

5. One *mu* = .0667 hectares. Around five percent of land is kept in "reserve" for new household members. When people leave by death or marriage their land flows back to the reserve.

6. Gini scores, which summarize income distribution, were .34 and .32 for Tranquillity and Middle village respectively.

7. Poor households cultivated 21.5 *mu* compared to 30.1 for the wealthy.

8. Gini scores for Great Pasture and Sandhill were .42 and .31 respectively.

9. Han think of livestock as a form of capital; the more they have and the heavier when sold, the better. They may hold animals longer than sensible, not simply because they value size and numbers, but because they anticipate need for capital—perhaps to pay for a wedding, purchase a house for the new couple, or endow them with a herd of their own. Families with many animals are also better able to weather fluctuations in earnings or expenditures. But their "more is better" strategy can also be environmentally problematic, especially if it involves sheep, which are particularly hard on pasture.

10. For a cross-cultural study that highlights how incompatible labor demands encourage family extension, see Burton Pasternak, Carol R. Ember, and Melvin Ember, "On the Conditions Favoring Extended Family Households," *Journal of Anthropological Research*, 32 (1976): pp. 109–123.

11. For a more extensive discussion of these issues see Myron L. Cohen, *House United, House Divided: The Chinese Family in Taiwan* (New York: Columbia University Press, 1976); and Burton Pasternak, *Guests in the Dragon: Social Demography of a Chinese District, 1895–1946* (New York: Columbia University Press, 1983).

SUGGESTED READINGS

Cohen, Myron L. *House United, House Divided: The Chinese Family in Taiwan*. New York: Columbia University Press, 1976. A penetrating analysis of Chinese family development and the factors that influence it, based on Taiwan fieldwork.

Lattimore, Owen. *Inner Asian Frontiers of China*. Boston: Beacon Press, 1962. A comprehensive history of Han Chinese expansion into Inner Mongolia prior to the Communist period.

Pasternak, Burton. *Guests in the Dragon: Social Demography of a Chinese District, 1895–1946*. New York: Columbia University Press, 1983. This study, based on fieldwork and an analysis of household registers, explores the connections between technology, family organization, and demographic behavior (fertility, mortality, divorce, adoption).

Pasternak, Burton and Janet W. Salaff. *Cowboys & Cultivators: The Chinese of Inner Mongolia*. Boulder, Colo.: Westview Press, 1993. A more extensive analysis of the data on Han herdsmen and farmers presented in this chapter.

Chinatowns: Immigrant Communities in Transition[1]

Richard H. Thompson

I first met Betty Luk in 1976. Then thirty-five years old, she lived in a modest but pleasant apartment in downtown Toronto where she managed a precarious existence as a free-lance writer. Independent, intelligent, and well educated, Betty fits well the image of the modern North American woman except for her Chinese ancestry. She, her two sisters and brother are among the very small number of Canadian and U.S.-born children of Chinese immigrants before the 1950s. They attended public schools, where Betty was an honor student, editor of the student newspaper and prom queen. Although she and her siblings were the only Chinese students in the school, Betty recalls no traumatic experiences of ridicule or humiliation from white students. It was understood, however, that dating Canadian boys was out of the question. "They would be stigmatized," she said, "even though I had crushes on Canadian boys all the time." Betty had one long-term relationship with a Canadian-born Chinese boy whose parents ended the relationship fearing their son's promising future might be derailed by an unwanted pregnancy. Since then Betty has dated only Caucasian men though she has never married despite "several opportunities." Her circle of friends is exclusively white save for her siblings with whom she remains close.

Betty is typical of the first generation of Chinese born in North America. She cannot speak or read Chinese, is completely acculturated and successfully assimilated to Canadian culture and society, and spends little time in Toronto's burgeoning Chinatown[2]. "Sometimes," she says, "I'm not even aware that I am Chinese. It's funny—I look in the mirror and I'm reminded that I'm Chinese, but it's not a conscious thing all the time." Betty is nevertheless reminded that she is Chinese in her relationship with her parents. She remembers being embarrassed by her parents' lack of fluency in English and ashamed of how their house looked compared to those of her friends. She recalls how her parents never praised her for doing well in school, nor ever said, "We're proud of you" or "We love you." Her parents were stern and reserved, not open and affectionate like Canadian parents. Unlike her parents, Betty values being open and straightforward but understands that they were "prisoners in a different society" who worked long hours in the family grocery store to make a better life for their children. Still, whenever Betty and her siblings have difficulty in relationships or in confronting personal problems, they attribute it to the "Chinese" in them.

Betty's brother Don, two years her senior and a supervisor with the postal service, has also never married despite constant pressure by his father to continue the family line. Mr. Luk wants Don to marry a Chinese woman, but Don does not want children and prefers to date Canadian women with whom he shares much more in common. Their elder sister, Eileen, did marry a Chinese-Canadian engineer but has recently divorced him and become involved in the women's movement. The youngest sister, Dorothy, married a Jewish boy after becoming pregnant, but they divorced after ten years of marriage and two daughters. Dorothy is deeply depressed by the divorce and thinks her Chinese upbringing and behavior patterns are responsible. "I do manifest Chinese patterns of submission," she remarked. "I am a low-profile person—I know how to be invisible. Playing the traditional Chinese wife role with Paul just didn't work."

Despite their successes, all of the Luk children trace their disappointments and difficulties to "the Chinese in us," even though their knowledge of Chinese culture has been gleaned mostly from books. They regard themselves as great disappointments to their parents who have continued to support them, sometimes economically as well as personally. The Luk children—educated, thoroughly anglicized, and seemingly well adjusted to Canadian life—still think of themselves as "marginal personalities" not fully at home in either the Canadian or Chinese worlds.[3]

The cultural gulf that separates the Luk children from their parents symbolizes the dramatically different circumstances faced by American- and Canadian-born Chinese from their immigrant parents. Mr. and Mrs. Luk are typical of how the first Chinese in North America were forced to live their lives. Mr. Luk was sixty-eight years old when I first met him, a retired green- grocer who maintained a comfortable living from rents on several buildings he owned in Toronto. His father had come to Canada in the early 1900s and, like the immigrants before him, left his family behind in China and sought his fortune in the gold mines of British Columbia. By this time the mining frenzy that had spawned the frontier boom towns of California and western Canada had subsided. Gold mining and newer industries such as canning, lumbering, and railroad construction were now in the hands of large companies who contracted Chinese and other immigrant labor, who were preferred over native whites because they worked reliably and performed rough and dangerous jobs.

After years of work in the mines in Nanaimo, British Columbia, the elder Luk sent for Mr. Luk, his middle son, who arrived in Victoria on the last ship carrying Chinese immigrants prior to the Immigration Act of 1923, which prohibited further Chinese immigration. Then fifteen years of age, Mr. Luk worked as a houseboy for a wealthy Vancouver family and was given the opportunity, rare at that time, to attend school. He left school after a couple of years, however, finding the language barrier too great to overcome and frustrated that the teachers made no attempt to teach him English. Like most of the early immigrants to North America, Mr. Luk speaks only broken English and associates almost solely with his Chinese-speaking friends.

In the late 1920s, Mr. Luk left Vancouver for Montreal where, in partnership with another Chinese, he opened a grocery stand specializing in fresh produce. Hostility towards the Chinese in western Canada had caused many to either return to China or to migrate eastward where they found economic niches as petty entrepreneurs or workers in laundries, restaurants, and grocery stands where there was little competition from whites. The same pattern had developed earlier in the United States due to anti-Chinese sentiment and legislation in California. In both countries, the Chinese were eventually excluded from citizenship and the vote, prohibited from owning farmland or gaining factory employment, and denied entrance into universities and technical and professional schools. Not wishing to arouse further hostility and denied participation in the U.S. and Canadian mainstreams, the Chinese moved to the growing cities where they found refuge and isolation in the form of ethnic enclaves that came to be known as "Chinatowns." To this day, even though all discriminatory legislation against the Chinese has been repealed, Chinese immigrants still pour into North America's cities where they continue to rely on Chinatowns for employment, housing, and other needs.

It was in Montreal that Mr. Luk met and married Mrs. Luk, a Canadian-born Chinese woman only several years his junior. Although Mrs. Luk was born in Canada, she was raised in the Chinatown community. Her father had worked for the Canadian National Railroad and later contracted with them to sell provisions as well as hire Chinese kitchen labor for the work crews. Because he had been classified a merchant, he was able to bring his wife to Canada, a "privilege" denied to other Chinese. Mrs. Luk's father disapproved of education for daughters and she was only permitted to complete primary school. She did learn some English, but after her school years she worked exclusively in Chinese businesses and today Chinese remains her primary language. Mrs. Luk, though Canadian-born, had her citizenship revoked upon her marriage to Mr. Luk, a Chinese "resident alien."

In Montreal, and later Toronto, the Luks established a domestic pattern that was to continue until retirement. Mrs. Luk worked full time in the store tending to customers, paying the bills, and keeping the accounts. Mr. Luk ordered and picked up the produce and supervised their preparation and display. Like most other Chinese small business families, they lived in the back of the store, worked extremely long hours, saved money that was later invested in a larger business and real estate, and raised four children. They worked such long hours that the family did little together and the children gradually became estranged and isolated from their parents as they adapted to white Canadian society. Two generations of one Chinese family, each typical of the respective Chinese communities in which they lived, yet poles apart linguistically, culturally, and personally.

Chinatowns today are populated by Chinese quite different in background and experiences from either Luk generation. There are thousands more living in the major Chinatowns of New York, San Francisco, Los Angeles, Toronto, Vancouver, and other large cities, which are now the main points of entry for recent Chinese immigrants.[4] Once small enclaves characterized by laundries, groceries, and restaurants scattered about the city and populated by men from rural China, Chinatowns today are thriving ethnic communities made up mostly of Chinese families emigrating from Hong Kong and other Chinese communities overseas.

It is useful to think of Chinatown history in three distinct periods; the "traditional community" spanning the years 1850–1945, the "transitional community" lasting from 1945–1965, and the "contemporary community" dating from 1965 to the present. Each period differs from the others in two ways: the characteristics of the Chinese themselves, and the American and Canadian policies and attitudes towards the Chinese. Understanding the relationship between these two factors is necessary for interpreting the Chinese experience in North America.

THE TRADITIONAL
CHINATOWN COMMUNITY

Nearly all of the earliest Chinese immigrants came to North America, first to California and later to British Columbia, in the latter half of the nineteenth century. Initially, they came in search of the gold rush riches that led them to refer to the United States as Gum Shan ("gold mountain") where they panned already worked-out claims abandoned by whites for the few nuggets and dust that remained. The migrants were married men and young bachelors, most of whom migrated from two agricultural regions known as Sze-Yap (pronounced "say-yap"; literally "four districts") and Sam-Yap ("three districts") that surrounded the port cities of Canton (Guangzhou) and Hong Kong in southern China. Perhaps as many as 60 percent came from the single district of Toisan ("elevated mountain"), a rocky, mountainous coastal area whose agricultural output could support its population of over half a million only four months out of the year.[5] Because of this, many men from Toisan made yearly journeys to Canton and Hong Kong where they worked on the docks or as middlemen between merchants and the fast-growing number of foreign seamen who were now entering the port cities recently forced open by the British.[6] Through their contacts with these seamen they learned of gold discoveries in America and how to secure passage for the three-month journey across the Pacific. Although the Chinese government prohibited emigration, peasants from Toisan and other poor districts in southern China had strong motivations to risk the journey to America. They were already accustomed to leaving their native villages many months of the year to supplement their family incomes through work in the city, and the opportunity to strike it rich in the gold mines of California, even if it meant several years away from village and family, was a sufficient economic lure to men already used to temporary sojourns.

Once men from a particular village or lineage became established in North America, they would occasionally return to China, usually to marry or visit the family they had left behind. Upon their return they might bring a teenaged son or lineage "brother" with them. Immigration laws favored the migration of relatives already resident in North America provided the sponsor could guarantee work and living quarters for the new immigrant. This established a pattern of chain migration that led many villages in rural southern China to become known as "emigrant communities."[7] These were communities where most of the working age men lived in North America and sent money (known as "remittances") to their families who remained. These remittances enabled Toisan to become the richest district in rural China with paved streets, electric lighting, and modern buildings and schools dotting its landscape.[8] The pattern of chain migration established more than a century ago continues today since immigration laws still favor the migration of relatives. In tracing the migration histories of two Chinese men who immigrated to Canada in the early 1900s, I discovered that thirty-five out of forty-four of their direct descendants were now citizens or permanent residents of Canada![9]

Very few Chinese struck it rich in the gold mines, of course, and most found themselves stranded in frontier mining towns with no money to return to China and few prospects for employment. Since the frontier populations of California and British Columbia contained few women, some Chinese made a living doing laundry and cooking, establishing the pattern of "women's work" that came to be the dominant economic adaptation of the traditional Chinatown community. As the mining towns went bust these Chinese moved to the growing cities of San Francisco, Sacramento, and Vancouver, where they established small hand laundries and cafes (the latter serving American, not Chinese, food in the beginning) that became the economic foundation of early Chinatowns.

Most Chinese in North America, however, found work constructing the Central Pacific Railroad in the U.S. in the 1860s and 1870s, and the Canadian Pacific Railroad in Canada during the 1880s and 1890s. A shortage of white labor due both to the U.S. Civil War and small native-born populations led the directors of the large railroad companies (including Leland Stanford in California and Andrew Onderdonk in British Columbia) to recruit Chinese labor. The Chinese responded by the thousands, a situation that led to increased emigration from China. Their work on the railroads can only be described as heroic, and they were praised for their industry as they blasted through rugged mountain passes and worked in temperatures, both extreme heat and cold, that European workers disdained.

After the railroads were built, the Chinese found work as farm laborers, domestics, and workers in cigar and woolen factories, canneries, and fisheries.

As both the mining and railroad booms ended and Chinese gradually entered into other laboring occupations, they encountered increasing discrimination and anti-Chinese hostility by native whites, who found the Chinese convenient scapegoats for the economic problems facing the West in the latter nineteenth century. The Chinese made up 10 percent of the populations of both California and British Columbia. Their Asian faces, lack of fluency in English, different modes of dress and culture, and lack of political power made them easy targets for groups such as Dennis Kearney's Workingmen's Party in California and the Knights of Labor in British Columbia.[10] These groups consisted of working class whites, many of whom were European immigrants, seeking farmland and other opportunities in the expanding West. But land and railroad monopolies held a political stranglehold on the western economy made worse by serious recessions. The Chinese thus came to be seen as foreign competitors for scarce jobs and they were falsely accused of accepting "slave wages" that prevented whites from employment.[11]

Throughout the last three decades of the nineteenth century, the Chinese were subjected to looting, robbery, arson, and even murder, not to mention name-calling, periodic beatings and other forms of harassment. Legislation discriminating against Chinese proliferated in the California and British Columbia assemblies. "Head" taxes ranging from $50 to $500 were levied on all Chinese entering North America. Chinese were prohibited from working on locally or state-funded public works projects and subject to other anti-Chinese ordinances. Most importantly, both California and British Columbia passed a series of exclusion acts designed to exclude the immigration of Chinese laborers and restrict Chinese immigration to officials, merchants, and students. What became known as "the Chinese question" dominated the politics of the West. Although many of the early exclusion laws were eventually vetoed or declared unconstitutional, both the United States and Canada succeeded in passing immigration acts that effectively halted Chinese immigration to North America.[12] These acts not only prohibited new Chinese immigration, but prevented Chinese laborers already in North America from sponsoring the immigration of their wives, children and other close relatives. Other laws were enacted at the local, state and federal levels preventing Chinese from securing citizenship, owning farmland, and working in trades and factories where white labor predominated. Although several thousand Chinese merchants, officials, teachers, and students immigrated in the late nineteenth and early twentieth centuries, few Chinese came to North America during those years when immigrants from Europe were coming by the millions. The Chinese had been effectively shut out.

Chinese who were already resident in North America reacted to the violence and discrimination they faced in several ways. Many thousands (the precise number is not known) returned to China when jobs became scarce and anti-Chinese hostility increased. Many of those who stayed gravitated to the San Francisco and Vancouver Chinatowns, while others gradually migrated eastward to the urban centers of New York, Boston, Philadelphia, Montreal, and Toronto, where they established themselves in the laundry, restaurant, and grocery businesses that were now the accepted forms of Chinese employment. Such enterprises were relatively cheap to start up and protected the Chinese from direct competition with whites. Of greatest importance, however, the Chinese organized themselves into various associations both to protest their treatment by the U.S. and Canada, and to unify and protect their economic and political interests.

These associations dominated the political, economic, and social organization of the early Chinatowns. They are referred to as family or district associations because membership in them was based on one's surname or district of origin in China. If your surname was Li or Wong, you belonged to the Li or Wong family associations; if you hailed from Toisan, you belonged to the Toisan district association. Such organizations had the effect of uniting all the Chinese in a city into a group of associations based on Chinese affiliations. These associations were grouped into a higher-level organization known in most cities as the Chinese Benevolent Association. The Benevolent Association was composed of the leaders of all the district and surname associations. It acted as a kind of government overseeing Chinese interests. It drafted specific regulations designed to prevent Chinese businessmen from direct competition with one another. Every business was required to register with the association and pay monthly dues based on their volume of business. The Benevolent Association was more than a business organization as it also undertook social welfare functions and fought against discrimination by the larger societies. The constitution of the Victoria, British Columbia, Benevolent Association is typical of those in other cities: "This association has been established in order to express our feelings of unity, to undertake social welfare, to settle disputes, to aid the poor and the sick, to eliminate evils within the community, and to defend the community against external threat."[13]

The Chinatown residents thus organized themselves into organizations that protected them from the often hostile U.S. and Canadian governments. These associations seem to have been modeled on organizations in China known as *hui guan* ("associations"). Hui guan were mutual aid and commercial organizations formed by peasant migrants to Chinese cities. Membership in a hui guan was based on one's surname, native village, or district. They were controlled by wealthy merchant leaders who possessed wide-ranging powers of judgment, arbitration and conciliation among association members and exercised powers of taxation, population registration, and political decision-making. Like the hui guan in Chinese cities, Chinatown family and district associations were dominated by the wealthiest merchants who exercised almost total social and legal control over their members, and who became the spokesmen for the Chinese in every North American city.[14]

Every large Chinatown also had fraternal and political or-ganizations that coexisted alongside the family and district associations. The two most important of these were the Cheekungtong, known as "Chinese Freemasons" in English, and the Guomindang, or "Nationalist Party." The Chinese Freemasons was established in the 1860s and traced its origins to a secret society in China known as the Triads. Chinese without ties to the family or district associations often belonged to the Freemasons, an organization involved in gambling and other illegal activities in the early Chinatowns. It was not primarily a criminal organization, however, as it performed welfare functions similar to the other associations and came to be viewed as a legitimate and progressive institution in Chinatown politics.

The Guomindang is another early political association that played a prominent role in Chinatowns. It was established by Dr. Sun Yat-sen to overthrow China's last dynasty, the Qing, and establish republican government in China. Sun traveled to the United States and Canada establishing overseas branches of the Guomindang to provide financial support for his war effort. Leaders of the Guomindang in Chinatowns, usually the wealthy leaders of the Benevolent Association, received charters from Sun as "official spokesmen" of the Chinese government overseas; a move that enhanced their prestige and legitimacy. The Chinatown Guomindangs had their greatest influence during the Sino-Japanese War in the 1930s and 1940s when it mobilized all Chinese residents in North America to send money to Chiang Kai-Shek's Nationalist Army. The fact that China was an ally of the U.S. and Canada greatly enhanced the prestige of Guomindang leaders who often used their power to undermine rival political groups such as the Freemasons.

By the end of World War II, then, most Chinese in North America were concentrated in urban Chinatowns where an ethnic economy based on laundries, restaurants, and groceries had developed. Other businesses such as import-export emporiums sprang up to serve increasing numbers of tourists who found Chinatowns a source of Oriental exotica and cheap food. The Chinese were socially organized into a pyramid-like structure of family and district associations headed by wealthier Chinese merchant elites who regulated business, carried out welfare functions, and represented Chinese economic and political interests to the dominant societies. The position of the Chinese in North America during the traditional period can be described as an "internal colony."[15] They were legally confined to economic adaptations which reinforced ethnic solidarity. It was not unusual for Chinese who had lived in the United States for thirty or more years to speak little or no English since their contacts with the larger society were limited to transactions over a laundry or lunch counter. Although the Chinese were in North America, they were not of North America.

THE TRANSITIONAL CHINATOWN COMMUNITY

Early Chinatowns were communities of Chinese men, not families, because immigration laws prevented men from bringing their wives and children with them. The bitterness felt by many is exemplified by a Chinese restaurateur who, when he related his story to me in 1976, had lived in Canada for sixty-two years.

> I remember looking out over the dining room of our restaurant on a busy day in 1946. I counted one hundred old Chinese men sitting out there and just six women, four Chinese and two Canadian. And I thought to myself, if Canadian culture has a Christian spirit, how could they deny Chinese their families? The whole city of Toronto didn't have a dozen Chinese women in 1946. You know, they talk a lot

about the Chinese gambling and all those things, but don't forget, this was all there was to do. I had family in China, but I couldn't bring them back with me. . . . I had been living here over thirty years and had contributed to the economy. I had worked hard and never asked the government for a nickel. And you know, because I didn't import thousands of dollars of goods from China . . . they wouldn't classify me as a merchant. And so I had to work hard all those years and I didn't have a family to help me. Canada never treated the Chinese very good then. Now it's different and my heart feels good to see so many Chinese families and women and children in Chinatown now. I have a son, a son-in-law, daughter-in-law, and wife here now and five grandchildren. Now that I'm old, I'm happy to see my family living in Toronto and they come and see me all the time. Now I think Canada is the greatest country in the world.[16]

The transitional period in Chinatowns dates from the end of World War II to the middle of the 1960s. During this twenty-year period the United States and Canada gradually dismantled the series of discriminatory laws that had been enacted against the Chinese. On December 17, 1943, President Roosevelt signed a law repealing all previous acts of Chinese exclusion, and four years later the Canadian Parliament followed suit by repealing the 1923 Chinese Exclusion Act. Other acts such as the U.S. War Brides Act, the Canadian Citizenship Act, and new immigration acts in both countries permitted the Chinese who had been resident in North America to become citizens and enter occupations and schools previously closed to them. Of greatest importance, however, were laws enabling the Chinese to sponsor their wives, children and, later, parents and other relatives to join them in North America. New Chinese immigration, however, was still strictly limited by both countries until the mid-1960s when discriminatory restrictions on Asian immigration were finally removed.[17] Chinatowns grew relatively little during this period as immigration was restricted to wives and children of Chinese already resident and a small number of Chinese professionals who did not enter the ethnic economy.

This period of Chinatown history is characterized by two features: the reunification of Chinese families, and the gradual appearance of a native-born Chinese population who would successfully assimilate into the American and Canadian mainstreams. The Chinese were thus divided into two groups: the immigrant Chinese and the North American-born Chinese. Comparisons between these two groups in Canada show how different their circumstances were. Canadian-born Chinese integrated into the occupations and professions of Canadian society and attained incomes and educational levels equal to or higher than other Canadians.[18] This integration even extended to marriage where Canadian-born Chinese had lower rates of endogamy (marriage within the ethnic group) than did the British Isles, French, and Jewish origin groups.[19] This is the group typified by Betty Luk and her siblings. Chinese immigrants, on the other hand, remained confined to the Chinatown community, which consisted of lower paying and less prestigious occupations, primarily those associated with the traditional ethnic economy of laundries and restaurants. Their language remained Chinese and they had little formal education, factors that prevented them from assimilating into the larger society. For them, Chinatown remained an internal colony. But for the small, yet increasing numbers of U.S.- and Canadian-born Chinese, their successful assimilation produced a new image of the Chinese in North America. They were now regarded as a model ethnic community.

CHINATOWNS TODAY:
THE CONTEMPORARY COMMUNITY

It is difficult to overstate the extent to which North America's Chinatowns today differ from those of the traditional and transitional periods. As a result of new immigration regulations of the mid-1960s Chinatowns have experienced explosive growth and the problems associated with such growth. The Chinese population of Toronto, for example, was about 8,000 in 1966, the year prior to Canada's removal of immigration restrictions against Asians. During my fieldwork in the late 1970s, the population was estimated at 80,000 and a newspaper report from 1990 gives 250,000 as a reasonable count. While Toronto's Chinatown has perhaps experienced the greatest growth, other major Chinatowns in North America such as San Francisco, New York, Los Angeles, and Vancouver have Chinese populations of well over 150,000. Whereas Chinese immigrants to North America made up only 1–2 percent of the total number of immigrants from 1950–60, they were nearly 7 percent of the total during the 1970s and 1980s. Growth in the immigrant population has led to an increasing reliance upon and a tremendous expansion of the ethnic community.

More important than growth itself is the diversity which now characterizes Chinatowns. New immigration regulations in both the United States and Canada favor the immigration of family members of Chinese already resident. These "family class" immigrants are usually non-English speaking, working class Chinese who must find jobs in the ethnic economy. Nearly 85 percent of all immigrants now come from Hong Kong, with the remainder emigrating from Taiwan, mainland China, or from other areas of Chinese settlement in Europe and Asia. Almost half of the Hong Kong emigres were born in China, primarily Guangdong Province, who made their way to Hong Kong, after the Chinese revolution of 1949. Most, however, had lived in Hong Kong for many years prior to coming to North America, were thus familiar with an urban lifestyle, and usually took jobs similar to those previously held in Hong Kong. The language spoken in Hong Kong is Cantonese, which is now the predominant language of Chinatowns. About 20 percent of all immigrants, those who have achieved university educations in Hong Kong or Canada, are bilingual in both English and Chinese.

Recent Chinese immigrants thus differ greatly from the first sojourning immigrants who came from rural China. They immigrate as families who intend to make North America their permanent home. They are accustomed to the crowded urban lifestyle of North America's cities and expect their children to integrate successfully into the larger societies. Because of this, the family and district associations which were so important in traditional Chinatowns have decreased in influence. Recent immigrants now rely on social service agencies, churches, clubs, and other immigrant services to meet their needs. Occupations have expanded beyond the old laundry/grocery/restaurant niches that employed the early immigrants to include clerical and professional positions and factory work, the latter mainly in garment factories that employ thousands of recent immigrants.

The Chinese Working Class

The immigrant working class is distinguished from the other classes by their positions in unskilled and semi-skilled occupations in the Chinatown economy, and by their inability to speak, read or write English. These immigrants must find jobs that require little knowledge of English and, as a result, are employed as garment workers, hotel domestics, or as waiters, cooks, cashiers, clerks, and other relatively low-paying and insecure jobs in Chinese restaurants or shops. Throughout North America, Chinese working class families earn only 60 percent of the average income of Americans and Canadians as a whole, and the poverty rate for Asian-American immigrants is twice that of non-Hispanic whites.[20] They usually live in Chinese neighborhoods where housing is substandard, rents are high, and overcrowding is the norm. Their children attend public schools where many of the other children are Chinese, but where little attention is given Chinese language or culture.

Few working-class Chinese families take part in organized groups such as unions, ethnic associations, and cultural groups. Linguistic barriers inhibit association with non-Chinese workers, and their employment in occupations with little job security make such associations hazardous at best. Chinese workers are completely dependent on Chinatowns for jobs, housing, social services, and the like. The adults will live out their lives in a Chinese world, but place great pressure on their children to become educated and assimilated into North American society.

The case of the Pan family, whom I met in Toronto, is typical of the adaptations and sacrifices which working class Chinese families must make. When I met the Pans in 1977 they lived in a small, four-room flat in downtown Toronto, which they rented for $130 a month. They had no car, a minimum of furniture, and no major appliances, such as a washing machine. Their prize possession was a portable color television. Mr. Pan worked as a cook in a Chinese restaurant six days a week on the night shift from 5 P.M. to 1 A.M. Mrs. Pan also worked six days a week, but from 7 A.M. to 4 P.M. as a laundress in a downtown hotel. Their combined weekly income was about $200. Like many Chinese families they were trying to save money for a down payment on a house, and they managed to save about $100 a month.

As is evident from their work schedules, Mr. and Mrs. Pan saw very little of each other. Mrs. Pan tried to sleep a few hours each evening after the children went to bed so she could spend some time with her husband when he came home from work. Mr. Pan also spent little time with his children since they were at school when he was at home. The children, two daughters aged 13 and 11 and two sons aged 10 and 8, were extremely self-sufficient. They arrived home from school two hours before their mother and while their father was asleep. The girls usually cooked supper for their father and did so with great delight since he had taught them how to cook. They also "mothered" the two boys, keeping tabs on them both at school and at home.

The children did very well in school. The girls especially spoke excellent English and were almost equal to their Canadian classmates in reading and writing. The boys also spoke good English, but were just learning how to read and write. At home, they usually spoke their native Fujian dialect, but increasingly the children conversed in English among themselves. Mr. and Mrs. Pan were very proud of their children's progress, but extremely anxious about several problems upsetting the household. The girls were becoming familiar with Canadian standards and saw how they stood out among their peers. Their clothes were out of style and they could not understand why their parents wouldn't buy them more. They were also beginning to view their family as quite "odd" in comparison to other families. The parents worried mostly about their sons, however, who were not learning as quickly as the girls and whose behavior they described as "wild." Nevertheless, the family is glad it came to Canada where, in the words of Mr. Pan, "There is always enough rice to eat."

The Pan family illustrates several patterns of working-class adjustments to Chinatown society. Like most families, both spouses work full time outside the home, most in laboring occupations in garment factories or restaurants.[21] The parents place extreme pressure on their children to succeed in school, since education has always been highly valued in Chinese culture. At the same time, however, the parents are ill-equipped to either help or monitor their children's progress. The extreme reverence for the family so characteristic of Chinese culture is both a blessing and a curse that children must psychologically navigate. Many children do succeed in school as evidenced by the large number of Asian-Americans who achieve college educations; 40 percent as compared to 23 percent among non-Hispanic whites in 1990.[22] But 20 percent drop out of high school, never develop fluency in English, have inadequate skills to find anything but marginal employment, and usually have strongly negative feelings about their Chinese heritage. Many of these get involved in youth gangs and have resorted to criminal activities to make a living.[23]

Recent evidence indicates that Asian-American populations are experiencing the same divisions as other American groups: the rich are getting richer and the poor are getting poorer.[24]

The younger the children are when they come to North America, the easier it is for them to acculturate and assimilate. Chinese who come as teenagers, however, find it extremely difficult to learn English or do well in school since they are already fully enculturated in Chinese language and culture. Most of these students drop out of school and are forced to seek the same low-wage employment in the ethnic economy as their parents. Husband-wife relations are also strained by differing work schedules, the frustrations of adjusting psychologically and economically to a new environment, and the unique problems associated with child-rearing. They want their children to assimilate but regret their loss of Chinese language and culture. A survey conducted in Toronto on the "family cohesiveness" of Chinese as perceived by married women's perceptions of the quality of their family life indicated that 150 of 177 women interviewed rated "low" on family cohesiveness. The most significant factor contributing to low cohesion was a severe lack of communication and interaction among all members of the family stemming from linguistic barriers between parents and children and relatively little time spent together among spouses.[25]

In spite of these problems, most working-class immigrants I knew were happy to be in Canada even though they had to work much harder to make a living than they thought they would have prior to immigration. The relative safety and security of Canada compared to Hong Kong and better opportunities for their children were the reasons. Nevertheless, the Chinese immigrant working class is still an "internal colony" whose low-wage labor and long working hours in the factories and Chinatown subeconomy make considerable profits for their employers. The North American economies have benefitted greatly from these immigrants. Our "Made in U.S.A" clothes are economically competitive with those made in Taiwan, Hong Kong, Singapore and other Asian sites because they are made by Chinese and other Asian immigrants who work very long hours for wages that non-immigrants would not accept.

The Chinese Educated-Professional Class

One of the major changes distinguishing contemporary China-towns from the traditional and transitional periods is the presence of thousands of young, college educated Chinese professionals who occupy key roles in the ethnic community as social workers, lawyers, counselors, and other "white-collar" employees. Many Hong Kong Chinese first came to North America as university students and achieved permanent immigrant status after graduation. These immigrants are unlike the educated North American-born Chinese in that they grew up in a culture (Hong Kong) in which both Chinese and English were necessary for educational success. They are bilingual and bicultural, knowledgeable about both Chinese and Anglo-European cultures, and do not experience the marginality of native-born Chinese.

Members of the educated class play important roles in Chinatown since they act as mediators or brokers between the Chinese working class and the institutions of American and Canadian society. Social workers, immigration and employment counselors, legal aid advisors, ministers, bank tellers, and other occupations in Chinatown require persons who can interpret the complexities of American life to Chinese-speaking immigrants. Effectively filling these roles requires an educated class that not only understands the Chinese immigrant community, but also has the education and training recognized by U.S. and Canadian universities. Because of this, their ability to speak and write in English is often equal to their abilities in Chinese, and their years of residence in North America, much of which was spent in university, has enabled them to learn and, in many cases adopt, the culture of North American society. This ability to interact effectively and creatively in both Chinese and North American contexts gives the educated-professional class its special distinction, and enables those of its members so inclined to assume influential and powerful roles in Chinatown. Chinese social workers in both the United States and Canada are a good example.[26] Their influence in Chinatowns is much greater than that of American or Canadian social workers for they are the primary interpreters of North American society to Chinese-speaking immigrants. The success of Chinese social services depends on their ability to articulate working-class needs to the state bureaucracies in order to secure funds to keep programs operating. Their jobs demand a knowledge of immigrant social problems, a great many of which stem from poverty and illiteracy in English.

The educated-professional Chinese have greatly altered the political landscape of Chinatowns. They have begun numerous community organizations that both stress and address the problems faced by recent immigrants in the areas of employment, housing, and schooling. They are "activist" in the sense that they sponsor voter registration drives, English language training, employee rights classes, and other activities designed to enhance the political participation and power of Chinese-speaking immigrants. They have also been leaders in organizing campaigns to protect Chinatown neighborhoods from development plans in Toronto, Vancouver, and New York that have threatened to displace needed services and housing for immigrants.[27] Such activism in support of working-class immigrants has brought Chinatown professionals into direct conflict with the traditional Chinatown leaders of the family associations. Recent immigrants have no use for the old associations so important to the early immigrants since their experiences and problems are so different. The associations have not recruited new members and thus remain the preserve of older immigrants rooted in the traditional Chinatown economy. In the Chinatowns of today, the professional class has effectively replaced the leaders of the Chinese Benevolent Association and other traditional associations as the spokespersons for the Chinese in North America. Their influence attests to the dramatic changes that have occurred in China-towns since the 1960s. The traditional associations were oriented inwardly to the special needs of a small entrepreneurial class who fought for removal of immigration restrictions and the reestablishment of family life in North America. Ironically, their successes in securing legislation that led to the influx of thousands of Chinese have also led to their own political and economic decline.

The Chinese Business Class

Despite the changes occurring in Chinatowns, Chinese businesses catering to tourists and immigrants alike remain the lifeblood of Chinatown communities. Although the hand laundries of the traditional community have disappeared due to the advent of home appliances and dry cleaning, restaurants retain their visibility as centerpieces of Chinese culture in North America. Next to the restaurants, however, are a wide array of new businesses not seen in previous times. Bookshops, gift shops, furniture stores, theaters, butchers, clothing stores, pet shops, beauty salons, Chinese groceries, real estate, automobile dealerships, professional offices, social service agencies, and more now crowd the Chinatown streets. A Chinese-speaking immigrant need never leave the confines of the community to meet his needs.

Chinese businesses are not only more diverse, but the scale of Chinese enterprise has greatly increased. In the traditional community, it was relatively inexpensive to start a laundry or small restaurant, but the cost of real estate and government regulations and restrictions have made it virtually impossible for any but the wealthy to establish a business. For many immigrants, however, the opportunity to start one's own business remains a dream. In every Chinatown small new businesses such as newsstands and tiny restaurants that represent the life savings of a few immigrant families crop up almost daily. Sadly, they are often out of business within a few weeks or months since they have neither the capital nor the credit to compete with the larger, more established businesses.

The Chinese business class is now dominated by a small, but wealthy and influential group of entrepreneurs, many of whom have recently immigrated from Hong Kong, London, Madrid, and other overseas communities where they established considerable fortunes. They have built multistory restaurants, shopping malls, and apartment complexes in Chinatown designed to attract tourists and upscale residents. They are viewed by the Chinese working class and their social worker allies as predators seeking to destroy housing and jobs. They are viewed as "businessmen first, Chinese second"; people who put profits ahead of their ethnicity and their responsibilities to the community. The businessmen, on the other hand, defend their actions by pointing to the number of jobs they provide Chinatown residents and the new businesses that attract tourists.

The "new entrepreneurial elite" with their business suits, car phones, and computers contrasts in both lifestyle and orientation with the "old merchant elites" who for years dominated the social and economic life of Chinatowns. This segment of the business class is represented by those successful Chinese of the traditional period who built their restaurants into large businesses and other enterprises that enabled them to gain considerable wealth. These older merchant elites controlled the family associations and the Chinese Benevolent Association, often to their own benefit, but they nevertheless saw themselves as representing the entire community. They were in the forefront of efforts to relax immigration and other restrictions against the Chinese and rightly viewed themselves as community leaders. The presence of the new immigrant business class has produced severe economic competition for these old elites whose economic resources pale in comparison. They consider themselves the guardians of "family business" who care about the Chinese community and thus also regard the new business class as predatory profit-seekers out to destroy the Chinese way of life. Toronto's most famous Chinese citizen and former leader of the traditional business elite summarizes their feelings:

> You know . . . the old restaurants, we all know each other and we're friendly with one another. We know none could survive alone, so we cooperate. When the Sai-Woo opened twenty-five years ago all the rest of us went to their opening. We were anxious to see them do well because we knew them and we knew they came up the hard way.
>
> But now this foreign money comes in and is so big that they can afford to take losses for two or three years. They say, "I'm not interested in your community. I don't care about the little man next door." And so they have price wars and pretty soon family business will be forced out.
>
> You know, we fought hard for the immigration law and for the civil rights of the Chinese in Canada, but immigration has come too fast, too soon. Foreign money [from Hong Kong] comes in and they think they know how to do everything the Chinese way. All this new money has created a false sense of security, and the small people are being eaten up. . . . I'm no longer a spokesperson for the community. I don't know anyone anymore, and I can't represent a community I don't know.[28]

In many ways, this statement is a brief social history of the nature and extent of changes which have affected Chinatowns. Foremost among these perhaps is a "loss of community"—the feeling among longtime residents that Chinatown is no longer a smoothly functioning ethnic community based on the ethnic solidarity of the old associations. What this loss of community signals, however, is the passage of power from the older merchant elites to recently immigrated groups such as the new business class and the educated professional class. The traditional structure of Chinatowns has been attacked on two fronts: economically by Chinese tycoons who compete for the tourist dollar, and politically by the educated class who now best represent the new working class immigrants. For those Chinese who came to North America prior to the 1960s, modern Chinatowns are nearly as foreign as the new countries to which they came.

THE FUTURE OF THE CHINESE IN NORTH AMERICA

Chinatowns today are best viewed as immigrant communities whose populations are mainly comprised of first-generation, foreign-born Chinese from Hong Kong, China, and other areas of Chinese settlement overseas. Their characteristics as ethnic communities thus reflect the diversity of the immigrants themselves, and the adjustments, hopes, and struggles that I have discussed. As the communities continue to grow, the Chinese will become increasingly dispersed geographically, a process that is already evident in the large metropolitan centers. Many smaller China-towns are thus springing up near the major ones as clusters of Chinese with particular origins, such as Taiwan, establish their own communities.[29]

Immigration has slowed appreciably since the mid-1980s, however, and if this trend persists Chinatowns will increasingly become communities of U.S.- and Canadian-born Chinese. Many of them will successfully integrate into the larger societies, but usually at the cost of losing—or never gaining—competency in Chinese language or an appreciation of Chinese culture.

NOTES

1. Much of the data for this article is based on my fieldwork in Toronto, Canada's Chinese community during 1976–1977 and a subsequent stay in 1983. All names mentioned are pseudonyms.

2. Acculturation is the process of learning the language, attitudes, and habits of another culture. Assimilation is a social process that leads people from one cultural group to integrate into the occupations and statuses of another group.

3. The notion of "marginal personality" was developed by sociologist Robert Park to refer to the psychological and social conflicts experienced by persons who are caught between the demands of their native culture (e.g., Chinese) and a very different culture to which they are attempting to assimilate (e.g., American culture).

4. Most Chinese today immigrate to large urban areas where "major" Chinatowns offer them opportunities for housing and employment. Major Chinatowns are those with Chinese populations over 100,000. There are also many mid-size and small Chinatowns scattered throughout North America's cities.

5. Betty Lee Sung, *The Story of the Chinese in America* (New York: Collier Books, 1967), p. 11.

6. Prior to the Opium Wars with Britain in the 1840s, China had strictly regulated trade with foreign countries and did not permit foreign vessels to enter its ports. The British were victorious in these wars, however, and required China to open its ports for the opium trade and other goods. China was also required to grant a leasehold over Hong Kong to the British. This expires in 1997 and Hong Kong will revert back to China.

7. Chen Ta, *Emigrant Communities in South China* (London: Institute of Pacific Relations, 1940).

8. Sung, *The Story of the Chinese in America*, pp. 16–17.

9. Richard H. Thompson, *Toronto's Chinatown: The Changing Social Organization of an Ethnic Community* (New York: AMS, 1989), p. 174.

10. For a history of this period consult Elmer Clarence Sandmeyer, *The Anti-Chinese Movement in California* (Urbana, Ill.: University of Illinois, 1939).

11. Sung, *The Story of the Chinese in America*, pp. 42–42.

12. In 1888 the United States passed the Scott Act which prohibited any Chinese laborers from immigrating. Only those classified as merchants, teachers, officials, and students were permitted entry. Canada passed a law with similar provisions in 1923 that has come to be known as the Chinese Exclusion Act.

13. Harry Con, Ronald J. Con, Graham Johnson, Edgar Wickberg, William E. Willmott, *From China to Canada: A History of the Chinese*

Communities in Canada, Edgar Wickberg, ed. (Toronto: McClelland and Stewart, 1982), p. 38.

14. For a description of the traditional segmentary structure in Chinese communities consult Lawrence W. Crissman, "The Segmentary Structure of Urban Overseas Chinese Communities," *Man,* N.S., 2 (1967): 185–204.

15. Michael Hechter, "Group Formation and the Cultural Division of Labor," *American Journal of Sociology,* 84 (1978): 293–318.

16. Thompson, *Toronto's Chinatown,* pp. 105–106.

17. Although the Chinese are racially distinct from Europeans, the discrimination and prejudice the Chinese faced are best thought of as forms of "social intolerance" rather than "race prejudice." Although whites in California feared competition from Chinese labor, they did not couch their opposition to the Chinese in terms of racial ideologies of inferiority. The latter form of "race prejudice" has been reserved for Native Americans and African-Americans. For a discussion of social intolerance and race prejudice see Oliver C. Cox, *Caste, Class and Race* (New York: *Monthly Review,* 1959), pp. 392–393.

18. Thompson, *Toronto's Chinatown,* p. 117.

19. Warren Kalbach, *The Impact of Immigration on Canada's Population* (Ottawa: Dominion Bureau of Statistics, 1970), p. 340.

20. William P. O'Hare and Judy C. Felt, *Asian Americans: America's Fastest Growing Minority Group* (Washington, D.C.: Population Reference Bureau, 1991), pp. 6–7.

21. Mary T. Ling, "Values and Voluntary Associations: The Chinese Community in Downtown Toronto," (Unpublished ms., 1975).

22. O'Hare and Felt, *Asian Americans,* p. 8.

23. For a discussion of Chinese youth gangs consult Chia-ling Kuo, *Social and Political Change in New York's Chinatown: The Role of Voluntary Associations,* (New York: Praeger, 1977); and Bernard P. Wong, *Chinatown: Economic Adaptation and Ethnic Identity of the Chinese* (New York: Holt, Rinehart and Winston, 1982).

24. O'Hare and Felt, *Asian Americans,* p. 7.

25. Ling, "Values and Voluntary Associations."

26. For the roles that Chinese social workers play in Chinatowns consult Bernard P. Wong, "Elites and Ethnic Boundary Maintenance: A Study of the Roles of Elites in Chinatown, New York City," *Urban Anthropology,* 6 (1977): 1–22; Richard H. Thompson, "Ethni-

city vs. Class: An Analysis of Conflict in a North American Chinese Community," *Ethnicity*, 6 (1979): 306–326.

27. Thompson, *Ibid.*

28. *Ibid.*, p. 274.

29. For an analysis of a Taiwan immigrant community in Queens, New York, see Hsiang-shui Chen, *Chinatown No More: Taiwan Immigrants in Contemporary New York* (Ithaca, N.Y.: Cornell, 1992).

SUGGESTED READINGS

Barth, Gunther. *Bitter Strength: A History of the Chinese in the United States, 1850–1870.* Cambridge, Mass.: Harvard University Press, 1964. A good history of early Chinese settlement in the United States.

Chen, Hsiang-shui. *Chinatown No More: Taiwan Immigrants in Contemporary New York.* Ithaca, N.Y.: Cornell University, 1992. A new study focusing on Chinese immigrants who establish communities apart from traditional Chinatowns.

Con, Harry, Ronald J. Con, Graham Johnson, Edgar Wickberg, William E. Willmott. *From China to Canada: A History of the Chinese Communities in Canada.* Edgar Wickberg, ed. Toronto: McClellan and Stewart, 1982. The best general study of the Chinese experience in Canada.

Loewen, James W. *The Mississippi Chinese: Between Black and White.* 2nd ed. Prospect Heights, Ill.: Waveland, 1992. An interesting study of race relations comparing African Americans and Chinese in a rural Mississippi community.

Nee, Victor and Brett DeBary Nee. *Longtime Californ': A Documentary Study of an American Chinatown.* (New York: Random House, 1972). An excellent and poignant account of Chinese life in San Francisco's Chinatown.